STRATEGIC ISSUES
IN HEALTH CARE MANAGEMENT

■ *Point and Counterpoint* ■

HSA 6107

KENT SERIES IN MANAGEMENT

Carland/Carland, *Small Business Management: Tools for Success*

Davis/Cosenza, *Business Research for Decision Making*, Second Edition

Duncan/Ginter/Swayne, *Strategic Issues in Health Care Management: Point and Counterpoint*

Duncan/Ginter/Swayne, *Strategic Management of Health Care Organizations*

Finley, *Entrepreneurial Strategies: Text and Cases*

Kemper/Yehudai, *Experiencing Operations Management: A Walk-Through*

Kirkpatrick, *Supervision: A Situational Approach*

Lane/DiStefano, *International Management Behavior*, Second Edition

Mendenhall/Oddou, *Readings and Cases in International Human Resource Management*

Mitchell, *Human Resource Management: An Economic Approach*

Nkomo/Fottler/McAfee, *Applications in Human Resource Management: Cases, Exercises, and Skill Builders*, Second Edition

Plunkett/Attner, *Introduction to Management*, Fourth Edition

Puffer, *Managerial Insights from Literature*

Punnett, *Experiencing International Management*

Punnett/Ricks, *International Business*

Roberts/Hunt, *Organizational Behavior*

Scarpello/Ledvinka, *Personnel/Human Resource Management: Environments and Functions*

Singer, *Human Resource Management*

Stahl/Grigsby, *Strategic Management for Decision Making*

Starling, *The Changing Environment of Business*, Third Edition

Steers/Ungson/Mowday, *Managing Effective Organizations: An Introduction*

Tate/Hoy/Stewart/Cox/Scarpello, *Small Business Management and Entrepreneurship*

Tosi, *Organizational Behavior and Management: A Contingency Approach*

STRATEGIC ISSUES IN HEALTH CARE MANAGEMENT

■ *Point and Counterpoint* ■

W. JACK DUNCAN
University of Alabama at Birmingham

PETER M. GINTER
University of Alabama at Birmingham

LINDA E. SWAYNE
University of North Carolina at Charlotte

PWS-KENT PUBLISHING COMPANY
■ BOSTON ■

PWS-KENT
Publishing Company

Sponsoring Editor: Rolf Janke
Assistant Editor: Marnie Pommett
Production Editor: Eve Mendelsohn Lehmann
Manufacturing Coordinator: Peter Leatherwood
Interior Designer: Eve Mendelsohn Lehmann
Cover Designer: Patricia Adams
Word Processing: Rita de Clercq Zubli
Cover Printer: John P. Pow Company, Inc.
Text Printer and Binder: Arcata Graphics/Halliday

Copyright © 1992 by PWS-KENT Publishing Company. All rights reserved. No part of this book may be reproduced, stored in a retrieval system, or transcribed, in any form or by any means, electronic, mechanical, photocopying, recording, or otherwise, without the prior written permission of the publisher, PWS-KENT Publishing Company, 20 Park Plaza, Boston, Massachusetts 02116.

PWS-KENT Publishing Company is a division of Wadsworth, Inc.

Printed in the United States of America.
1 2 3 4 5 6 7 -- 95 94 93 92

ISBN: 0-534-92918-4

■ PREFACE ■

Management of health care organizations has become an extremely complex and difficult task, primarily because of the rapid and dramatic changes that have occurred. Indeed, the dynamics of the industry, may be measured by the number of strategic issues that health care organizations have to address. No other industry faces this number and diversity of challenging strategic issues.

In many cases, strategic issues are ill-structured, ambiguous, multifaceted, and complex. Rational arguments may be presented supporting either side. Regardless of their form, strategic issues shape the future of the industry and represent the major "forces" affecting organizations. Health care organizations of all types (hospitals, HMOs, nursing homes, medical equipment manufacturers, drug distributors, regulators, and so on), regardless of their mission, will be affected by these issues. Therefore, health care managers must understand the various issues and their current and potential impact on organizations.

Based on extensive review of the health care literature, personal interviews with health care professionals, and formal surveys of public and private health care experts, we have identified ten major strategic issues health care managers will face in the 1990s. Explicit decisions concerning these issues will have to be made by these managers in this decade. The fundamental approach of this book is a point and counterpoint debate in which health care professionals and researchers present pro and con positions concerning these ten issues.

In the following discussions of the ten strategic management issues facing health care organizations, twenty-four leading scholars, practitioners, and consultants in the field have engaged in lively debates. Our goal has been to preserve to the greatest extent possible the individual style and approach of each scholar. As you read through the issues, a number of different approaches will be evident.

Some have chosen to passionately debate the issue using insights from experiences and perspectives gained in the study and practice of health care management. Others have chosen to carefully develop and document their arguments with citations and references to original works. We encouraged this diversity because it is appropriate in light of the present controversies faced in the strategic management of health care organizations.

The book can appeal to health care administration students, managers, and executives. It may be used effectively as a supplementary text in graduate and undergraduate health care strategic management and health policy courses. The book provides a basis for class discussion concerning the most important management issues facing the industry. After a review of the pro (point) and con (counterpoint) positions, the class can attempt to reach a synthesis position. Through this process, students gain an in-depth understanding of the issues and the rationale underlying each position. This pedagogy asks students to grapple with issues they will definitely face after graduation.

This book is a valuable tool for health care managers as well. The important contemporary health care issues are brought into focus and the advantages of each side of the issue are provided. What better way to understand the major issues facing the industry than to be presented with the rationale for each side of the issues by the top authorities in the field?

With this appreciation for diversity ever present, we encourage the reader to engage in the spirit of the debate. The authors who participated in this project have been instrumental in crafting much of the current thinking in health care — so take advantage of their intellect. We hope you find reading this material as exciting as we found collecting and organizing it.

We would like to thank all the contributors who allowed us to include their essays in this text. We would also like to thank our reviewers for their helpful and insightful comments: Gary N. Armistead, of North Carolina Medical Society, and Paul T. Bruder, of the University of Houston at Clear Lake.

W. Jack Duncan

Peter M. Ginter

Linda E. Swayne

■ CONTENTS ■

INTRODUCTION

Strategic Issues Facing Health Care Managers 1

STRATEGIC ISSUES IN HEALTH CARE MANAGEMENT

Point and Counterpoint   11

ISSUE ONE: Diversification is a successful strategy for health care organizations because it allows faster entry into growing markets, higher returns, and better financial support for core operations. 11

Point: Beaufort B. Longest, Jr. 14
Counterpoint: Jeffrey A. Alexander 25

ISSUE TWO: Cooperative strategies enhance the competitive capabilities of health care organizations to provide quality services in a dynamic environment that is characterized by increasing service expectations and limited resources. 34

Point: Arnold D. Kaluzny and Howard S. Zuckerman 36
Counterpoint: James W. Begun 44

ISSUE THREE: The growth of investor-owned, for-profit hospital chains has been a positive influence in the health care industry by increasing competitiveness and lowering costs. 51

Point: Stephen James O'Connor 53
Counterpoint: Samuel C. Webb 63

ISSUE FOUR: The extension of prospective payment systems to all health care providers will stimulate efficiency in the delivery of health care services and prove to be an effective means of cost control. 72

Point: E. Greer Gay and Richard H. Nordquist 74
Counterpoint: Robert W. Broyles 85

ISSUE FIVE: Vertical integration is a useful strategy that allows health care organizations to control patient flow, enter fast-growing markets, and better acquire the returns necessary to survive in competitive environments. 94

Point: Douglas A. Conrad 96
Counterpoint: Jan P. Clement 103

ISSUE SIX: Employers should be required to provide health insurance for employees as a means of ensuring that all citizens have access to health care. 112

Point: Myron D. Fottler 114
Counterpoint: Michael A. Morrisey 124

ISSUE SEVEN: Certificates of need and other regulations are necessary to limit the number of competitors and facilities in a market so that existing organizations can achieve sufficient economic returns to ensure survival. 132

Point: Howard L. Smith and Neill F. Piland 134
Counterpoint: John D. Blair and Susan Marie Long 145

ISSUE EIGHT: Hospitals play an important role in meeting the goals of society by providing health care services to all people, regardless of their ability to pay. 158

Point: Stephen S. Mick 160
Counterpoint: Reuben R. McDaniel, Jr. 170

ISSUE NINE: Rural hospitals are important parts of their communities and provide essential health care services not otherwise available, therefore federal and state governments should provide the support necessary to ensure their survival. 182

Point: Gerald A. Doeksen 184
Counterpoint: James E. Rohrer 192

ISSUE TEN: The shortage of allied health professionals is due to relatively low salaries, long working hours, fear of infectious diseases, and the inability of physicians to create a health care team. 200

Point: Barbara A. Mark 202
Counterpoint: R. Scott MacStravic 210

STRATEGIC ISSUES
IN HEALTH CARE MANAGEMENT

■ *Point and Counterpoint* ■

INTRODUCTION

Strategic Issues Facing Health Care Managers

The paradox of planning suggests that the less we can predict the future the more we need to plan for it. Health care is one industry where we most directly confront that paradox. Because of the industry's dynamic nature, strategic planning tends to be more complex, difficult, and frustrating than it is in more stable environments. Our thinking becomes, "Why bother? Things will change before we can even complete the planning process." Yet the more potential for change, the more important the planning effort becomes to envision the potential changes and to develop appropriate responses for the myriad of possibilities. Strategic planning continues to be crucial in health care because the opportunities are boundless and the threats are catastrophic. The paradox remains.

UNDERSTANDING STRATEGIC ISSUES

The best hope for the health care strategist is to cultivate a method of examining and studying the strategic issues in the external environment and then to position his or her organization to take advantage of the opportunities while avoiding the threats as much as possible. This book addresses ten of the current strategic issues facing health care decision makers. Each issue is multifaceted and complex, and although a few are relatively clear, most of them are ambiguous and ill-structured.

Admittedly, there are numerous strategic issues in health care, and any attempt to identify only ten is subject to errors of omission. We have taken the task of issue delineation seriously and have attempted to be as systematic as possible in selecting the issues. More than 400 articles in strategic management and health care journals, as well as published studies of issues facing health care (Amara, Morrison, and Schmid, 1988; Arthur Andersen and Company, 1987; Foster, 1989; Institute of Medicine, 1988), were reviewed. In addition, attendees at health-related professional meetings and county, state, and federal health officials were polled for their opinions. Although the list is not all-inclusive, we believe these ten issues represent the general types of strategic issues facing health care managers in the 1990s.

The focus in this book will be on the critical examination of the selected strategic issues. We recognize, of course, that action-oriented managers will demand more: a means of converting this discussion into performance. Therefore, in this first chapter, we will briefly present the general process by which strategic issues are recognized, defined, formulated, diagnosed, and eventually addressed within a health care organization.

DEFINING STRATEGIC ISSUES

A *strategic issue* is an external or internal condition or pressure that is likely to affect the extent to which a health care organization — a hospital, health maintenance organization, or nursing home — can accomplish its goals (King, 1982). Strategic issues demand action. This book is intended to provide health care managers a means to understand strategic issues and anticipate environmental changes. Such an understanding can help both students and managers to organize proactive strategies that will assist them in achieving a better strategic fit between the organization and its environment.

Role of the Strategic Decision Maker

Unfortunately, strategic issues do not have unique and explicit meanings. Instead, they are "plastic" and without well-defined intrinsic structures until they are "molded into different shapes" by the decision maker, the organization, and the environment (Ramaprasad and Mitroff, 1984). The identification and significance of a strategic issue is affected by the internal environment of the organization, which includes its culture, ideology, and structure (Daft and Weick, 1984; Meyer, 1982).

The role of the decision maker in defining strategic issues is particularly important because problem formulation is not a "disinterested, impassioned process" (Lyles and Mitroff, 1980). In fact, the way strategic issues are defined, identified, and interpreted is influenced by at least three important characteristics of the decision maker (Dutton, Fahey, and Narayanan, 1983):

1. Cognitive maps, or the lens through which the strategic decision maker sees the world;
2. Political interests, or attempts by the strategist to influence the strategic process for his or her own self-interest;
3. Issue-specific characteristics such as availability of information and time pressures.

The cognitive maps of strategic decision makers are influenced by many things — education, experience, and even heredity. Political interests are equally unique to each individual and his or her aspirations and values. Although issue-specific characteristics are less personalized, the type of information a decision maker seeks and analyzes is related to the individual's cognitive map and political interests. This book focuses on issue-specific characteristics by increasing information about selected strategic issues and by providing a systematic approach that can be used to address all strategic issues.

Formulating Strategic Issues

The manner in which strategic issues are recognized and formulated is a complex process. Lyles (1981) proposed a seven-step model:

INTRODUCTION

1. *Awareness* begins to develop concerning a possible issue.
2. *Triggers* (persistent patient complaints, declining bed occupancy rates, resignation of a key physician, escalating incidence of a disease) surface the issue.
3. *Exploration* begins and facts are gathered and organized.
4. *Diplomacy* occurs when decision makers look beyond the facts to the political dimensions of the issue.
5. *Rationalization* follows as data are collected to support the view of the strategist.
6. *Confrontation* takes place when all views are aired and examined.
7. *Resolution* is reached when a choice is made among the views expressed.

The dialectic approach (to be discussed later) focuses on confrontation and resolution.

Unfortunately, when decision makers attempt to formulate strategic issues, the complexity of the environmental analysis limits the scanning process. This limitation can be addressed by restricting information sources to a relatively few that relate specifically to the issue or issues under examination, by limiting the signals monitored to a few critical events, or by limiting the number of issues that are tracked at any particular time (El Sawy, 1985; El Sawy and Pauchant, 1988).

Strategic Issue Diagnosis

Recognizing and formulating strategic issues is important and must be skillfully applied; however, strategic management requires that the issues be properly conceptualized and diagnosed. Strategic issue diagnosis (SID) is important to all aspects of strategic decision making because it "constrains the domain of strategic alternatives, serves to facilitate or mobilize behavioral and political forces toward action, and has potential impact on the course of future diagnoses" (Dutton, Fahey, and Narayanan, 1983, p. 320).

SID includes all the activities and processes by which data and stimuli are translated into issues. It is a dynamic process in that issues are continually defined and redefined. It is complex because issue recognition involves focusing, filtering, and organizing data into meaningful concepts with the expectation that eventually the concepts will be formulated into cause and effect relationships.

Finally, because issues arise from the interaction of a number of organizational players, SID relies on group processes. The outcomes of the processes are assumptions (premises that must be taken as "given" when addressing a particular issue), cause and effect understandings (beliefs about causal connections relative to a particular issue), predictive judgments (assessments regarding the future of the issue), and language and labels (reflections on the understanding of the strategic issue from the perspective of those conducting SID).

SID is an iterative, cyclical process that involves two major events: recognition and assessment. It begins when a strategic issue is recognized. Once recognition occurs, issue assessment requires interpretation of the urgency of taking action relative to the issue and the feasibility of dealing with the issue. The assessment creates momentum for change. If the momentum is great, radical change occurs; if the momentum is weak, incremental change takes place (Dutton and Duncan, 1987).

Issue Urgency and Feasibility

Pragmatically, strategic issues are important because they influence management actions. Research indicates that the type of action a manager takes depends primarily on urgency and feasibility. Feasibility refers to the manager's expectations that any action may result in a constructive outcome.

The following relationships between urgency, feasibility, and action have been proposed relative to strategic issues (Dutton, Fahey, and Narayanan, 1983):

- The more decision makers believe they understand the strategic issue and the more they perceive the organization to have the capability to deal with it, the greater the momentum for change.
- The more the issue is diagnosed by decision makers as urgent and feasible to resolve, the greater the momentum for change and the more radical the resulting change will be.
- The more diverse the beliefs of decision makers, the more frequently strategic issue diagnosis will be triggered.
- The more dissimilar the beliefs of decision makers, the greater the perceived feasibility of change and the greater the momentum for change.
- The greater the organizational resources, the less the perception of urgency, the less the perceived need to change, and the less the momentum for change.
- The greater the available organizational options and the greater the perceived feasibility of resolving the issue, the greater the momentum for change.

Strategic Issue Management Systems

Not all organizations have the capability to deal with strategic issues in the same way. For this reason, several strategic issue management systems (SIMS) have been identified. SIMS are sets of organizational procedures, routines, personnel, and processes devoted to perceiving, analyzing, and responding to strategic issues (Dutton and Ottensmeyer, 1987).

SIMS are either passive, in that they make little or no attempt to alter internal or external forces, or active, in that they aggressively shape strategic decision outcomes and attempt to influence environmental forces. Using this framework, we can identify four types of SIMS (Dutton and Ottensmeyer, 1987):

1. *Collectors* detect internal strategic issues and adopt a passive set of activities for SIMs participants. These resemble management information and budgetary systems.
2. *Antennas* perform passive roles but focus on external issues. These resemble traditional environmental scanning activities.
3. *Activators* monitor and act on internally generated strategic issues. These also resemble management information and budgetary systems and, similar to collectors, focus on the identification of internal business issues for purposes of control (Rhyne, 1985).

4. *Interveners* perform active roles in the external environment. In this type, the system actually becomes a tool of the organization to obtain greater control over its environment.

These four types of strategic issue management systems form a continuum ranging from passive (collectors) to active (interveners). All four types of SIMS are found in the health care industry. Organizations with passive systems react to issues as they surface through the internal information system (usually seen in the organization's financial statements). Thus, when profits or revenues decline, or costs escalate, management searches for the reasons, which become issues. Organizations with active systems, on the other hand, attempt to shape their environment by identifying issues early and becoming a part of their momentum or by actually creating external issues. For example, a public health department may recognize a growing trend of acute nutritional problems in a segment of the population and work to create an issue by making the public and legislature more aware of the problem. In this case, the SIMS has become a tool of the health department to control environmental events.

Before moving to the issues, we need to say more about the dialectic method and how it will be applied in this book.

DIALECTIC INQUIRY: POINT AND COUNTERPOINT

The scholastic tradition of dialectic has its roots in Aristotle's *Topics* in which he attempted to codify the Socratic style of arguing. Aristotle contended that a dialectical disputation arises from a problem that has widespread disagreement among the wise. "In dialectic disputation, one participant is a questioner and the other is an answerer; each participant upholds one side of the problem as true" (Stump, 1989). Although the questioner and answerer have opposite aims, they have a common task because neither one has the ability to resolve the issue alone.

Israel (1979) has characterized the dialectic relationship as one in which:

1. Elements form a whole.
2. These elements are separate and different.
3. They are opposite and mutually exclusive.
4. They are mutually dependent.
5. They have something in common.

Dialectical thought has been referred to as "negative thinking." Its function is to break down self-assurance and self-contentment and to develop internal contradictions that lead to qualitative change (Marcuse, 1960). The systematization of dialectic brings into proximity different individuals with differing opinions, working toward some kind of "rapprochement" or truth (Kainz, 1988).

Frederick Hegel, the nineteenth-century German philosopher, reestablished dialectic as a central theme of modern philosophy and suggested that the use of dialectic was the surest path to truth. Hegelian dialectic is the attempt to show that some apparently incompatible ideas may be compatible when they are put in the context of a larger set of categories. Hegel began with some basic category, showed how it conflicted with an equally basic category, and then offered a speculative explanation, using a new category to illustrate how the conflict is only apparent (Pinkard, 1988).

In contemporary terms, dialectic inquiry is the "point and counterpoint" process of argumentation. It is an intellectual exchange in which a *thesis* (pro) is pitted against an antithesis (con). Truth emerges from the search for a *synthesis* of apparently contradictory views (Karmel, 1980). Hegel stressed the historical element in all understanding and the relativity of that understanding to its surrounding intellectual and cultural environment (Pinkard, 1988). In other words, our understanding of an issue is time and culturally dependent.

Dialectic Inquiry and Strategic Issues

In strategic issue assessment, dialectic inquiry is the development, evaluation, and synthesis of conflicting points of view through separate formulation and refinement of each point of view (Webster, Reif, and Bracker, 1989). For instance, one person may argue that health care costs will be declining by the year 2000 (point) because of the prospective payment system, pressure by businesses and labor, physician reimbursement reform, and so on. Another individual may argue that health care costs will continue to rise (counterpoint) because of hospital failures, the costs of new technology, increased costs of malpractice insurance, an end to the reductions in relatively easy to control costs, and so on. Debating this issue should unearth the major factors influencing health care costs and the implications for the future.

To discover the major factors influencing issues and their implications, we have asked experts to debate specific issues. Many of the best thinkers, researchers, practitioners, and consultants in health care have willingly contributed and forcefully argued the pro and con positions for the selected issues. It has always been our opinion that informed scholars are equally qualified to argue either side of controversial issues. The reader should understand at the outset that participants were asked to make their arguments in the "spirit of the dialectic" and not necessarily to state their own personal points of view. Thus, the reader should not assume that the pro or con debater is a proponent of the argument he or she is making. The charge was to make a passionate and logical plea for or against the issue and allow the reader to decide.

Using the Point and Counterpoint Approach

Managing organizations is difficult because there are at least two equally plausible alternatives for addressing complex issues. In managing the strategy, the situation becomes more complex because the issues have more variables, seem to be more ambiguous, and shift over time. For such issues the best management can do is to be extremely well informed about the issue and make the best judgment possible. Management, after all, is a process of making informed judgments in the face of uncertainty and doubt.

INTRODUCTION

For most really complex issues, managers must formulate opinions and make judgments. It is difficult to rely solely on facts, because there are conflicting facts and rational, logical arguments (opinions) supporting each side of the issue. Opinions give meaning or weight to facts. Understanding the argument underlying each side of an issue can help managers to understand the salient variables and conflicting facts surrounding the issue. Thus, from the opinions of others (their interpretations of the facts), we can better formulate our opinions and make necessary judgments.

As Peter F. Drucker has pointed out:

> The effective decision does not, as so many tests on decision making proclaim, flow from a "consensus of the facts." The understanding that underlies the right decision grows out of the clash and conflict of divergent opinions and out of the serious consideration of competing alternatives. (Drucker, 1974, p. 471)

It is not surprising that many policymakers have advisers with radically different points of view — some conservative, some liberal, some low-risk takers, some high-risk takers, and so on. The point and counterpoint approach provides passionate and informed opinions for each side of a complex issue. Through a critical assessment of these arguments, observers can weigh the information presented, form their own opinions, and, supplemented with their own values, beliefs, attitudes, perceptions, and experience, make a judgment.

THE STRATEGIC ISSUES

The ten strategic issues selected for this book have many subissues, variables, facts, and subtitles. They are ten of the most significant issues facing health care managers in the 1990s. Rational arguments may be made, and opinions presented, supporting either the pro or con side of each issue. As a health care administrator or a student of health care administration, however, you should have informed, well-articulated, and supportable opinions concerning these issues.

Through this book, you have the opportunity to be challenged intellectually by some of the best thinkers and advisers in health services administration. Use their pro-and-con arguments to formulate your own opinion. Do not blindly accept one side or the other, but instead apply your own independent, critical intelligence and make judgments in a world of different and conflicting points of view. Good luck.

REFERENCES

Amara, R., J. I. Morrison, and G. Schmid. 1988. *Looking Ahead at American Healthcare.* New York: McGraw-Hill.

Arthur Andersen and Company. 1987. *The Future of Healthcare: Changes and Choices.* Chicago: American College of Healthcare Executives.

Daft, Richard L., and Karl E. Weick. 1984. "Toward a Model of Organizations as Interpretation Systems." *Academy of Management Review*, 9(2): 284-296.

Drucker, Peter F. 1974. *Management: Tasks, Responsibilities, Practices.* New York: Harper & Row, Publishers.

Dutton, Jane E., and Robert B. Duncan. 1987. "The Creation of Momentum for Change Through the Process of Strategic Issue Diagnosis." *Strategic Management Journal*, 8(3): 279-295.

Dutton, Jane E., Liam Fahey, and V. Narayanan. 1983. "Toward Understanding Strategic Issue Diagnosis." *Strategic Management Journal*, 4(1): 307-323.

Dutton, Jane E., and Edward Ottensmeyer. 1987. "Strategic Issue Management Systems: Forms, Functions, and Contexts." *Academy of Management Review*, 12(2): 355-365.

El Sawy, Omar A. 1985. "Personal Information Systems for Strategic Scanning in Turbulent Environments: Can the CEO Go Online?" *Management Information Systems Quarterly*, 9(1): 53-60.

El Sawy, Omar A., and Thierry C. Pauchant. 1988. "Triggers, Templates, and Twitches in the Tracking of Emerging Strategic Issues." *Strategic Management Journal*, 9(5): 455-473.

Foster, John T. 1989. "Hospitals in the Year 2000: A Scenario." *Frontiers of Health Services Management*, 6(2): 3-42.

Institute of Medicine, Committee for the Study of the Future of Public Health. 1988. *The Future of Public Health.* Washington, D.C.: National Academy Press.

Israel, Joachim. 1979. *The Language of Dialectics and the Dialectics of Language.* Munksgaard, Copenhagen: Billing & Sons Limited.

Kainz, Howard P. 1988. *Paradox, Dialectic, and System: A Contemporary Reconstruction of the Hegelian Problematic.* University Park, PA: The Pennsylvania State University Press.

Karmel, Barbara. 1980. *Point and Counterpoint in Organizational Behavior.* Hinsdale, IL: The Dryden Press.

King, William R. 1982. "Using Strategic Issue Analysis." *Long Range Planning*, 15(4): 45-49.

Lyles, Marjorie A. 1981. "Formulating Strategic Problems: Empirical Analysis and Model Development." *Strategic Management Journal*, 2(1): 61-75.

Lyles, Marjorie A., and Ian I. Mitroff. 1980. "Organizational Problem Formulation: An Empirical Study." *Administrative Science Quarterly*, 25(1): 102-119.

Marcuse, Herbert. 1960. *Reason and Revolution: Hegel and the Rise of Social Theory.* Boston: Beacon Press.

Meyer, Alan D. 1982. "Adapting to Environmental Jolts." *Administrative Science Quarterly,* 27(4): 515-538.

Pinkard, Terry P. 1988. *Hegel's Dialectic: The Explanation of Possibility.* Philadelphia: Temple University Press.

Ramaprasad, Arkalgud, and Ian I. Mitroff. 1984. "On Formulating Strategic Problems." *Academy of Management Review,* 9(4): 597-605.

Rhyne, L. C. 1985. "The Relationship of Information Usage Characteristics to Planning System Sophistication: An Empirical Examination." *Strategic Management Journal,* 6(4): 319-337.

Stump, Eleonore. 1989. *Dialectic and Its Place in the Development of Medieval Logic.* Ithaca, NY: Cornell University Press.

Webster, J. L., W. E. Reif, and J. S. Bracker. 1989. "The Manager's Guide to Strategic Planning Tools and Techniques." *Planning Review,* 17(6): 4-13.

STRATEGIC ISSUES
IN HEALTH CARE MANAGEMENT

Point and Counterpoint

> **ISSUE ONE**
>
> *Diversification is a successful strategy for health care organizations because it allows faster entry into growing markets, higher returns, and better financial support for core operations.*

The health care industry has faced increasing financial pressures throughout the past decade as a result of fundamentally new forces that affect the very viability of many health care organizations. Such forces include prospective payment, increased competition, diminished federal monies, new technological developments (especially those emphasizing outpatient care), the increased growth and bargaining power of preferred provider organizations (PPOs), and growing employer and consumer demands for more cost-effective care. Strategies have had to change from internally focused operations to externally focused, market-driven operations (Shortell, Morrison, and Hughes, 1989). Today's marketplace is highly competitive, and health care organizations experience greater risks as they attempt to control costs and increase volumes (Walker and Rosko, 1988).

Health care organizations have responded to these environmental forces by diversifying into new services and new markets (Coddington, Palmquist, and Trollinger, 1985). Such diversification most often has been into health-related areas, such as outpatient diagnosis and surgery centers, rehabilitation, industrial medicine, home health care, nursing facilities, trauma centers, wellness and health promotion, and health maintenance organizations (HMOs). This type of diversification is sometimes referred to as concentric or related diversification. In some instances, however, health care organizations have invested in areas not directly related to health, such as restaurants, hotels, office buildings, retirement housing, and parking lots. This type of diversification is often referred to as conglomerate or unrelated diversification. Both concentric and conglomerate diversifications have been implemented through acquisitions, mergers, internal developments, joint ventures, and licensing.

Although health care strategists have several rationales for pursuing diversification, the primary motive is to increase revenues (profits). Many administrators see diversification as a necessary defensive strategy to support the core business in light of shrinking demand and declining reimbursements (Graham, 1987). Health care organizations that have attempted both concentric and conglomerate diversification cite as reasons the need to expand into new markets, distinguish themselves from competition, and enter less regulated markets. Diversification efforts that have been most profitable include freestanding outpatient surgery, outpatient diagnosis, rehabilitation, home health services, industrial medicine, and women's medicine. Diversification strategies that have been largely unprofitable include wellness and health promotion, trauma centers, pediatrics, obstetrics, and retirement housing (*Hospitals,* 1991).

Concentric diversification has been used to build integrated health care systems that offer a wide range of services (Graham, 1987). These integrated systems, which are usually regional in scope, provide a variety of health care and nonhealth care services, including acute care, management consulting, real estate companies, nursing home facilities, insurance, and so on. It is hoped that such a system will produce greater capacities and reduced costs (synergy) for both the new unit and the core business.

Within the health care industry, the issue of diversification has generated considerable controversy. Although diversification appears to be a major strategy for health care organizations for the 1990s, it is seen as risky and has met with mixed results. Is diversification appropriate for health care organizations? Have the expected additional revenues been realized? Have the costs of health care been reduced? Have the additional revenues generated rescued core health delivery areas, thus better serving the public? Does diversification dilute specialization and divert concentration on quality?

Examining the issue of diversification, Beaufort B. Longest, Jr., of the University of Pittsburgh, examines the extent of diversification over the past decade and argues that diversification has been a necessary and successful coping strategy for many health care organizations. On the other side of the issue, Jeffrey A. Alexander, of the University of Michigan, questions the wisdom of mimicking business sector organizations by adopting diversification strategies and argues that this managerial diversion avoids more central health care problems.

REFERENCES

American Hospital Association. 1991. "Home Health, Diagnostic Centers Were Financial Winners in 1990." *Hospitals,* 65(1): 27-29.

Coddington, Dean C., Lowell E. Palmquist, and William V. Trollinger. 1985. "Strategies for Survival in the Hospital Industry." *Harvard Business Review,* 63(3): 129-138.

Graham, Judith. 1987. "Diversified Hospitals Review Plans After Some Bumpy Rides." *Modern Healthcare,* 17(17): 30-40.

Shortell, Stephen M., Ellen Morrison, and Susan Hughes. 1989. "The Keys to Successful Diversification: Lessons from Leading Hospital Systems." *Hospital & Health Services Administration,* 34(4): 471-492.

Walker, Lawrence R., and Michael D. Rosko. 1988. "Evaluation of Health Care Service Diversification Options in Health Care Institutions and Programs by Portfolio Analysis: A Marketing Approach." *Journal of Health Care Management,* 8(1): 48-59.

POINT

Diversification is a successful strategy for health care organizations because it allows faster entry into growing markets, higher returns, and better financial support for core operations.

BEAUFORT B. LONGEST, JR.
University of Pittsburgh

Beaufort B. Longest, Jr. is a professor of Health Services Administration at the Graduate School of Public Health and a professor of Business Administration at the Joseph M. Katz Graduate School of Business at the University of Pittsburgh. He also serves as director of the University's Health Policy Institute. He received a master's of Health Administration and a Ph. D. in Business Administration from Georgia State University. Longest was a faculty member of the Kellogg Graduate School of Management at Northwestern University before assuming his present position in 1980. He has conducted research and published extensively in the fields of health care management and policy. One of his coauthored books, *Managing Health Services Organizations*, is the most widely used text in graduate programs in health administration in the United States. He is a board member of four health organizations and a Fellow of the American College of Health-care Executives. Dr. Longest has consulted widely with provider organizations, associations, and government agencies in the health sector. His special expertise is in the area of strategic management.

In order to defend this assertion properly, we must make clear what we mean by *diversification*. It is a process whereby organizations add to their existing product/service mixes and/or enter new markets with their existing and/or new products/services. As this definition implies, product/service diversifications can be differentiated from market diversifications, but these types of diversifications are interrelated and have become commonplace strategic initiatives in health care organizations.

In fact, one of the most readily identifiable trends in the health industry in recent years has been the propensity of many health care organizations, especially hospitals, to diversify. Diversification has become a basic component of the strategic behavior of hospitals in the United States. In their recent landmark study of the strategic choices the leaders of these organizations make, Shortell and his colleagues went so far as to conclude that "diversification must be a part of each hospital's strategy regardless of its specific strategic orientation" (Shortell, Morrison, and Friedman, 1990, p. 232).

In order to appreciate the importance of diversifation for hospitals, as well as the magnitude of their success with this strategy, it will be useful to organize our thoughts around several aspects of the diversification phenomenon. First, we will explore the impetus for hospital diversification in the past decade. There are rather clear-cut reasons for the volume of this activity for hospitals; these reasons are key to understanding the extent of this activity and the urgency with which it has been pursued. Second, we will consider the context within which diversification has taken place in hospitals. The form and patterns of diversifications in these organizations are functions of the interactions between the opportunities for engaging in this activity and the constraints hospital managers face when they consider diversifying. We will examine both the opportunities and the constraints briefly. Third, we will review the basic types of diversification strategies open to any organization and consider why hospitals strongly favor some types and certain specific activities within these types. Finally, with this background, we will be a position to examine the available information on the outcomes of hospital diversifications and to judge the degree of success.

THE IMPETUS FOR HOSPITAL DIVERSIFICATION

Almost without exception, hospitals that have undertaken diversifications in the past decade have done so in the hope that these activities would provide new revenues to help offset declines in revenues from their core acute care inpatient activities. The relative attractiveness of new sources of revenue for health care organizations — indeed, the necessity of them for many organizations — is a function of what has happened to their traditional sources of revenue.

In brief, the once-generous hospital reimbursement policies that were based on actual costs have been supplanted, for the most part, by capitation, negotiated rates, and fixed payment schemes. This has had the effect of slowing the growth in, if not reducing, hospitals' revenues. Further, these institutions continue to face other, unrelenting cost-control pressures from both the public and private sectors, often in the form of schemes that closely monitor and manage the utilization of hospital services.

Among the direct consequences of these more stringent policies has been a precipitous decline in the production of inpatient days, a hospital's traditional core product/service and its most important source of revenue. The magnitude of this decline is a key to explaining the appeal of diversification strategies to hospitals. After years of steady growth, the volume of inpatient days began to decline in 1982. The average daily census of inpatients in the nation's hospitals has decreased nearly 20 percent since then (American Hospital Association, 1990). Reflecting this decline in volume, almost 60 percent of the nation's community hospitals had negative net patient margins (i.e., they lost money on patient care services) by the late 1980s (American Hospital Association, 1988a).

Utilization declines and the resultant revenue problems have made it more difficult — in some cases impossible — for affected hospitals to maintain physical plants and technology at state-of-the-art levels, to compete for a dwindling pool of skilled labor, or to provide charity care. Not surprisingly, hospitals have aggressively followed the path of diversification into activities that offer opportunities for new revenues and expanded markets. They have pursued diversification strategies as means of supporting their core activities in the face of reduced demand for, and declines in the profitability of, many of their traditional activities. Favorite diversification activities have included freestanding outpatient surgery centers, women's health centers, various outpatient programs, industrial medicine programs, and a variety of services for the elderly, including home health services.

In essence, diversification has been a strategic response to the less munificent environment that has faced most hospitals since the early 1980s. For many hospitals, these strategies have been a matter of survival. During the 1980s, 508 hospitals in the United States closed (*Hospitals*, 1990). Viewing these closings as the beginning stages of a Darwinian winnowing of those institutions least able to survive, many hospital managers have come to believe that the ability of their institutions to diversify into profitable new products/services and/or markets may well determine who wins and loses the survival game.

Although revenue enhancement and profitability are the most important reasons for diversification, there are other important motives that are often only indirectly economic in nature. For example, some hospitals have viewed diversification as "a means of building an integrated health care system" that will enhance the quality of each phase of care represented in the system (American Hospital Association, 1988a). In theory, the synergies gained in this way will provide a significant competitive advantage for these systems and for their component parts. Coddington and Moore (1987) offer a more elaborate set of possible motives for diversification that include the following:

- *Community service.* Health care needs of a particular population may go unmet without an organization diversifying to respond to this unmet need.
- *Innovation.* By operating at the cutting edge of new products/services, organizations may be positioned to identify emerging business opportunities.
- *Risk management.* Health care organizations can minimize overall organizational financial risk by spreading risks among a variety of activities and markets.
- *Medical staff relations.* Diversification into services that members of a medical staff either want to provide or want to have available to their patients (e.g., a substance abuse treatment unit) can improve the relationship between an organization and its medical staff.

While these and other factors have contributed to the impetus to pursue diversification strategies, we must not forget that diversification is spurred most forcefully by the need to improve the bleak financial picture that can face a hospital that relies solely on traditional revenue sources. This fact must be kept in mind later when we are considering the success or failure of hospital diversifications.

THE CONTEXT OF HOSPITAL DIVERSIFICATION

Contributing to the enormous volume of hospital diversifications in recent years is the fact that hospitals have been relatively unfettered in their attempts to diversify into new products/services or into new markets. Given the tremendous stock of technology, human resources, and management and patient care expertise present in most hospitals, it is quite natural for hospital managers to seize opportunities to deploy these assets, especially when they are closely related to core patient care activities. Furthermore, because many diversifications are programmatic in nature and may not need large amounts of expensive physical space, regulatory constraints, which tend to focus on "brick and mortar" projects in the health sector, have been rather limited.

Obviously, however, hospitals wishing to diversify are not completely unfettered. They face the same capital, competitive, and market opportunity constraints that any firm faces when contemplating diversification. Beyond this, health care organizations face certain other unique constraints. Two of these — one that has been in effect for quite a long time and another that is just emerging — deserve comment here because they help explain some of the choices hospital managers make in their diversification strategies.

A longstanding constraint on strategies to fit hospitals to the opportunities inherent in existing markets or to expand markets lies in the fact that voluntary (i.e., private, nonprofit) ownership and control predominates in the hospital industry. Of the 5,455 community hospitals in the United States, 3,220 of them are voluntary, 1,466 are under state or local government control, and only 769 are investor-owned (American Hospital Association, 1990). Thus, of the total stock of community hospitals, only a few (some of the investor-owned ones) are able to diversify their products/services or to expand into new markets without consideration of the nonmarket issues that accompany their ownership and control. Even among the investor-owned hospitals, which may have more flexibility in strategic decisions, many are the sole providers of care in their communities and can ill-afford to make product/service mix or market adjustments without considering the preferences of the communities they serve.

Hospitals under public or voluntary control are literally locked into certain courses of action and precluded from others. A publically sponsored hospital is subject to a public agenda, which may have little direct relationship to the need to reshape the hospital's product/service mix or to redefine its markets. A voluntary hospital is a social charity, for which it has been granted tax-exemption. But, this privileged status carries with it certain responsibilities and obligations that include providing all the charitable services it can afford; turning away no one it is equipped to serve; and making real efforts to identify and fill unmet community needs, even when this cannot be done profitably. Taken literally, these are very restrictive burdens. They represent limits on the freedom of hospital managers to make diversification decisions on strictly financial grounds.

A much more recent constraint — in fact, an emerging constraint — on the diversification options available to hospitals lies in a recent ruling by the 11th U.S. Circuit Court of Appeals in Atlanta, Georgia (Key Enterprises of Delaware, Inc. v. Venice [FL] Hospital). This ruling could place diversified hospital subsidiaries at risk of antitrust complaints (Green, 1991). The court ruled that Venice Hospital's medical supply business, an activity into which the hospital had diversified, had an unfair competitive advantage in gaining customers when compared to competing businesses not directly associated with the hospital. Many of the most popular types of hospital diversifications in recent years (e.g., home-care services, durable medical equipment services, rehabilitative units, and hospices) could be affected by this decision because of the ability of a hospital's managers and physicians to influence or direct potential customers to these services.

Obviously, diversifications that yield antitrust complaints for hospitals are not likely to be popular. This is not to say that all diversifications will be threatened by this ruling. In fact, while it is a market-by-market situation, in many circumstances it may be possible for hospitals to avoid antitrust difficulties simply by carefully honoring patient and physician choice in selecting from among competing providers of services, never disparaging competitors, and making no claims for their services that cannot be fully substantiated. On the other hand, it is likely that this ruling, which grows from the unique relationship between hospitals and their "customers," will have a chilling effect on some hospital diversification plans.

In the next section we will explore in more detail the nature of the specific diversification activities hospital managers have undertaken. Then, we will be in a position to make some judgments about the outcome achieved through these activities.

TYPES OF HOSPITAL DIVERSIFICATION ACTIVITIES

While hospitals have a large menu of diversification opportunities, there are only four basic categories, or types, of diversification strategies open to any organization (Holt, 1990). As we will see in this section, over the past decade hospitals have exhibited considerable activity in three of the four categories.

Product/Service Diversification

This strategy entails expanding into new product/service lines, either through internal development or through acquisition. Product/service development is the most common form of hospital as well as business diversification. Hospitals have also diversified by acquiring organizations with products/services that they wish to add to their existing mix. The opportunity for product/service diversification, whether by internal development or acquisition, is limited only by the range of products/services the diversifying hospital does not already offer.

Prominent examples of product/service diversifications seen in the past decade include outpatient therapeutic services such as chemotherapy and radiation therapy, outpatient diagnostic services such as computerized tomography scans and magnetic resonance imaging, and outpatient health promotion services such as health screening and fitness centers. In addition, hospitals have a vast array of inpatient services that can be added to allow them to offer an expanded set of products/services to the markets they serve. For example, hospitals that do not already provide such services can diversify into rehabilitation, psychiatric, obstetrical, pediatric, or trauma services.

Market Diversification

This strategy entails locating and entering new markets for existing and/or new products/services. Many of the product/service diversification opportunities previously noted carry with them the opportunity to enter new markets. For example, the addition of obstetrical or pediatric services may open whole new population groups to the services provided by a hospital. Services targeted to the elderly, such as geriatric day care, home-delivered meals for home-bound elderly people, the provision of durable medical equipment, and in-home skilled nursing services, are especially good examples of what can be done simply by targeting a new population group to serve.

Market diversification strategies for hospitals often involve establishing primary care or urgent care centers as satellites of the main facility. These centers serve as sources of new customers both for the new center and for existing services. This form of market diversification works especially well when the centers are located in areas that are not fully served by another hospital, such as in a new population growth center in a metropolitan area.

Market diversification strategies may also mean the establishment of new referral patterns to generate patients for existing services. This widely used strategy for achieving a larger market share for a hospital's existing set of products/services is based on the fact that markets for hospital products/services can be redefined through patient referral patterns. Driven by certain changes in the health sector, opportunities to reshape referral patterns are improving in many hospitals. One such change, for example, involves the direction in which patient referrals flow. In the past, referrals flowed almost exclusively from routine care to specialty care. This meant that teaching hospitals were the prime beneficiaries of patient referrals. This is now changing. As price sensitivity to medical care increases, relatively expensive referral centers need to be able to refer some of their more routine cases to less expensive affiliated settings. Hospitals that recognize this change and develop workable *quid pro quo* referral arrangements can expand the markets for their existing and new products/services.

Concentric Diversification

This strategy entails developing or acquiring products/services that specifically complement existing ones in order to expand sales to existing markets and/or to penetrate new ones. Characteristically, in pursuing this diversification strategy, the organization remains close to its distinct competencies (Rue and Holland, 1989). Because the provision of health care services involves a remarkably distinctive set of competencies, often protected by licensure and professional dominance and rarely substitutable, it is not surprising that most product/service and market diversification in the health industry tends to be concentric in nature. This proclivity for concentric diversification distinguishes diversification in health care organizations from diversification in other organizations in which sticking to distinct competencies may not be as important.

Most of the examples that have been given here for product/service and market diversifications are concentric, because they revolve around the common core of technologies inherent in providing health care services. Even when health care organizations diversify into nonhealth services, they tend to stick to activities that are related to the activities they undertake in support of their patient care services. For example, hospitals sometimes diversify into businesses that appear to be indirectly related to their core patient care missions but in which they have expertise by virtue of their patient care support operations. These businesses may include providing computer or laundry services or food catering.

Hospitals sometimes enter into extremely complex and extensive forms of concentric diversification. One hospital collaborated with a large multispecialty group practice, a skilled nursing facility, and an insurance carrier to design, produce, and market a managed-care program (Longest, 1990). In this case, the four organizations actually formed what has been termed a quasi-firm (Luke, Begun, and Pointer, 1989). This arrangement permitted each organization to operate independently of one another in accomplishing other objectives but to add a new concentric diversification product (i.e., the managed-care program) to its product/service mix. The hospital in this arrangement was able to diversify without the expense, restrictions, or possible diminution of autonomy and identity that would have been associated with acquiring or merging with the other organizations.

Conglomerate Diversification

A fourth type of diversification, one much less used by health care organizations to date, is *conglomerate diversification*. This strategy entails a conscious effort to develop *unrelated* products/services in unrelated markets. Usually, the motive for conglomerate diversification is the ability of a newly acquired or developed firm or operating unit to meet rather stringent standards of profitability once it is under the control of the diversifying organization (Holt, 1990). In the hospital sector, which is predominantly nonprofit at the institutional level, conglomerate diversification has the purpose of producing money that can be plowed back into activities directly supporting the organization's core mission. Hospitals that have been involved in this type of diversification have usually limited their activity to real estate development.

Having examined the reasons for diversification by hospitals, the context in which they occur, and the types of diversifications undertaken by these organizations, we are now in a position to explore their relative success. Have the outcomes of their diversification strategies been what hospital managers wanted them to be?

OUTCOMES OF HOSPITAL DIVERSIFICATION

In ascertaining the success of hospital diversification strategies, we must first decide what criteria to use in making the assessment. The first impulse might be to conclude that the massive volume of diversification over the past decade is evidence that the strategies are achieving the purposes established for them. Assuming rational decisions are driving this activity, this is probably a reasonable conclusion, at least in the aggregate (across the industry).

At the level of individual institutions, however, a relatively large volume of diversification activity is not necessarily a good indicator of success. In fact, no matter which type of diversification is undertaken by a hospital, there is evidence that a strategy of *fewer* diversifications improves the chances for success in those that are undertaken. It has been shown, for example, that hospitals enjoying relatively good financial health, as reflected in such indicators as increasing operating margins, are less diversified and make more money from their diversifications by concentrating on priority programs where they can gain market share (Moore, 1990). This suggests that the hospitals that succeed with their diversification strategies apparently recognize that

> Danger arises from diversification when the new products or markets differ radically from those the organization has previously known. Management may be unable to function effectively if it employs technology and expertise that is not appropriate for the new endeavor. (Kaluzny and Hernandez, 1988, p. 400)

Clearly, especially at the level of individual institutions, a larger volume of diversification activity does not necessarily equate to greater success in pursuing this strategy. As we noted earlier in considering the impetus for hospital diversifications, the overriding, although not exclusive, objective for these activities rests on their potential to provide new sources of revenue when traditional sources become inadequate. Therefore, the most appropriate way to judge the degree of success of hospital diversification strategies may well be whether or not diversifications contribute needed revenues that exceed the expense involved in their production. That is, are the diversifications profitable or at least offer the promise of profitability if the activity can be sustained through its developmental stages?

Fortunately, some data now exist with which to assess performance along the parameter of contributions to profitability. For the past four years, the consulting firm of Hamilton/KSA has undertaken an annual survey in which this information has been collected. The results of these surveys are reported in *Hospitals* magazine and provide a rather comprehensive picture of the degree of success of hospital diversification strategies.

Drawn from the 1990 version of this series of surveys, Table 1 contains a ranking of the relative ability of various diversifications to generate a profit or to break even for sponsoring hospitals in that year. As can be seen in this table, for more than 60 percent of the hospitals providing them, freestanding outpatient surgery centers, freestanding outpatient diagnostic centers, inpatient physical rehabilitation units, and home health services generated profits in 1990. In all of the other categories of diversification surveyed, except wellness/health promotion programs, the majority of hospitals at least broke even. This suggests that in many cases hospitals may continue these activities until they do produce profits. Yet, as the data in Table 1 indicate, not all diversifications meet the financial objective of profitability in and of themselves. Perhaps some of them never will.

TABLE 1 *Relative Financial Performance of Hospital Diversifications, 1990*

PRODUCTS/SERVICES	PERCENTAGE PROFITABLE +	PERCENTAGE AT BREAK EVEN	= SUCCESS RATE
Freestanding Outpatient Surgery Center	76.4%	18.1%	94.5%
Freestanding Outpatient Diagnostic Center	71.7	18.3	90.0
Physical Rehabilitation	60.5	28.0	88.5
Home Health Service	60.4	27.2	87.6
Cardiac Rehabilitation	42.2	38.5	80.7
PPO	33.9	46.4	80.3
Industrial Medicine	45.5	34.5	80.0
Women's Medicine	39.3	38.5	77.8
Skilled Nursing Unit	39.7	32.9	72.6
Psychiatric	49.0	22.5	71.5
Substance Abuse Treatment Unit	39.2	30.9	70.1
HMO	38.9	27.8	66.7
Intermediate Care Facility	34.2	32.5	66.7
Satellite Urgent Care Facility	41.6	24.7	66.3
Retirement Housing	29.4	35.3	64.7
Obstetrics	37.6	23.2	60.8
Pediatrics	24.7	34.3	59.0
Trauma Center	26.1	31.8	57.9
Wellness/Health Promotion Program	11.0	35.1	46.1

Source: Adapted from American Hospital Association. 1991. "Home Health, Centers Were Financial Winners in 1990." *Hospitals*, 65(1): 27-29.

In some instances, the original decision to provide a new product/service or to enter a new market may have been flawed. In others, circumstances, including the actions of competitors, may have changed along the way. When, through careful screening and selection from among options, good marketing, and effectively managed implementation, a diversification does work, it is clear that it can contribute significantly to the viability of a health care organization by making a direct financial contribution.

Even in the case of wellness/health promotion programs, in which only 11 percent of the responding hospitals had diversified profitably, we can see the capacity to meet objectives other than direct contributions to profitability. Although hospitals were unlikely to make a profit on these activities, and fewer than half of them could break even, more than 70 percent of hospitals surveyed had diversified into health promotion/wellness programs as early as 1987. When asked why in the Hamilton/KSA survey of that year, the answer was that while these services may not make money in a direct way, "they can benefit a hospital by enhancing its reputation in the community and generating referrals" (American Hospital Association, 1988b, p. 64). Over time, these results can translate into a stronger financial position just as surely as does a product/service that is making a more direct and immediate contribution to profitability.

To conclude, product/service diversifications and market diversifications have been undertaken by hospital managers on a massive scale in the past decade. Often these diversified activities have been profitable, or they have achieved break even status with the promise of future contributions to the financial good health of the institutions initiating them. Indeed, against a troubling backdrop of declining revenue from their traditional inpatient sources, diversification into a host of revenue producing activities has become a necessary and successful coping strategy for many hospitals.

REFERENCES

American Hospital Association. 1988a. *Hospital Statistics*. Chicago: American Hospital Association.

American Hospital Association. 1988b. *Vision, Values, Viability: Environmental Assessment 1989/1990*. Chicago: American Hospital Association.

American Hospital Association. 1990. *Hospital Statistics*. Chicago: American Hospital Association.

American Hospital Association. 1991. "Home Health, Diagnostic Centers Were Financial Winners in 1990." *Hospitals*, 65(1): 27-29.

Coddington, Dean C., and Keith D. Moore. 1987. *Market-Driven Strategies in Health Care*. San Francisco: Jossey-Bass Publishers.

"Data Watch." 1990. *Hospitals*. 64(12): 16.

Green, Jeffrey. 1991. "Will Claims of Unfair Competition Hold Up Against Subsidiaries?" *AHA News*, 27(6): 1 and 5.

Holt, David H. 1990. *Management: Principles and Practices*, 2nd ed. Englewood Cliffs, NJ: Prentice Hall.

Kaluzny, Arnold D. and S. Robert Hernandez. 1988. "Organizational Change and Innovation," in Stephen M. Shortell and Arnold D. Kaluzny, eds. *Health Care Management: A Text in Organization Theory and Behavior*, 2nd ed. New York: John Wiley & Sons, pp. 379-417.

Longest, Beaufort B., Jr. 1990. "Interorganizational Linkages in the Health Sector." *Health Care Management Review*, 15(1): 17-28.

Luke, Royce D., James W. Begun, and Dennis D. Pointer. 1989. "Quasi-Firms: Strategic Interorganizational Forms in the Health Care Industry." *The Academy of Management Review*. 14(1): 9-19.

Moore, W. Barry. 1990. "Hospitals Win Healthy Margins by Following Business Basics." *Hospitals*, 64(8): 56-58.

Rue, Leslie W. and Phyllis G. Holland. 1989. *Strategic Management: Concepts and Experiences,* 2nd ed. New York: McGraw-Hill, p. 57.

Shortell, Stephen M., Ellen M. Morrison, and Bernard Friedman. 1990. *Strategic Choices for America's Hospitals: Managing Change in Turbulent Times.* San Francisco: Jossey-Bass Publishers.

> **COUNTERPOINT**
>
> *Diversification is **not** a successful strategy for health care organizations because it does not allow faster entry into growing markets, higher returns, or better financial support for core operations.*

JEFFREY A. ALEXANDER
University of Michigan

Jeffrey A. Alexander received a Ph.D. in Sociology (organization theory) from Stanford University in 1980, after earning a master's degree in Health Services Administration from Stanford in 1976. Before going to the University of Michigan, he taught in a number of academic settings, including the University of California at Berkeley, Northwestern University, and the University of Alabama at Birmingham. Dr. Alexander also served as assistant director and senior researcher at the Hospital Research and Educational Trust, an affiliate of the American Hospital Association. His teaching and research interests focus on the organization, management, and performance of health delivery organizations, including hospitals, multihospital systems, and patient care units. Within this broad area, he is interested in questions concerning the relationship of organizational environments and structural change, interorganizational relationships (e.g., multi-institutional systems, contract management arrangements), professionals in management roles, and health care governance.

INTRODUCTION

In the eyes of many, diversification has been the dominant strategy of the 1980s among health care organizations — a response to the downsizing of inpatient care and increased competition from alternative providers (Cottington, Palmquist, and Trollinger, 1985; Vraciu, 1985; Clement, 1987, 1988a, 1988b; Conrad, et al., 1988; and Shortell, et al., 1987). Theoretically, the motivations for diversification among health care organizations are compelling. Offering products and services that differ in their production technology and markets from those related to the core business of the organization has been touted to be an effective means of changing the environmental circumstances under which an organization operates. Health care organizations faced with increasing competition and scarce resources may seek more munificent, less competitive domains for their operations. The establishment of new lines of business with new technologies, markets, or both, in effect, shifts the organizational domain and, presumably, establishes a more hospitable environment in which to operate (Aldrich, 1979; and Scott, 1981).

In a similar vein, as environments grow more competitive and less munificent, organizations may seek to lessen dependence on a single market or product and spread their risk by operating different lines of business in a number of different environmental domains (Rumelt, 1982). Because many health care organizations are compelled by increasing complexity and uncertainty to establish interdependent relationships with other organizations, diversification may afford these organizations the opportunity to obtain resources with less interdependence, thereby preserving their autonomous status (Pfeffer and Salancik, 1978). Finally, when conditions preclude further growth in an industry through an existing market or product, organizations may seek to expand through the development of new products and markets. Conditions inhibiting growth may include market saturation, intense competition, or resource scarcity (Mintzberg, 1979).

Like many other strategies borrowed from the business sector, diversification has gained credence among health care managers largely through the persuasiveness of its logic as opposed to the results it has attained, both in the area of reducing risk and increasing revenue. Unfortunately, mimicry of corporate business practices and strategies has become the norm among health care organizations. Mimetic practices are particularly common when means/ends relationships are difficult to establish, when operating uncertainty is high, or when borrowing becomes more expedient than a close, critical examination of the fit between a particular strategic practice and the conditions under which such practices are adopted. In the remainder of this essay, I will attempt to highlight, in critical fashion, problems with the strategy of diversification that suggest that "diversification is not the panacea that its popularity among some health care managers and consultants seems to imply" (Clement, 1988a, p. 13).

TRANSACTION COSTS OF DIVERSIFICATION

The first, and perhaps most fundamental, point is that diversification varies in the extent to which new markets, products, and technologies are involved. Some have correctly pointed out that diversification might be best seen as a continuum ranging from new business activities that closely correspond to the health care organization's core business to businesses with wholly different technologies and markets (Clement 1988a, 1988b). There is an inherent paradox in the approaches to diversification espoused for hospitals and other health care organizations. On the one hand, unrelated diversification may offer the greatest potential for financial gain and increased revenue streams from businesses that are clearly distinct from the hospital's core line of activity. On the other hand, such activities are fraught with a number of costs and risks, which I will enumerate later. In related diversification efforts, benefits stem largely from the similarity of the technologies, markets, and management skills required to run these activities. Potential gains, however, may also be reduced, owing to the very attributes that make this type of diversification easier to manage. For hospitals and other health care organizations, therefore, the risk/reward trade-off associated with different degrees of diversification would appear to be similar to those in other types of investment opportunities. Greater risks may translate into potentially higher rewards. Thus, the appropriateness of diversification as a strategy for hospitals and other health care organizations must center in part around the answers given to a series of questions: How well is the hospital able to read the market? Who should take primary responsibility for decisions about new lines of business (e.g., individual hospitals, corporate headquarters of systems, CEOs)? How far should the hospital venture out beyond its primary business? Are the management skills, technology, and capitalization of the organization adequate to successfully operate a new line of business?

I submit that the costs and risks associated with diversification (particularly unrelated diversification) are higher than most hospitals and health care organizations can afford and that such costs and risks have not been taken into consideration adequately by organizations engaging in diversification strategies. For many organizations, in fact, diversification may make the already chronic problems related to downsizing, reduced revenue streams, and maturation of the core business of hospitals and health care organizations acute.

The transaction costs of managing a diversified enterprise are considerable. Although those costs associated with managing either market exchanges or interunit transfers inside an organization are usually associated with vertical integration strategies, diversification carries its own set of transaction costs. First, and perhaps most fundamental, is the issue of the adequacy of management skills to operate a new line of business. Health care organizations that have traditionally focused on acute inpatient care may fall victim to a type of organizational hubris if they assume that the management skills required to operate a new line of business can be easily transferred from an existing core business. By definition, new products, markets, and technologies require new management skills, orientations, and training if they are to be an effective part of a diversified array of business activities. More than one diversified organization has failed because it has lacked the management talent to operate multiple types of businesses effectively. Operating the inpatient care side of a hospital, for example, does not equip an organization for running a restaurant or for managing extensive real estate transactions.

ORGANIZATIONAL AND GOVERNANCE COSTS

Beyond the difficulties of managing new lines of business are the costs associated with integrating such businesses into the organization as a whole. These difficulties include the incongruence of goals and objectives between one line of business and another, inappropriate or nonexistent control systems, and inappropriate organizational designs and structures. The case of governance is a good illustration of such dilemmas. For years hospitals have struggled with the questions of the most appropriate governance structures, composition, and roles for effective accountability, strategic direction, and monitoring activity. In diversified health care organizations, these governance issues become compounded and more complex with the addition of new organizations, each of which requires its own governance mechanism and board. How do these boards interrelate? What is the division of responsibility and authority among them? How should the structure and composition of these various governing bodies be constituted? Thus, the already complex, internal transaction costs associated with running any health care organization become exacerbated with the addition of new lines of business that require not only new management approaches and skills but also organizational and governance integration with the core business.

Corporate restructuring also serves to illustrate the costs and problems associated with diversifying. Because of governmental regulations and legal restrictions, health care organizations interested in diversifying often must undergo corporate restructuring or legal rearrangement of the organization's assets and activities into separate corporations before diversifying (Gerber, 1983). The restructuring process often entails a long period of legal groundwork involving attorneys, consultants, and the state in order to make diversification through subsidiary add-ons feasible. The costs and organizational complexities associated with restructuring may often exhaust the health care organization's resources even before the diversification effort begins. Thus, the infrastructure required for diversification can be costly, time-consuming, and add a layer of complexity to the health care organization that may offset any anticipated advantages associated with the diversification effort. Unfortunately, these costs are often not recognized until the organization has invested heavily in the restructuring effort. The past five years have been witness to a number of re-restructurings in which health care organizations have simplified their organizational structures and returned to a business-as-usual approach to delivering health care, because of the operational problems and transaction costs of diversification.

STRATEGIC LIMITATIONS OF DIVERSIFICATION

A second paradox facing diversification efforts concerns the viability of such strategies for particular types of hospitals or health care organizations. Essentially, the dilemma here is that those organizations most in need of enhanced revenue streams from diversification may be least able to engage in such strategies. Rural hospitals are good examples. Many rural hospitals are currently struggling with declining inpatient revenues, aging physical plants, underinsured patient populations, and declining occupancy rates. Some leaders in the health care industry have touted a strategy of diversification for these organizations, advocating entry into long-term care and psychiatric or drug/substance abuse rehabilitation. Whereas there is little doubt that these organizations desperately require enhanced revenues, diversification may not be the panacea and, in fact, may hasten their downfall. One reason why diversification strategies may be inappropriate for rural hospitals has to do with the amount of risk born by these institutions. A rural hospital with $50,000 in operating revenues stands to lose much more from diversifying than a large tertiary care center with $10 million in operating revenues. Given the managerial and transaction costs, coupled with the start-up period for many new ventures, most rural institutions cannot afford to engage in such a risk-laden enterprise. Often, these institutions do not have the sources of capital available to larger facilities and thus do not have access to nonoperating sources of diversification capital.

Hospitals and health care organizations contemplating diversification must also consider the nature and availability of markets for new businesses. For many hospitals, including rural institutions, markets simply do not exist to support a new line of business, however novel or attractive it may appear. This was demonstrated in the 1980s when many hospitals attempted to go into the HMO business only to find out that the population base was not sufficient to sustain a managed-care enterprise. During this period, many other institutions abandoned efforts to operate nursing homes and other long-term care facilities because existing competition had established a firm foothold and had a competitive advantage over hospital-based nursing homes. Admittedly, these constraints may not be faced by larger, better-funded, and better-capitalized health care organizations. However, if these organizations can afford the start-up costs associated with the restructuring and shake-down periods for new enterprises, it would seem that diversification may simply be a way for the rich to get richer, not a survival strategy for hospitals and other health care organizations that operate at the margin.

Other important contextual constraints serve to limit the usefulness of diversification as a strategy for health care organizations. Many, if not most, health care organizations currently operate under the corporate aegis of a multihospital system or parent holding company. These hierarchically structured systems serve to constrain the strategic options available to their operating units (e.g., hospitals) through the imposition of corporate strategies. Indeed, some would argue that diversification is the prerogative of the corporate headquarters of these M-form organizations, not the operating units. At the corporate level of a hospital system, for example, a fundamental strategic consideration is the business or businesses in which the organization should be engaged. The scope and nature of business activity becomes the primary strategic variable to be manipulated at the corporate level. Corporate decisions may impose strategic constraints on the system as a whole and therefore directly influence the operations and strategies of member hospitals in their local markets. The diversification efforts of local operating units must conform to the corporate strategies of the system. At the system level, diversification considerations are made largely in relation to the firm as a whole, as opposed to any one of its operating units. At issue here is the question of whether diversification represents a corporate strategy (What business should we be in?) or a competitive strategy that manifests itself at the local operating level. In the business sector, such considerations have assumed the corporate strategy position, but in the health care sector, many have viewed diversification as a competitive strategy. The feasibility of diversification as a competitive strategy, as we have seen, is subject to numerous constraints and may be available to only a select few health care organizations.

EXPECTATIONS OF DIVERSIFICATION

Many of the problems inherent in diversification among health care organizations relate to the process and uncertainty associated with implementing and following through on new ventures. A recent *Harvard Business Review* article reported that initial expectations about diversification are often too high (Coddington, Palmquist, and Trollinger, 1985). Many organizations fail to anticipate the time it takes to develop a successful new business, and these unrealistic expectations often lead to the failure of the diversification effort. The "diversification as panacea" orientation in many health care organizations causes them to abandon many diversification efforts before sufficient time has passed to achieve profitability. Examples from business suggest that the lead time from idea generation to implementation of a new business is twelve to eighteen months. Additional time is needed to reach a break-even point (two to three years in most cases), and a large portion of new ventures fail all together. These data suggest that health care organizations attempting to diversify need to be sufficiently capitalized to endure long start-up periods and possibly several years of losses from these ventures.

Can health care organizations afford a diversification strategy? In most cases, the answer would seem to be no. The degree of change and turbulence in the health care environment is so great that three-to-five year time horizons are largely unrealistic for many health care organizations. Strategic planning under these conditions bears little resemblance to the methodical formulation and articulation of deliberate, premeditated actions that are then implemented in a systematic fashion. This view of organizational strategies, and of diversification strategies in particular, is unduly restrictive and inconsistent with contemporary forms of organizational operation in the health care sector. Diversification strategies tend to resemble a dynamic process that consists of trial and error attempts at initiating new lines of business with products being added or eliminated on a regular basis with decidedly mixed degrees of success. My position is that only a select few health care organizations can afford to engage in such activities. For the vast majority of hospitals, for example, the notion of engaging in such risky business is clearly beyond the financial and strategic capabilities of these institutions.

Unwarranted expectations regarding the rapidity of returns on investment in diversification activity are exacerbated by inflated notions regarding the rate of such returns. Recently reported evidence in the *Harvard Business Review* suggests that revenues from nonhospital activities will normally "not exceed 10 to 15 percent of total hospital revenues over the three to five years following intensive diversification" (Coddington, Palmquist, and Trollinger, 1985, p. 131). Other evidence on diversified corporations in the business sector suggests that profitability from diversification is not guaranteed (Clement, 1988a). For many health care organizations, therefore, a strategy of diversification becomes considerably less compelling if the expected returns in additional revenue do not justify the transaction costs, risks, and capitalization requirements associated with their start-up and implementation periods.

Diversification, finally, represents a larger issue concerning mission for many health care organizations, particularly those that would consider engaging in unrelated diversification. Diversification ultimately raises the question: What business are we in? That is, diversified health care organizations run the risk of becoming real estate development firms, insurance companies, group purchasing plans, or health care management consulting enterprises to such a point that the core activities of the organizations are subsumed in a broader, and certainly more convoluted, set of activities. At what point, therefore, does the tail begin to wag the dog? Do the intermediate objectives of escaping overdependence on a declining market, moving toward more profitable businesses, avoiding business cycles, achieving economies of scope, and realizing lower debt financing become ends in themselves? Under these conditions, might not the core business of providing high quality medical care to patient populations become subsumed under the larger, revenue-enhancing or profit-maximizing objectives of the diversification effort? Losing track of the mission or core purpose of health care organizations is another, more insidious but no less important, form of risk undertaken by hospitals considering diversification. Health care managers, governing boards, and policymakers concerned with maximizing the community benefits of health services delivery must attend to the risk of diffusing the hospital's core mission and even supplanting that mission with a set of objectives that bear uncanny and uncomfortable resemblance to the profit maximization goals held by firms in the business sector.

Beyond the implications that diversification may have for mission displacement, such strategies may also trigger adverse responses from policymakers who are closely scrutinizing the tax-exempt status of many not-for-profit health delivery organizations. If diversification places these organizations in a precarious position by operating businesses only tangentially related to health care (e.g., hotels, restaurants, office building management), they will become increasingly hard pressed to justify to the GAO and others their claims that their activities are centered on improving the health status of the community as opposed to generating revenue for the organization. There is little doubt that as more nonprofit health delivery organizations come to resemble their counterparts in the corporate sector through diversification, it will become increasingly difficult to maintain the credible position that their activities result in tangible community benefits. For many health care organizations, this hidden cost can never be offset by the gains that may be realized through enhanced revenues resulting from diversification.

CONCLUSION

In this essay, I have enumerated a number of arguments that suggest that the cost and risks of diversification are greater than the potential gains. Those advocates of diversification may dismiss each argument individually with the claim that organizations must procede cautiously, must employ diversification strategies in a logical, strategic framework, and must be sensitive to the conditions under which diversification can and cannot work. My view, in contrast, is that the collective arguments against diversification are so great as to impose almost overwhelming constraints and costs in this strategy for health care organizations. Whereas any one of the arguments cited in this paper may be countered through logical remedies, most organizations will be confronted with multiple constraints on their actions that will severely reduce the potential efficacy of diversification strategies. The weight of the arguments indicates, in sum, that none but the most well-endowed, financially secure, and market-dominant health care organizations can successfully engage in this strategy. At best, then, diversification might be thought of as a strategy not to increase competition and financial viability among health care organizations, but to secure the dominance of few health care organizations already enjoying powerful positions in their local markets.

I began this essay by claiming that hospitals and other health care organizations tend to mimic the organizational strategies of the business sector. This is perhaps unavoidable for a sector that is undergoing wrenching changes and looks to models of supposedly successful organizational actors. A careful scrutiny of the business sector, however, would reveal that many of the most widely diversified conglomerates have begun to sell off their businesses because of management problems, overextension, and debt-servicing problems. If there are models to be adopted from the corporate sector, health care organizations would do well to view these events as the harbingers of things to come for diversified organizations. Diversification is not the answer for the problems facing many health care organizations today. It is only an elaborate managerial diversion to avoid the more central problems of increasing productivity and accountability in organizations that have traditionally been exempt from such demands.

REFERENCES

Aldrich, H. 1979. *Organizations and Environments.* Englewood Cliffs, NJ: Prentice Hall.

Clement, J. P. 1987. "Does Hospital Diversification Improve Financial Outcomes?" *Medical Care,* 25(10): 988-1001.

Clement, J. P. 1988a. "Corporate Diversification: Expectations and Outcomes." *Healthcare Management Review,* 13(2): 7-13.

Clement J. P. 1988b. "Vertical Integration and Diversification of Acute Care Hospitals: Conceptual Definitions." *Hospital & Health Services Administration,* 33(1): 99-110.

Coddington, D. C., L. E. Palmquist, and W. V. Trollinger. 1985. "Strategies for Survival in the Hospital Industry." *Harvard Business Review,* 63(3): 129-138.

Conrad, D. A., S. S. Mick, C. W. Madden, and G. Hoare. 1988. "Vertical Structures and Control in Health Care Markets: A Conceptual Framework and Empirical Review." *Medical Care Review,* 45(1): 49-101.

Gerber, L. 1983. *Hospital Restructuring: Why, When, and How.* Chicago: Pluribus Press.

Mintzberg, H. 1979. *The Structuring of Organizations.* Englewood Cliffs, NJ: Prentice Hall.

Pfeffer, J., and G. Salancik. 1978. *The External Control of Organizations.* New York: Harper and Row.

Rumelt, R. P. 1982. "Diversification Strategy and Profitability." *Strategic Management Journal,* 3(4): 359-369.

Scott, W. R. 1981. *Organizations: Rational, Natural, and Open Systems.* Englewood Cliffs, NJ: Prentice Hall.

Shortell, S. M., E. M. Morrison, S. L. Hughes, B. S. Friedman, and J. L. Vitek. 1987. "Diversification of Health Care Services: The Effects of Ownership, Environment, and Strategy." *Advances in Health Economics and Health Services Research,* 7(3): 3-40.

Vraciu, R. A. 1985. "Hospital Strategies for the Eighties: A Mid-Decade Look." *Healthcare Management Review,* 10(4): 9-19.

> **ISSUE TWO**
>
> *Cooperative strategies enhance the competitive capabilities of health care organizations to provide quality services in a dynamic environment that is characterized by increasing service expectations and limited resources.*

Conventional thinking in the United States suggests that each organization is responsible for its own success. In actuality, every organization is part of a collection of organizations that influence one another. Increased awareness of this interdependence is giving new importance to these links. More and more, health care managers are realizing that strategic alliances and cooperative strategies may be used to reinforce key partners, facilitate strategic networks, and link with others to inhibit major competitors (Lewis, 1990).

Alliances and cooperative strategies are contractual agreements between two or more parties that pool resources for specific projects to achieve common purposes. Strategic alliances are different from formal joint ventures because alliances typically do not establish a new corporate entity (Paap, 1990). Although the allied organizations work closely together and cooperate, they remain independent.

Typically, the rationale underlying strategic alliances and cooperative strategies has been to obtain grant monies, strengthen suppliers to project long-term supply, simplify logistics, share technological know-how, develop new products and markets, provide more bargaining power, block access to scarce resources, raise market entry barriers, and force competitors to follow an organization's lead (Lewis, 1990). Cooperative strategies may be initiated with suppliers, customers, universities, governments, or competitors.

In the past decade, there has been significant restructuring within the health care industry. Strategic alliances, organizational networks, and cooperative strategies have become commonplace. Cooperative strategies have been formed under such names as voluntary multi-institutional systems, partnerships, cooperatives, affiliations, consortia, confederations, coalitions, councils, networks, and alliances. Such cooperative efforts have influenced the nature of competition within the health care industry.

Several alliances, such as the Voluntary Hospitals of America (VHA) with 831 not-for-profit hospitals and American Healthcare Systems (AmHS), a private, for-profit alliance owned by 38 not-for-profit systems, are multimillion-dollar businesses wielding considerable purchasing clout (Lutz, 1990). Recently, however, formation of strategic alliances and cooperatives has been most pronounced among rural health care organizations, principally hospitals, that have associated in record numbers. These cooperative strategies offer the advantages of multihospital systems while avoiding many of the problems and financial risks of these systems. Rural health care alliances typically have about fifteen member institutions and often have an urban member linkage (Lutz, 1991).

It appears that strategic alliances and cooperatives will continue to be formed and will alter the competitive balance within the health care industry. Have such strategies benefited the public? Have such alliances created unfair advantages for alliance members? Have the benefits of the increased power of alliance members been passed on to consumers? Are there antitrust issues that should be considered?

In exploring the issue of cooperative strategies, Arnold D. Kaluzny, of the University of North Carolina, and Howard S. Zuckerman, of Arizona State University, propose that new organizational forms and configurations of resources are required to address today's health care challengers. James W. Begun, of Virginia Commonwealth University, takes the other side of the issue, suggesting that cooperative strategies are the result of a lack of marketplace discipline and that such alliances are too complex, inflexible, inefficient, and slow moving.

REFERENCES

Lewis, Jordan D. 1990. "Using Alliances to Build Market Power." *Planning Review,* 18(5): 5-9, 48.

Lutz, Sandy. 1990. "Tracking America's Two Largest Alliances." *Modern Healthcare,* 20(14): 26-36.

Lutz, Sandy. 1991. "Hospital Alliances Are Taking Root in Rural America." *Modern Healthcare,* 21(5): 41-42.

Paap, Jay E. 1990. "A Venture Capitalist's Advice for Successful Strategic Alliances." *Planning Review,* 18(5): 20-22.

POINT

Cooperative strategies enhance the competitive capabilities of health care organizations to provide quality services in a dynamic environment that is characterized by increasing service expectations and limited resources.

ARNOLD D. KALUZNY
University of North Carolina

Arnold D. Kaluzny is a professor in the Department of Health Policy and Administration, School of Public Health at the University of North Carolina at Chapel Hill, and directs the program on health care organizations at the University's Cecil G. Sheps Center for Health Services Research. His research interests involve technology assessment, implementation, program evaluation and organizational innovation and diffusion. Dr. Kaluzny received his undergraduate education in economics and chemistry at the University of Wisconsin at River Falls and a master's degree in Hospital Administration from the University of Michigan, where he also earned a Ph.D. in medical care organization/social psychology. He has been the principal and/or co-investigator of several large studies and currently serves as the principal investigator for a large National Cancer Institute (NCI) funded contract to evaluate the implementation and impact of the Community Clinical Oncology Program (CCOP).

Kaluzny is the author of numerous articles and has coauthored several books, including *Evaluation and Decision Making for Health Services* with James Veney, *Health Care Management: A Text in Organizational Theory and Behavior* with Steve Shortell, and *The White Labyrinth: A Guide to the Health Care System* with David B. Smith.

HOWARD S. ZUCKERMAN
Arizona State University

Howard S. Zuckerman's teaching, research, and publications have centered on the strategy, structure, and performance of multihospital systems and alliances. He recently completed a study of alternative models of collaboration among Catholic health care organizations and an evaluation of hospital mergers and consolidations in two-hospital communities. He is continuing his work on the development and growth of strategic alliances in health care and other industries. In addition to journal articles and chapters in various books, he has authored a book entitled *Multi-Institutional Hospital Systems*.

Dr. Zuckerman serves as a consultant to several multihospital systems and alliances across the United States and is a frequent lecturer to health care groups. Before his academic career, he was an administrator with Bethesda Hospitals in Cincinnati, one of the early satellite hospital systems.

Consider a few of the challenges facing health service organizations:

- Changing disease patterns that transcend existing organizational entities, which require new configurations of resources to meet emerging needs.
- Limited access to resources and increased emphasis on cost containment and accountability.
- Increased interdependency between research and clinical service to assure rapid diffusion and utilization of new technology.

These and other challenges cannot be met effectively with the existing organizational arrangements. A new organizational form is required to meet the unrelenting demands of cost containment, improved quality, and technology transfer. Increasingly, this role is being assumed by strategic alliances, those loosely coupled arrangements among existing organizations designed to achieve some long-term strategic purpose not possible by any single organization (Zuckerman and Kaluzny, 1991). These alliances vary in configuration, ranging from fairly simple exchange networks in which there is an informal, loosely linked group of organizations having relationships of preferred exchanges to formal interorganizational units jointly producing a product or service in pursuit of a common goal (Alter and Hage, 1991). Moreover, these forms cover a wide variety of service areas. Most are hospital alliances that represent formally organized groups of hospitals or hospital systems that have come together for specific membership purposes with specific membership criteria. Alliances are pervasive, however, in other service areas, including human service agencies and the procurement and distribution of organs (Alter and Hage, 1991; Prottas, 1989). Alliances are also used to accrue patients for cancer treatment and control trials and in the study of clinical research on AIDS (Fennell and Warnecke, 1988; Kaluzny et al., 1989; Veney, Simpson, and Jacobson, 1991).

In part, the emergence and prominence of alliances in all service areas at this point in time is a function of individuals and technological environments (Alter and Hage, 1991). As a result of educational achievements and exposure to the world through travel and the media, individuals have developed more complex cognitive processes and structures, making them better able to conceptualize and implement network arrangements. Moreover, the emergence of new knowledge, technology, occupations, and changing environments have stimulated the search for new organizational forms. Given the complexity and uncertainty of the future, strategic alliances provide a set of characteristics that uniquely qualify them to meet these challenges. These characteristics include partnership arrangements, the ability to transcend existing structural inertia, and a fundamental emphasis on commitment, not control.

PARTNERSHIP ARRANGEMENTS

The complexity of the problems clearly facing health services demonstrates that existing organizational forms do not have the required resources to resolve many of the challenges. In the area of cancer treatment and control, for example, the difficulty of providing state of the art therapy, let alone appropriate early detection and control regimens, requires a new organizational form beyond existing hospital, HMO, and other provider configurations. What is required is a configuration that accommodates the growing need for interdependency between relevant providers and organizations while still permitting a substantial amount of organizational and provider independence and autonomy. Thus, to meet this need, we have seen emerge the Community Clinical Oncology Program (CCOP), sponsored by the National Cancer Institute (NCI), which is designed to link the development and application of protocols for cancer treatment and control with service delivery organizations. Each component — individual CCOPs, designated research bases, and NCI Division of Cancer Prevention and Control (NCI/DCPC) — in this three-part alliance has a complementary role in the overall mission of the program. Close interdependencies exist among these components. The research bases are responsible for developing specific protocols for treatment and control. In turn, these are reviewed by the NCI/DCPC and then implemented within the CCOPs. Each component is critical to overall success, and the success results from the interdependencies among the components.

Interdependencies are also demonstrated through several initiatives of hospital alliances. American Healthcare Systems (AmHS) and SunHealth, for example, have engaged in corporate partnerships with major vendors, characterized by long-term, close relationships in rather sharp contrast to traditional buyer-seller arrangements. These two alliances are building a relatively small and exclusive group of vendors who provide a broad range of products at competitive prices as well as other value-added services. General Medical, for instance, provides SunHealth hospitals with just-in-time and stockless inventory systems while serving as product distributor. Baxter International is exploring venture opportunities to enhance revenues of AmHS member systems.

The development of regional networks, initiated by Voluntary Hospitals of America and SunHealth, also speaks to the notion of interdependency. In this case, the interdependencies arise from relationships between the alliance members and other organizations in the same service area. Thus, the effort is to link several levels of the production process to create a regional integrated delivery system.

In each of these illustrations, it is worthwhile to note that the partnerships are built on relationships between organizations within a given alliance and also between alliance members and other stakeholder organizations. It is especially instructive to note that such interdependencies are based not on common ownership, but on high interdependency and mutual benefit. This is the thrust of what have been referred to as "value-adding partnerships" (Johnston and Lawrence, 1988). In such partnerships, each unit in the value-adding chain has a stake in the success of the others, and it is recognized that threats to any part of the chain effects the entire chain.

TRANSCENDING EXISTING STRUCTURAL INERTIA

Existing organizational forms have the potential for change; however, such change capability is usually inhibited by structural inertia. That is, the very complexity of the existing structures and the vested interest within these structures make it very difficult to initiate needed activities. Under the demands for control, even well-meaning managers usually limit the development of needed activities within the organization. The alternative is to develop a new configuration that will add value to the activities of existing organizations. Clearly, then, alliances are in a position to assist their members in a variety of ways. Alliances can add value to their members by taking advantage of economies of scale through such efforts as group purchasing or by making available state-of-the-art technology to individual communities that would not have the advances without the alliance. While such programs may provide a threshold of performance, alliance activities beyond this base may be equally important. To the extent that alliances can add value by helping their partners cope with key strategic issues, there can indeed be enduring value added.

Strategic alliances provide the structure necessary to go beyond the current functions or perspective of existing organizations. For example, alliances can use economies of scale to accrue value to members in a variety of ways. Group purchasing, which takes advantage of the size and power of the buying group, has proven to be a compelling argument for alliance participation. Returns in the form of cost reductions and dollar savings from joint purchasing of medical/surgical supplies, pharmaceuticals, and capital equipment among other things are reported to be substantial. Likewise, premium dollars for various types of insurance coverage are reduced through group efforts. Economies of scale are observable not only in terms of reducing costs but also in generating revenues. Centralized cash management programs, for example, command high rates of interest for the large sums deposited by alliance members. Further, alliances may use their scale in an attempt to wield political power and gain influence in public policy.

Alliances also add value through a broad array of programs and services available to the membership. These may include management services (planning, marketing, management, engineering), technical services (equipment repair and maintenance), human resources services (recruitment, education, training), and financial services (tax-exempt financing, bond insurance).

In an increasingly technological age, alliances serve the participating members by increasing their knowledge of new clinical and managerial technologies. For example, through the clinical trials and technology assessment programs, the Premier Hospitals Alliance and the University Hospital Consortium, help member hospitals to remain at the forefront of technological development, innovative therapies, investigational drug treatments, and new drug delivery systems. Similarly, the CCOP program provides a vehicle by which to assure the availability of state-of-the-art cancer treatment and control to local communities.

Alliances further benefit members by helping to cope with key strategic issues. To illustrate, several alliances, notably Voluntary Hospitals of America and SunHealth, have embarked on the development and support of integrated regional networks, often with the member hospital as the hub of the network. Such networks are designed to enhance the market position of alliance members.

Often overlooked as a value of strategic alliances is the role that such organizations can play in the adoption and diffusion of innovation. E. M. Rogers (1983), defining diffusion as the process by which innovation is communicated among organizational members, suggests that organizations with both *ad hoc* and routinized linkages among members will be able to more rapidly diffuse innovation. It follows that alliances, which often have both mechanisms in place, will be in a position to more rapidly disseminate information concerning innovation, new technology, new management approaches, and the like.

The notion of "pooled interdependence" describes nicely the relationships that often exist within an alliance. The performance of each individual organization, at least to some extent, affects that of the alliance. Such pooled interdependence often leads to stronger communication linkages, which in turn are often found in organizations characterized as tending to learn about innovations sooner, have stronger diffusion effects, and adopt innovations more rapidly (Anderson and Jay, 1985; Becker, 1970; Coleman, Katz, and Menzel, 1966; Rogers, 1983). Information linkages in alliances are strengthened if they are horizontal or lateral (among members) as well as vertical (between members and the corporate office) (McKinney, Kaluzny, and Zuckerman, 1991). In these situations, alliances can further influence innovation awareness and the range of innovation choices available to members by increasing the opportunities to share innovations that evolve from within the membership as well as innovations from outside the alliance.

Finally, it is evident that many alliances seek to facilitate the diffusion of innovations through a variety of integration-enhancing mechanisms, such as newsletters, forums and councils, educational programs, joint projects among members, and other vehicles to share information. Research by Anderson and Jay

(1985), Kimberly (1978), Zmud (1983), and McKinney, Barnsley, and Kaluzny (in press) all indicate that the greater the availability of such mechanisms and activities, the greater the likelihood that there will be greater use and earlier implementation of innovations.

COMMITMENT NOT CONTROL

To meet the future challenges within health services, organizations must make a fundamental shift in how they do business. The complexity and dynamics of present and future environments require an internal fluidity. Managing such complexity requires more than a set of rules and regulations. It requires a unified vision based on commitment to common values and an accountability exacted through communications and information.

This notion of commitment represents a paradigm shift in management thinking, which has been long dominated by control models (Kaluzny, 1989; and Walton, 1985). In other industries and in other countries, this shift has been driven by the globalization of markets, the emergence of foreign competitors, and the costs, complexity, time, and risk involved in the development of new technology. Thus, one observes an array of cooperative strategies emerging among organizations. Such strategies involve not ownership or control, but rather trust, commitment, shared risk, and common purposes. As Ohmae has noted, "companies are beginning to learn what nations have always known — in a complex uncertain world, filled with dangerous opponents, it is best not to go it alone" (Ohmae, 1989, p. 145).

Health care organizations are not immune from such environmental and market forces. Pressures to reduce the rate of increase in costs, improve quality, and increase access and availability, while attempting to respond to changes in payment systems, conflicting regulatory and competitive initiatives, and limited resources, have led organizations to seek new ways of managing. Alliances have emerged as an attractive organizational alternative, calling for interdependence among partners but allowing retention of substantial degrees of flexibility, autonomy, and independence.

Commitment is the underlying philosophical base and organizing principle for strategic alliances. Commitment can prove to be a powerful force in alliance cohesiveness over time. However, alliance members will have to strive constantly to maintain commitment. In turn, the alliance will have to demonstrate value added as the criteria against which commitment will be measured.

Thus by the nature of their structure, alliances illustrate that the resolution of these challenges requires a management built on a commitment to common values and accountability. Strategic alliances provide a means of sharing risks and control with partners in the alliance. As described by Ohmae:

> Good partnerships, like good marriages, don't work on the basis of ownership or control. It takes effort and commitment and enthusiasm from both sides if either is to realize the hoped for benefits. You can not own a successful partner any more than you can own a husband or a wife (Ohmae, 1989, p. 154).

SUMMARY AND CONCLUSION

Health services face unprecedented change; the problems are unique and the resolution of such problems require unique solutions. Strategic alliances provide the vehicle whereby it is possible to access existing resources in a timely fashion and address critical problems with a new configuration of resources. Whether strategic alliances will be effective or whether they represent the optimal model is unclear. Nevertheless, strategic alliances represent unique opportunities that have proven effective in other sectors of our society. Failure to apply these concepts to health services would be a missed opportunity for meeting the challenges of the future.

REFERENCES

Alter, C., and J. Hage. 1991. "Organizations Working Together: Coordination in Interorganizational Networks." Unpublished manuscript.

Anderson, J. G., and S. J. Jay. 1985. "The Diffusion of Medical Technology: Social Network Analysis and Policy Research." *The Sociological Quarterly*, 26(1): 49-64.

Becker, M. H. 1970. "Factors Affecting Diffusion of Innovations Among Health Professionals." *American Journal of Public Health*, 60(2): 294-305.

Coleman, J. S., E. Katz, and H. Menzel. 1966. *Medical Innovation: A Diffusion Study*. Indianapolis, IN: Bobbs-Merrill.

Fennell, M., and R. Warnecke. 1988. *Diffusion of Medical Innovation: An Applied Network Analysis*. New York: Plenum Press.

Johnston, R., and P. R. Lawrence. 1988. "Beyond Vertical Integration: The Rise of Value-Adding Partnerships." *Harvard Business Review*, 66(4): 94-101.

Kaluzny, A. D. 1989. "Revitalizing Decision Making at the Middle Management Level." *Hospital & Health Services Administration*, 34(1): 39-51.

Kaluzny, A. D., T. R. Ricketts, R. Warnecke, L. Ford, J. Morrissey, D. Gillings, E. J. Sondik, H. Ozer, and J. Goldman. 1989. "Evaluating Organizational Design to Assure Technology Transfer: The Case of the Community Clinical Oncology Program." *Journal of the National Cancer Institute*, 81(22): 1717-1725.

Kimberly, J. R. 1978. "Hospital Adoption of Innovation: The Role of Integration into External Informational Environments." *Journal of Health and Social Behavior*, 19(4): 361-373.

McKinney, M. J., J. Barnsley, and A. D. Kaluzny. In press. "Organizing for Cancer Control: The Diffusion of a Dynamic Innovation in a Community Cancer Network." *International Journal of Technology Assessment in Health Care*.

McKinney, M. M., A. D. Kaluzny, and H. Zuckerman. 1991. "Paths and Pacemakers: Innovation Diffusion Networks in Multihospital Systems and Alliances." *Healthcare Management Review*, 16(1): 17-23.

Ohmae, K. 1989. "The Global Logic of Strategic Alliances." *Harvard Business Review*, 67(2): 143-154.

Prottas, J. 1989. "The Organization of Organ Procurement." *Journal of Health Politics, Policy, and Law*, 14(1): 41-55.

Rogers, E. M. 1983. *Diffusion of Innovations*, 3rd ed. New York: The Free Press.

Veney, J. E., K. N. Simpson, and J. C. Jacobson. August 27, 1991. Evaluation Design for Community Programs for Clinical Research in AIDS. Final Report under Contract No. MD12048, submitted to the Community Clinical Research Branch, Division of AIDS. NIAID, NIH, Bethesda, MD. The North Carolina Public Health Foundation, School of Public Health, University of North Carolina at Chapel Hill.

Walton, P. E. 1985. "From Control to Commitment in the Workplace." *Harvard Business Review*, 85(2): 76-84.

Zmud, R. W. 1983. "The Effectiveness of External Information Channels in Facilitating Innovation Within Software Development Groups." *MIS Quarterly*, 7(2): 43-58.

Zuckerman, H. and A. D. Kaluzny. 1991. "Strategic Alliances in Health Care: The Challenges of Cooperation." *Frontiers of Health Services Management*, 7(3): 3-23.

ADDITIONAL REFERENCES

Cohen, A. R., and D. L. Bradford. 1990. *Influence Without Authority*. New York: John Wiley.

Kanter, R. M. 1983. *The Change Masters: Innovations and Entrepreneurship in the American Corporation*. New York: Simon and Schuster.

Kanter, R. M. 1989. *When Giants Learn to Dance: Mastering the Challenges of Strategy, Management, and Careers in the 1990s*. New York: Simon and Schuster.

Lewis, J. D. 1990. *Partnerships for Profit: Structuring and Managing Strategic Alliances*. New York: The Free Press.

Ohmae, K. 1990. *The Borderless World: Power and Strategy in the Interlinked World Economy*. New York: Harper Business.

> **COUNTERPOINT**
>
> *Cooperative strategies weaken the competitive capabilities of health care organizations to provide quality services in a dynamic environment that is characterized by increasing service expectations and limited resources.*

JAMES W. BEGUN
Virginia Commonwealth University

James W. Begun is a professor in the Department of Health Administration, Medical College of Virginia, Virginia Commonwealth University, where he teaches organization theory and design. He received a Ph.D. in sociology from the University of North Carolina at Chapel Hill. Dr. Begun has authored numerous book chapters and journal articles. He is also the author of *Professionalism and the Public Interest.* He is past chairman of the Health Care Administration Division of the Academy of Management and serves on the Dissertation Grants Review Committee of the Agency for Health Care Policy and Research as well as the editorial board of *Medical Care Review*. Begun's interests include the management of clinical professionals and the strategic behavior of health occupations and professions.

The management field, including health administration, is continually swept by faddish ideas that begin with a grain of truth, explode into a frenzy of application, and then retreat quietly from the scene as managers learn that their expectations have significantly exceeded reality. In the past decade, U.S. firms have sought panaceas for success in Theory Z management, the pursuit of "excellence," and most recently, total quality management. Health care organizations in large numbers have pursued these fads, along with a number of ideas specifically peddled to health care managers.

Guest relations and product-line management are among the latest ideas to cycle through the health care industry. Needless to say, a cadre of academics and consultants (or, worst of all, academic consultants) is always available to push the latest fad onto organizations.

Into the quick-fix management grab bag has entered the notion that cooperative strategy, rather than competitive strategy, will lead troubled firms to wealth and stability. The notion was popularized in the late 1980s in Rosabeth Moss Kanter's book, *Dancing with Giants* (1989). Health care academics and consultants have now seized the opportunity to press the case for cooperative strategy in the health care industry.

My reaction to this proposal is a big yawn. Cooperative strategies are joint ventures, affiliations, and other arrangements in which the participating organizations retain their separate legal identities. To the extent that cooperative strategy does improve competitive capability in the health care industry, it has been employed in the industry for decades and is the product of common sense. If, however, cooperative strategy is pursued as something new and important for health care organizations, it can dangerously distract managers from the basic driving pressure in all economic exchanges in our society: the need to clobber your competitors, or at least to behave as if you have that need. This basic driving pressure operates even if an organization holds a monopoly or oligopoly in a market, as many health care organizations do. Even monopolistic markets are contestable. If the current organization does not do the job, the job will be turned over to another organization, or the market will be opened up to greater competition. To maximize effectiveness, the monopolist organization must act as if it were continually threatened. Even the U.S. Postal Service, an extremely entrenched monopoly, has been threatened with loss of its position.

The basic task of strategists in health care organizations is to create competitive advantages for their organizations. To do so, strategists must focus on the goals of their own organizations, not the goals of other organizations. To complicate an organization's vision of its self-interest can cause all kinds of problems inside and outside the organization. Pursued on a widespread basis, cooperative strategies undermine the very nature of an organization and the nature of a competitive economic system. Several illustrations of the folly of cooperative strategy follow.

LEGAL CONCERNS

A quite practical reason for avoiding cooperative strategy is that its pursuit will contribute to the nation's outlandish oversupply of lawyers. In defining the principles of a free-market economic system, our legislators have set a few rules that are in concert with free-market economic theory. They have passed laws that will discourage collusion among competitors. There is an obvious reason for this. What's comfortable for competitors (collusion) does not benefit society in the form of greater efficiency, innovation, and abundance of services. The pursuit of cooperative strategy can lead to prosecution for price-fixing, boycotting, and division of territories or services (Montgomery, 1991).

A hoard of tax attorneys and health antitrust experts is available to assist organizations in creating complex cooperative arrangements that help to minimize tax liabilities, legal liabilities for the actions of cooperative groups, and antitrust problems. These problems can include charges of fixing prices, lessening competition, dividing markets, limiting expansion into new markets, and restricting cooperative members from competing with the cooperative venture (Rosenfield, Mancino, and Miller, 1987; and Sneed and Marx, 1990). Well-paid lawyers no doubt can construct joint venture and affiliation agreements that skirt around the edges of laws and regulations, but the risk of legal challenges and their resulting expensive litigation should be sobering to any organization.

Antitrust laws are procompetition laws. Their purpose is to allow the free-market system to work effectively. If the board and CEO of Hospital X want to shape a more rational health care system in their community, cooperation and collusion with competitors is not the answer. Their job is to run a better hospital than Hospital Y down the street so that consumers flock to Hospital X. If Hospital Y loses business, then good for Hospital X and good for the community.

COOPERATIVE STRATEGY IS COSTLY

Cooperative arrangements are extremely costly to maintain. Mechanisms for decision making among representatives of legally autonomous organizations must be invented, often by trial and error. Turnover in the personalities involved can sabotage relationships. Monitoring of participants is often necessary, and if slackards or frauds are discovered, the question of sanctions must be addressed. The process hassles are tremendous. Even in group purchasing cooperatives, members often will forsake the group vendor for better deals, which forces the cooperative to develop sanctions. For example, American Healthcare Systems, an alliance representing over 1,000 nonprofit hospitals, recently had to design a sanctioning system and its attendant bureaucracy to deal with violators of its group purchasing plan.

Because cooperative strategies introduce new bureaucracy, conflict, and indecision, they raise health care costs. Conflict resolution, communication, and coordination among legally autonomous entities are all quite expensive. The bottom line benefits of many cooperative strategies are easily offset by the costs of initiating them and managing the process.

COMMITTEES CAN'T RUN BUSINESSES

In actuality, cooperative groups are just other types of committees, and we all know how effective committees are at running businesses. Cooperative strategies transfer organizational control from a legally responsible, financially integrated, hierarchically structured entity to a loosely coupled, unstable, undisciplined entity.

Cooperative groups have all the normal problems of committees that function within single organizations as well as additional problems brought about by the fact that the members represent separate organizations. New committees spend endless time working on mechanics of process and developing trust. Because the members of a cooperative group committee represent different organizations, the organizations may replace their representatives from time to time or may attempt to change the rules of the game. The cooperative group committee often lacks a hierarchical reporting relationship to one decision maker. No one individual is given responsibility and accountability for the committee's work. The performance of members, or the committee as a whole, is rarely assessed. Robert Montgomery, an experienced health care alliance executive, recently cited several examples of failed cooperative ventures and observed that "the graveyard of businesses sponsored by alliances of all types continues to grow" (Montgomery, 1991, p. 26).

COOPERATIVE ARRANGEMENTS FALL APART EASILY

Everyone acknowledges that cooperative arrangements are fragile. Most cooperative arrangements require the active support of CEOs of member organizations. CEO turnover, however, is very high, up to 25 percent per year in the hospital industry. The high turnover in part reflects the fact that organizational strategies in health care are volatile and different sets of strategic skills are required at different times in the same organization. For these same reasons, cooperative arrangements are likely to be appropriate for only short periods of time.

An organization's commitment to its own goals will supercede its commitment to the goals of a cooperative group. Under these circumstances, it is very probable that a significant number of a cooperative group's members will change their strategic goals and modify or withdraw from a cooperative venture. Cooperative enterprises that look phenomenal on paper can dissolve before any of the benefits of cooperation ever emerge.

COOPERATIVE STRATEGY REDUCES FUTURE STRATEGIC FLEXIBILITY

In the turbulent environment faced by most health care organizations, executives are advised to move quickly to create competitive advantages and to maintain the organization's strategic flexibility. Cooperative arrangements inhibit both speed and flexibility. Cooperation slows down or constrains a firm's ability to begin rapid strategic moves. If Joe or Jane Manager is presented with a great short-term opportunity for his or her organization but needs to secure Cooperative Group 6-B's permission to proceed, the deal may disappear. Indeed, Cooperative Group 6-B may not even approve the deal. This is a danger that managers often overlook in the haste to take advantage of a quick opportunity for cooperation. The costs of signing into a cooperative arrangement can be huge when the reduction in future strategic flexibility is considered.

COOPERATIVE STRATEGY IS BORING

Let's face it — cooperation is boring. American managers are trained to look out for themselves and their organizations. To ask managers to give up the thrill of the chase and to cooperate rather than compete with neighboring institutions may appeal to some of those who are in management positions awaiting an academic appointment, but successful managers will strive to further their organization at the expense of other organizations, not with others. That is the nature of capitalism. Competition creates loyalty and team spirit within an organization. It unleashes incredible creativity, drive, and pride not just among the leadership, but throughout the organization. Cooperative strategies, on the other hand, lead an organization's employees to wonder who they really work for and to question their own commitment to the organization.

SYSTEMIC EFFECTS OF COOPERATIVE STRATEGY

Cooperative strategy is attractive to lazy organizations that are not particularly interested in competition. The systemic effects of such organizational laziness are observable from the past history of the hospital industry. Hospitals did not compete. In markets with more than one hospital, cooperation encouraged collusion (e.g., mutual efforts to keep nurses' wages low), the splitting-up of markets, and a benign and comfortable life. Cost increases were passed along to consumers and third-party payers. In such an industry, there was little organizational learning and little incentive for efficiency and innovation. New technologies were purchased with no attention to cost or cost-effectiveness.

In a more competitive market, cooperative strategy is also harmful. It allows weak organizations to survive longer than they should. The whole system suffers because weak organizations are allowed to "feed" off of stronger ones rather than being swallowed up by the stronger ones.

COOPERATIVE STRATEGY MAKES MORE SENSE IN OTHER INDUSTRIES

Cooperative strategy has been oversold to the health care industry. It is another example of a strategy uncritically imported from the business world into the world of health care, as was the case (mistakenly) with product line management. Much of American industry faces significant challenges from foreign competitors. In seeking to enter new foreign markets, it makes eminent sense to temporarily cooperate with foreign partners in order to penetrate those markets. It also makes sense to temporarily band together with competitors to offset the market power of a large, new international competitor or to invest jointly in expensive research and development. Even in those situations, however, the conditions for successful outcomes of a strategic alliance are very limited (Hamel, Doz, and Prahalad, 1989).

International industrial markets bear very little resemblance to health care markets where competitive advantage is established in local geographic areas. Consumers do not travel to foreign countries for most of their health care services. Indeed, they rarely travel outside local markets. The factors that affect the strategic position of a health care organization — the demographic traits of the service population, rival organizations, physician referral patterns, major employers — are found largely within the local geographic area.

In addition, unlike international industrial firms, health care organizations do not have significant investments to make in research and development. Health care organizations rarely need to combine with each other to finance such research. To the extent that local markets are the battleground for health care organization strategy, cooperative strategies are largely irrelevant.

APPROPRIATE ROLE FOR COOPERATIVE STRATEGIES

Health care is clearly not the cutthroat competitive industry that fast foods or automobiles are, nor should it be. There is a place for cooperation among competitors in the health care industry, but it is at the *margins* or in times of *transition*. For decades, cooperative strategy has been at work at the margins of the industry as organizations have legally pooled resources for group purchasing, sharing of expert services, group insurance, and lobbying. These types of cooperative strategies are labeled "service alliances" in the literature, and cooperative organizations like SunHealth and Voluntary Hospitals of America are involved in such service alliance activities (Kanter, 1989; and Zuckerman and Kaluzny, 1991). There is nothing new or controversial or particularly interesting about service alliances. If costs are low, strategic flexibility barely reduced, and other disadvantages minimal, it would be simply foolish not to participate in an alliance.

Opportunistic and stakeholder alliances, the other two types of cooperative alliances differentiated in the literature, occasionally may offer transitory or marginal competitive advantages to health care organizations. Opportunistic alliances — arrangements to take advantage of sudden opportunities — usually only provide transitory benefits, if any, because the market conditions that give rise to sudden opportunities are the same conditions that replace sudden opportunities with new ones. Thus, it is not suprising that opportunistic alliances often fail, as has been the case with many of the joint ventures between hospital organizations and insurance companies to provide managed-care products.

Stakeholder alliances involve more complex inter-organizational arrangements between an organization and its suppliers, customers, or employees. As with other alliances, stakeholder alliances are dangerous if they represent more than a marginal aspect of an organization's strategy. Stakeholder alliances should be a minor aspect of competitive strategy and should be pursued only when they are in congruence with, and subordinate to, preexisting organizational goals and overall competitive strategy. For example, who's to argue if a hospital wishes to enhance its reputation for quality in oncology care, and participation in the Community Clinical Oncology Program of the National Cancer Institute will enhance that goal at low cost (an example of a stakeholder strategic alliance) (Zuckerman and Kaluzny, 1991)? The important points are that such stakeholder strategic alliance participation is really quite marginal to the organization as a whole and that participation flows from previously defined competitive strategy. The appropriate role for cooperative strategy in a health care organization is a marginal and transitory one.

CONCLUSION

The health care system is incredibly bloated with inefficient, underutilized, noninnovative facilities because health care organizations historically have been exempt from marketplace discipline. To exacerbate that situation further through widespread pursuit of cooperative strategies is a recipe for long-term disaster at the managerial, organizational, and societal levels. At the managerial level, health care executives may find themselves facing antitrust suits, boring jobs, and confused organizational allegiances. At the organizational level, health care firms may find themselves too interdependent with other organizations, too complex, and absurdly slow, inflexible, and inefficient. At the societal level, cooperative strategies in the health care sector will contribute to further cost escalation and lost opportunities to improve social welfare through competition. Cooperative strategy is weak from the perspective of public policy, organizational performance, and managerial satisfaction. Let's move on to the next fad.

REFERENCES

Hamel, G., Y. L. Doz, and C. K. Prahalad. 1989. "Collaborate with Your Competitors and Win." *Harvard Business Review,* 89(1): 133-139.

Kanter, R. M. 1989. *When Giants Learn to Dance: Mastering the Challenges of Strategy, Management, and Careers in the 1990s.* New York: Simon and Schuster.

Montgomery, R. L. 1991. "Alliances — No Substitute for Core Strategy." *Frontiers of Health Services Management,* 7(3): 25-28.

Rosenfield, R. H., D. M. Mancino, and J. N. Miller. 1987. "Health Care Joint Ventures." In L. F. Wolper and J. J. Pena, eds., *Health Care Administration.* Rockville, MD: Aspen, pp. 197-213.

Sneed, J. H., and D. Marx, Jr. 1990. *Antitrust: Challenge of the Health Care Field.* Washington, D.C.: National Health Lawyers Association.

Zuckerman, H. S., and A. D. Kaluzny. 1991. "Strategic Alliances in Health Care: The Challenges of Cooperation." *Frontiers of Health Services Management,* 7(3): 3-23.

> **ISSUE THREE**
>
> *The growth of investor-owned, for-profit hospital chains has been a positive influence in the health care industry by increasing competitiveness and lowering costs.*

The purpose of the investor-owned hospital is similar to the purpose of any other private for-profit corporation in that its ultimate goal is to make money for its owners. To some, the growth of for-profit hospitals is no reason for concern. Medicine, after all, has always had some profit orientation. In 1910, for example, almost 20 percent of the medical schools in this country were stock companies, and another 33 percent were "operated by entrepreneurs" who were primarily concerned with making money (Ginzberg, 1988).

Those who believe for-profit organizations are as legitimate in health care as they are in any other industry customarily cite the success of competitive enterprises in gaining access to capital markets without government subsidies, their faster reaction to changing customer needs resulting in a broader range of more relevant services, and the efficient delivery of services resulting from competitive pressures. Critics of a hospital industry dominated by not-for-profit organizations point to an industry that they contend is overbuilt, overequipped, and overstaffed (Cook, 1990).

There are, however, those who are concerned about the growth of for-profit hospitals and health care organizations. Fein (1990) argues that these businesses do not address two of the most important issues in health care: equity in the access to care and consensus about the appropriate level of national health expenditures. The first is not a part of the agenda of for-profit organizations, and the second is believed to disappear in the presence of competition and efficiency.

In addition to the arguments of access and national consensus, critics question the quality of care available in for-profit as opposed to not-for-profit hospitals. Some maintain that the quest for profits provides incentives to cut corners, take shortcuts, and engage in other measures that will reduce the quality of medical care but increase profits. Although the argument is clearly complicated by our inability to agree on precise measures of quality, advocates of for-profit hospitals point to existing research. M.T. Koska quotes an executive with Hospital Corporation of American (HCA) who argues that "there is no reason to believe that hospitals that strive for higher quality will be less profitable . . . it's a mistake to believe high quality care will mean low margins" (Koska, 1990, p. 62). Arrington and Haddock (1990) found no basis for believing that not-for-profit hospitals were more accessible to the indigent and uninsured, invested less in capital improvements, operated any less to maximize physician benefits, or provided superior services.

There are other issues relating to the relative merits of for-profit and not-for-profit hospitals that have potential impact on the quality and quantity of health care in the United States. There is the assumption that for-profit hospitals have inherently better managers because the competitive system attracts the best and most creative administrative resources while the not-for-profit area attracts security seekers and bureaucrats. One of the reasons for-profit hospitals have grown so fast is their acquisition of not-for-profit community hospitals that are in serious financial difficulty. Many smaller communities and rural areas are able to obtain adequate health care only because larger and more financially stable for-profit chains have acquired the local not-for-profit hospital. The for-profit hospital wins because the cost of an ailing facility is often quite favorable, thus allowing substantial profit potential (Manheim, Shortell, and McFall, 1989).

Who really profits from for-profit hospitals? Do not-for-profit hospitals really provide better quality medical care? Are for-profit managers better than not-for-profit managers? Have for-profit hospitals really improved access to care in communities where they have "saved the day" for a dying rural facility? Are costs really lower in for-profit hospitals?

These are the types of important questions that must be addressed in the debate over the relative merits of for-profit and not-for-profit hospitals. This controversy is pursued in greater detail in the discussion by Stephen J. O'Connor, of the University of Wisconsin at Milwaukee, who presents a case in favor of for-profit hospitals not only on the basis of operational efficiency and innovation but also as a possible solution to the problem of some rural hospitals. Samuel C. Webb, of Wichita State University, is not convinced. It is his contention that decision makers in not-for-profit hospitals may have even greater incentives for efficient behavior than managers of for-profit enterprises.

REFERENCES

Arrington, Barbara, and Cynthia C. Haddock. 1990. "Who Really Profits from the Not-For-Profits?" *Health Services Research*, 25(2): 291-303.

Cook, James. 1990. "How Good Are Our Non-Profit Hospitals?" *Forbes*, 145(9): 104-110.

Fein, Rashi. 1990. "For Profits: A Look at the Bottom Line." *Journal of Health Care Policy*, 11(1): 49-61.

Ginzberg, Eli. 1988. "For Profit Medicine: A Reassessment." *New England Journal of Medicine*, 319(12): 757-760.

Koska, Mary T. 1990. "High Quality Care and Hospital Profits: Is There a Link?" *Hospitals*, 64(5): 62-64.

Manheim, Larry M., Stephen M. Shortell, and Stephanie McFall. 1989. "The Effect of Investor-Owned Chain Acquisitions on Hospital Expenses and Staffing." *Health Services Research*, 24(4): 461-481.

> **POINT**
>
> *The growth of investor-owned, for-profit hospital chains has been a positive influence in the health care industry by increasing competitiveness and lowering costs.*

STEPHEN JAMES O'CONNOR
University of Wisconsin – Milwaukee

Stephen J. O'Connor is an assistant professor of Health Care Management in the School of Business Administration at the University of Wisconsin – Milwaukee. He received a Ph.D. in health services administration with a concentration in health care marketing from the University of Alabama at Birmingham. Dr. O'Connor is interested in health care management, quality, and marketing. His articles have appeared in *Journal of Health Care Marketing, Hospital & Health Services Administration, Medical Care Review, Health Services Management Research, Journal of Hospital Marketing, Clinical Laboratory Management Review,* and *Academy of Management Proceedings.*

The American hospital industry is composed of both investor-owned (for-profit) and nonprofit ownership forms. The nonprofit form, which includes both private (voluntary) and public (tax-supported) organizations, has been the mainstay of the industry. During the 1970s and early 1980s, however, for-profit hospital chains experienced phenomenal growth, thus launching an acerbic controversy that continues to this day.

Although each camp has its own vocal supporters, much of the unfavorable commentary has been directed at for-profit hospital chains. Most of these denunciations, which are laden more with emotion than fact, come from physicians — especially physicians in academic medicine (Herzlinger, 1989).

In this essay, I will argue that both the nonprofit and for-profit forms serve necessary and important functions and that the presence of for-profit hospital chains is especially valuable in strengthening the health of the industry and the communities served by promoting competitiveness and cost efficiencies. Furthermore, I will demonstrate that the unwarranted criticisms leveled at for-profit hospital chains have been grossly misdirected. The energy wasted on criticizing could be better used in searching for and demanding comprehensive plans, policies, and laws that address the fundamental inadequacies of our health care system rather than squabbling over the issue of for-profit hospital ownership.

PREVALENCE OF THE NONPROFIT OWNERSHIP FORM

The American hospital industry has always been characterized by a strong nonprofit sector. Why society has been favorably predisposed to this extensive nonprofit presence is an extremely interesting question, especially when we consider that the prevailing ideology of market forces, competitiveness, and the pursuit of profits has worked so well in other enterprises.

The voluntary nonprofit hospital form of ownership has been encouraged and granted tax-exempt status because:

1. It provides a substantial community benefit (i.e., providing and paying for health services to the poor) without the need for much in the way of public expenditures and taxation.
2. It furnishes a setting that supports professional prerogatives, a patient orientation, and high-quality medical care.
3. It allows a diverse assortment of religious organizations and other private community sponsors an opportunity to carry out their ecclesiastical missions and social agendas.
4. It serves as a mechanism by which dissimilar value orientations and contradictory social interests can be accommodated against a backdrop of unclear, unquantifiable, and value-laden public goals (Stevens, 1989).
5. It provides a strong symbolic means by which citizens and community groups can contribute, in the best tradition of volunteerism, time and money to a private organization committed to an unalloyed social good without being forced to do so through taxation (Stevens, 1989; and Sloan, 1988).

AN EXPANDED FOR-PROFIT PRESENCE

Over the past century, a variety of factors and circumstances have emerged to alter drastically the character of American hospitals. First, hospitals no longer serve only an impoverished clientele. Changes in the extended family due to increased urbanization and astounding advances in medical technology have allowed the hospital to supplant the home as the preferred place to receive care. As a consequence, the middle and upper classes, who had previously shunned hospitals, began to use them routinely. Second, by the 1960s, the widespread acceptance of employer-subsidized health insurance along with government's enormously expanded role in paying for health services through Medicare and Medicaid, gave most people (as a virtual benefit of being employed, poor, or elderly) a financial backer willing to pay for their hospital care. Because these people had sponsors, hospitals began *charging* them for care. As charity became socialized through Medicare and Medicaid, the provision of free care naturally declined as did voluntary charitable contributions. The focus of hospitals became less centered on social benevolence and more on the business side of the enterprise.

As financing for hospital services became more widespread and abundant during the late 1960s and 1970s, the health care system witnessed the emergence of a number of for-profit multi-institutional hospital systems or chains. The most notable among these are Hospital Corporation of American (HCA) and Humana. Their astonishing growth and success have provided them with both supporters and detractors.

In 1980, a landmark article by Arnold Relman, entitled "The New Medical-Industrial Complex," appeared in *The New England Journal of Medicine*. Relman described this complex as an expanding "network of private corporations engaged in the business of supplying health-care services to patients for a profit — services heretofore provided by nonprofit institutions or individual practitioners" (Relman, 1980, p. 963). Finding this phenomenon disturbing, he emphasized that the medical-industrial complex should not be permitted to "distort our health-care system to its own entrepreneurial ends" (p. 969). His commentary clearly stated almost all of the fears and criticisms that have since been directed at investor-owned hospital chains. Included among these criticisms is the fear that a single-minded fixation on profits will compromise physicians, negatively impact medical research and teaching, increase costs, endanger the quality of care, and eschew the poor. This fixation on profits, critics argue, could lead to cream-skimming, offering only a profitable mix of services, emphasizing highly lucrative procedures at the expense of personal care, and improperly influencing health policy.

THE PROFIT MOTIVE

Critics fear that for-profit chains with their all-consuming attention to the bottom-line will corrupt physicians, reduce their autonomy, and jeopardize the physician-patient relationship. It is argued that physicians who may be investors in the corporation they work for, will be guided more by self-interest than client needs. Moreover, many people feel that it is unethical for hospitals or physicians to make any profit from sick people (Mershon, 1986). Even though the medical profession has been one of the most entrepreneurial of occupations, reality dictates that, unless heavily subsidized, both for-profit and nonprofit hospitals need to earn profits. Profits are required for such things as asset growth and replacement, debt repayment, periodic staff salary increases, and adjustments for inflation. Profits become especially important when technology is changing swiftly and inflation is high (Sloan and Vraciu, 1983).

Nonprofit hospitals earn what economists call "accounting profits." Accounting profits represent excess revenue over accounting expenses. Because a nonprofit hospital has no shareholders to whom these excess revenues are owed, they can accrue to the organization as "fund balances" (Conrad, 1984). For-profit chains, on the other hand, have shareholders who contribute capital and who expect a return on their investment in the form of dividends and/or growth in the value of their shares. While some sort of profit is necessary in both the for-profit and nonprofit forms, profit is not the principal *objective* of any hospital. According to Levitt (1983), profit is never a purpose but always a requisite. An old saying states, "We must eat to live, not live to eat." Likewise, any hospital, regardless of its ownership form, must earn a profit in order to sustain itself and carry out its mission. However, no hospital (including for-profit hospitals) exists solely for the purpose of making a profit (Bromberg and Goodwin, 1987). David Jones, the chief executive of Humana, explains this issue as follows:

> Profit need not be an end, but it is always a requirement. To offer on a continuous basis high quality service, state-of-the-art technology, stable employment and secure pensions in an uncertain future, any hospital's revenues must exceed expenses. This is true without regard to sponsorship or tax-paying status. (Mershon, 1986, p. 243)

Also, far from corrupting and negatively coopting physicians, for-profit hospitals have done an excellent job in responding to their needs. Recognizing that physicians play a key role in enhancing the hospital's image and in meeting the needs of patients and the community, they have undertaken enormous steps to attract new physicians and maintain excellent relations with those already on staff (Siegrist, 1983).

Case Mix, Service Mix, and Charity Care

Critics have also accused for-profit hospitals of being uniquely prone to cream-skimming and of offering only profitable services. Cream-skimming is the practice of attracting patients who are well insured and whose cases offer high-profit margins while leaving to others the higher-cost, Medicare, Medicaid, or nonsponsored patient. However, empirical evidence indicates that for-profit chains are scarcely different from nonprofit hospitals in this regard (Biggs, Kralewski, and Brown, 1980; Pattison and Katz, 1983). Other evidence indicates for-profit hospitals do not price gouge the favorable patients they are able to attract (Herzlinger and Krasker, 1987). In addition, research in this area has revealed no significant differences between investor-owned and nonprofit hospitals in terms of providing free care (Sloan and Vraciu, 1983; Shortell et al., 1986).

As a matter of survival, both ownership forms are forced to send expensive cases and unsponsored patients primarily to public hospitals. The argument that for-profit chains are more apt to skim cream and avoid unfavorable patients is clearly false. Although the overall amount of free care is not uniformly balanced among all hospitals, "investor owned institutions seem no worse in this regard than voluntaries" (Luft, 1985, p. 15).

Concerns that investor-owned chains will be more reluctant to render unprofitable or highly sophisticated services is also unsupported. Sloan and Vraciu (1983) found no differences in the level of service sophistication available or the propensity to provide unprofitable services between for-profit and nonprofit hospitals.

Quality of Care

Although difficult to square with a strong consumer (physician, patient, payer) orientation and the fact that an association exists between high-quality care and hospital profitability, for-profit chains have been accused of sacrificing quality and necessary patient care to a healthy bottom line (Koska, 1990). Gross indicators of patient-care quality as measured by mortality statistics, however, have shown no significant difference between investor-owned chains and nonprofit (voluntary and public) hospitals (Shortell and Hughes, 1988). Because purchasers have become extremely serious about looking at quality in terms of value, the incentives inherent in the for-profit form of ownership serve to provide patients and purchasers with what they are demanding: the suitable blend of cost and quality that results in greatest value (Lewis, 1989). As many hospitals become immersed in the quality improvement processes professed by W. Edwards Deming and his disciples, the investor-owned Hospital Corporation of America has taken the lead in successfully adopting this process (McEachern and Neuhauser, 1989). Any organization thinking about committing itself to a program of continuous quality improvement would do well to emulate HCA's experience.

Medical Education and Research

Many in the medical profession view a for-profit presence in medical education as a threat to their fundamental value orientation, especially when they have procured a considerable amount of their own training in nonprofit academic medical centers (Feder and Hadley, 1987; Friedman, 1989). Until recently, for-profit hospitals have shied away from connecting teaching with patient care, not because medical education and research are inherent money losers, but instead a remnant of the very high entrance barriers they have had to face since Abraham Flexner's *Bulletin Number Four* assailed proprietary medical schools (Flexner, 1910; Sloan, 1988). In addition, many teaching hospitals have been reluctant to adopt a for-profit presence. The attempt by Hospital Corporation of America to purchase the McLean Hospital psychiatric facility in 1983 is a good example of this reluctance. The practitioners at McLean were so forcefully opposed to a for-profit orientation that they prevailed upon the governing board of Massachusetts General Hospital to reverse the purchase the board had previously approved (Herzlinger and Krasker, 1987).

Since that time, more than twenty teaching hospitals have become affiliated with for-profit chains. Examples of these affiliations are the University of Louisville Hospital and Humana, St. Joseph's Hospital (Creighton University) and American Medical International, and the Lovelace Medical Center (University of New Mexico) and HCA. Humana recently purchased Chicago's Michael Reese Hospital and promises to maintain the hospital's mission of research, teaching, and service to the poor (*AHA News*, 1991). Humana made this pledge even though the hospital lost over $1 million in 1989 and is projected to continue losing money in the near future (Mullen, 1990).

Teaching hospitals will sell to, or contract with, investor-owned chains because of their proven ability to:

1. Sustain high quality services.
2. Continue accessibility to the patient (Bromberg, 1985).
3. Provide needed capital for research, education, and renovation.
4. Increase availability of funds to the medical school.
5. Sustain (not thwart) traditional academic activities.
6. Maintain adequate patient revenues.
7. Provide marketing expertise for maintaining or improving the patient base (Feder and Hadley, 1987).

NONPROFITS: AN ABSENCE OF OVERSIGHT

Many suggest that profitability and efficiency should not be used to judge the performance of voluntary hospitals, especially when these organizations provide good and necessary services to their communities in a spirit of commitment, altruism, generosity, and benign ecumenicism. Indeed, this is why society has granted these institutions tax-exemptions and other favorable legislation in the first place. In reality, however, these institutions misallocate resources, ignore consumer demands (Newhouse, 1970), serve the self-interests of physicians (Herzlinger and Krasker, 1987), and have been largely "income-oriented, exclusionary, and self-serving" (Stevens, 1989, p. 360). The cause is a lack of incentives for the provision of efficient services that are responsive to the broader needs of consumers or the community. Because private nonprofit hospitals lack shareholder or government ownership, there is an absence of scrutiny from equity owners or legislators (Herzlinger, 1987). The net result is that nonprofit hospitals are disciplined by no one.

In contrast, for-profit hospitals are overseen by the equity markets. If efficiency drops and costs become excessive, investors will take their money somewhere else, and more efficient competitors will see an opportunity they can fulfill. This benefits not only investors but also purchasers and users of health care. The continual probing of the equity market forces for-profit hospitals to compete effectively and ceaselessly for markets and earnings. This in turn inspires innovation and change, enhances operational efficiencies, lowers costs, improves access to capital, and provides patients and purchasers with a wider choice of hospital providers.

TAKING THE STRESS OUT OF DISTRESSED HOSPITALS

For-profit chains have been instrumental in breathing new life into rural communities. Numerous nonprofit hospitals in these locales have faced chronically low occupancy rates, expenses that invariably exceed revenues, an inability to raise sufficient capital (Stevens, 1989), and difficulty in interpreting and responding to a rapidly changing environment. For-profit chains not only have nursed these hospitals back to health but also have provided additional benefits to the community.

For-profit hospitals find it easier to gain access to capital than nonprofit hospitals (Ermann and Gabel, 1984). Thus, a distressed rural hospital acquired by a for-profit chain is no longer starved for the capital it needs to service debt and to upgrade its physical equipment and plant. Further, for-profit hospitals provide access to well-trained managers who are knowledgeable in operations, finance, industrial engineering, human resources, marketing, strategic planning, and other important management functions. These managers can improve cash flow by understanding the reimbursement system, being sure they are appropriately reimbursed by payers, and by being aggressive in collecting unpaid bills. They also can help the hospital monitor and control performance through updated budgeting processes and access to state-of-the-art financial sophistication that permits comparisons with other institutions in the chain and to benchmark norms.

Usually, experts in industrial engineering and operations can enhance internal efficiencies and productivity; former staff levels can be substantially reduced. Specialists in strategic planning and marketing can help the hospital decipher the external environment, chart the future, and determine the proper mix of services necessary to meet the health care needs of the service area and to ensure profitability.

Through economies of scale, the for-profit chain is able to permit a newly acquired hospital to spend far less on administrative overhead and still have access to a broad range of excellent managerial talent. The centralized services of the chain leverage the hospital's purchasing power by allowing it to take advantage of enormous volume discounts. In addition, an assortment of other specialized areas, such as law and risk management, computer information systems, and technology assessment, become available to the hospital.

In short, for-profit chains have been able to turn many financially distressed hospitals into attractive, profitable, high-quality, well-managed facilities that are responsive to the needs of the community. When for-profit chains acquire a nonprofit hospital not only do they provide a source of stable jobs that helps to strengthen the economy but the proceeds of the sale usually are used to establish a community foundation. These new funding organizations, freed from the ordeal of having to operate a hospital, have formidable resources available for other pressing needs in the community. Finally, the for-profit hospital serves as a sizeable source of previously unavailable tax revenues. The for-profit hospital, unlike the nonprofit hospital, pays taxes that can be used to fulfill community needs.

CONCLUSION

In this essay I have argued that for-profit hospitals serve a meaningful purpose in the health care system. Proprietary hospital chains provide comparable quality and similar amounts of charity care as nonprofit hospitals. However, for-profit hospitals seem better able than nonprofit hospitals to create efficiencies, access capital, respond to consumer (patients, physicians, payers) and community needs, aid in cost containment, improve overall levels of management sophistication, develop useful innovations, revive distressed hospitals, and restore ailing academic medical centers, including their teaching, research, and indigent care functions. As they do all of this, for-profit hospitals pay a significant amount of tax dollars to the public coffers.

The Best of All Worlds

Clearly, investor-owned hospital chains are an indispensable element of the American health care delivery system. Stevens (1989) claims that competitiveness in this system is enriched by maintaining a plurality of ownership types. She further suggests that voluntary organizations "continue to be the natural alternative to socialism in the United States" (Stevens, 1989, p. 361). But is this the case with voluntary hospitals? A number of factors have contributed to making hospitals operate more like businesses and less like charities. As environmental forces cloud the traditional distinctions between for-profit and nonprofit ownership forms, society increasingly questions why nonprofit hospitals continue to receive extraordinary public benefits, especially tax-exemptions. Like any paradigm that has outlived its usefulness, the model that champions nonprofit hospitals while denigrating for-profit chains is as anachronistic in the 1990s as the belief that the world is flat. Because these outdated world views are encouraged and tend to persist, many modern nonprofit hospitals become increasingly hypocritical in their attempts to rationalize the status quo. According to Fein (1990), just because a hospital has nonprofit status "does not confer the right to claim that it is a paragon of virtue, fully responsive and responsible to the community it claims to serve" (p. 54). In fact, most nonprofit hospitals could switch to for-profit status "without missing a beat" (Friedman, 1989, p. 33).

Society's Responsibility

As I pointed out earlier, a great deal of energy has been expended blaming proprietary hospital chains for the many ills afflicting the health care system. To the extent that this view lingers and society continues to consider health policy primarily within the context of the federal budget, the ills will remain (Bromberg and Goodwin, 1987).

When a health system is guided chiefly by budget deficits, hospitals (both nonprofit and for-profit) are required to bear much of the brunt for those in the population who are unable to pay. All of the competition and pluralism in the health care system will never be able to deal properly with the seemingly endless amounts of free care required if adequate remuneration remains unavailable. Society needs to come to terms with this quandary and may do so in the near future. In the meantime, " 'free' care is free only to those who receive it" (Bromberg, 1985, p. A11).

Society does not expect supermarkets to supply food to those who cannot afford it. Instead, it has permitted for-profit grocery stores to accept food stamps (Fein, 1990). Likewise, access problems are not solely the obligation of those who deliver health care. We should keep this thought in mind the next time we feel inclined to blame for-profit hospitals for the shortcomings of our health care delivery system.

REFERENCES

AHA News. 1991. "Humana Finalizes Its Purchase of Chicago's Michael Reese Hospital." *AHA News,* 27(10): 3.

Biggs, E., J. Kralewski, and G. Brown. 1980. "A Comparison of Contract Managed and Traditionally Managed Non-Profit Hospitals." *Medical Care,* 18(6): 586-595.

Bromberg, M. D. 1985, April 8. "The Business of Health Care: The Profit Motive Can't Hurt." *Washington Post,* p. A11.

Bromberg, M. D., and T. G. Goodwin. 1987. "Ethics and Health Care: The Importance of the Profit Motive." In G. R. Anderson and V. A. Glesnes-Anderson, eds., *Health Care Ethics: A Guide for Decision Makers.* Rockville, MD: Aspen Publishers, Inc., pp. 250-253.

Conrad, D. A. 1984. "Returns on Equity to Not-For-Profit Hospitals: Theory and Implementation." *Health Services Research,* 19(1): 41-63.

Ermann, D., and J. Gabel. 1984. "Multihospital Systems: Issues and Empirical Findings." *Health Affairs,* 3(1): 50-64.

Feder, J., and J. Hadley. 1987. "A Threat or a Promise: Acquisition of Teaching Hospitals by Investor-Owned Chains." *Journal of Health Politics, Policy, and Law,* 12(2): 325-342.

Fein, R. 1990. "For Profits: A Look at the Bottom-Line." *Journal of Public Health Policy,* 11(1): 49-61.

Flexner, A. 1910. *Medical Education in the United States and Canada.* Bulletin 4. New York: The Carnegie Foundation for the Advancement of Teaching.

Friedman, E. 1989. "The For-Profits: Sorting Myth from Reality." *Medical World News,* 30(4): 32-43.

Herzlinger, R. E. 1987, March 23. "Nonprofit Hospitals Seldom Profit the Needy. *Wall Street Journal,* p. 22.

Herzlinger, R. E. 1989. "The Failed Revolution in Health Care — The Role of Management." *Harvard Business Review,* 67(2): 95-103.

Herzlinger, R. E., and W. S. Krasker. 1987. "Who Profits from Nonprofits?" *Harvard Business Review,* 65(1): 93-106.

Koska, M. T. 1990. "High-Quality Care and Hospital Profits: Is There a Link?" *Hospitals,* 64(5): 62-63.

Levitt, T. 1983. *The Marketing Imagination.* New York: The Free Press.

Lewis, S. W. 1989. "Achieving High-Value Health Care in the Hospital Setting." In P. L. Spath, ed., *Innovations in Health Care Quality Measurement.* Chicago: American Hospital Publishing, Inc., pp. 87-100.

Luft, H. S. 1985. "For-Profit Hospitals: A Cost Problem or Solution?" *Business and Health,* 2(3): 13-16.

McEachern, J. E., and D. Neuhauser. 1989. "The Continuous Improvement of Quality at the Hospital Corporation of America." *Health Matrix,* 7(3): 5-11.

Mershon, K. M. 1986. "Dispelling Myths about For-Profit Health Care." *Nursing Economics,* 4(5): 240-244, 264.

Mullen, P. 1990. "Humana's Reese Buyout Stirs Windy City." *Healthweek,* 4(1): 1, 38.

Newhouse, J. P. 1970. "Toward a Theory of Nonprofit Institutions: An Economic Model of a Hospital." *The American Economic Review,* 60(1): 64-67.

Pattison, R. V., and H. M. Katz. 1983. "Investor-Owned and Not-For-Profit Hospitals: A Comparison Based on California Data." *The New England Journal of Medicine,* 309(6): 347-353.

Relman, A. S. 1980. "The New Medical-Industrial Complex." *The New England Journal of Medicine,* 303(17): 963-970.

Shortell, S. M., and E. F. X. Hughes. 1988. "The Effects of Regulation, Competition, and Ownership on Mortality Rates Among Hospital Inpatients." *The New England Journal of Medicine,* 318(17): 1100-1107.

Shortell, S. M., E. M. Morrison, S. L. Hughes, B. Friedman, J. Coverdill, and L. Berg. 1986. "Hospital Ownership and Nontraditional Services." *Health Affairs,* 5(4): 97-109.

Siegrist, R. B. 1983. "Wall Street and the For-Profit Hospital Management Companies." In B. H. Gray, ed., *The New Health Care for Profit: Doctors and Hospitals in a Competitive Environment.* Washington: National Academy Press, pp. 35-50.

Sloan, F. A. 1988. "Property Rights in the Hospital Industry." In H. E. Frech III, ed., *Health Care in America: The Political Economy of Hospitals and Health Insurance.* San Francisco: Pacific Research Institute for Public Policy, pp. 103-141.

Sloan, F. A., and R. A. Vraciu. 1983. "Investor-Owned and Not-For-Profit Hospitals: Addressing Some Issues." *Health Affairs,* 2(1): 25-37.

Stevens, R. 1989. *In Sickness and in Wealth: American Hospitals in the Twentieth Century.* New York: Basic Books, Inc.

> **COUNTERPOINT**
>
> *The growth of investor-owned, for-profit hospital chains has **not** been a positive influence in the health care industry and has not increased competitiveness nor lowered costs.*

SAMUEL C. WEBB
Wichita State University

Samuel C. Webb is professor of economics at the W. Frank Barton School of Business at Wichita State University where he has taught since 1966. He received his Ph.D. in economics from the University of Kansas and his M.S. in business administration and B.S. in civil engineering from the University of Missouri. He teaches managerial economics to graduate students and money and banking to undergraduates. He is the author of *Managerial Economics*. Most notable among his recent journal articles in the area of health care is "Physician Goals: Impact on Hospital Performance" in *Healthcare Management Review*. He is a consultant in the fields of local banking in the area of compliance with the Community Reinvestment Act and economic damages resulting from personal injury and wrongful death.

Wisdom from the past:
>All general judgments are loose and imperfect.
>   Michael De Montaigne, *Essays*, III
>General propositions do not decide concrete cases.
>   Oliver Wendell Holmes, Jr., Dissent, Lockner Case
>No generalization is wholly true, not even this one.
>   Attributed to Oliver Wendell Holmes, Jr.

This paper benefited from comments on previous drafts by several of the author's colleagues at Wichita State University: Randall B. Haydon, Philip L. Hersch, Edwin A. Sexton and John D. Wong. They are not responsible for the paper's shortcomings.

Hospitals are not identical. Diversity among them is so great that blanket statements about them are almost always misleading, especially those alleging that for-profit organizational forms are superior to not-for-profit forms. Some hospitals specialize in certain types of treatment; some emphasize education; some are staffed by persons with altruistic motivations, that is, by persons who are more interested in serving society than in helping themselves. However, when model-building researchers (including myself) turn their attention to comparing the relative merits of different types of hospitals, they stereotype the hospitals in ways that are frequently too narrow. Diversity is subordinated to simplicity, and investigators tend to rely much too heavily upon their training and indoctrination in standard economic theory. Thus, empirical work based upon simple, elegant models is used. Sometimes, the results of associated multiple regressions indicate some degree of statistical significance in selected variables that tends to support the notion that for-profit hospitals increase competition and lower costs in the health care industry. Without doubt, some for-profit hospitals are more efficient in some ways than some not-for-profit hospitals. In other cases, however, the reverse is true, and not-for-profit facilities should be preserved where they serve in superior fashion, especially in markets that are neglected by profit maximizers. As these words are written, there is not enough empirical evidence to support the case for the superiority of for-profit hospitals. Indeed, the preservation of not-for-profit hospitals appears to be in the public interest.

A fundamental problem with many profit-maximizing hospitals is their managers' inherent proclivity to focus narrowly on the bottom line by shirking on quality in the short run and ignoring other important considerations, especially those associated with social costs and benefits (e.g., the careless handling of radioactive wastes). These considerations can have a major impact on profitability over a longer time horizon.

It is possible for an exploitive entrepreneur to take over a public-spirited organization and to squeeze that organization's mission and goals from "providing community service" to maximizing short-run stockholder returns. Costs can be cut dramatically by concentrating on the production of the simplest, easiest-to-provide, and most-profitable services that have the greatest demand. Less-profitable and more complex services to the few can be dropped. Cream-skimming promotes short-run profits; forget the customer/patients who can't pay.

In the limited space that can be devoted to the subject in this essay, a wide range of institutional and managerial goals believed to exist among health care organizations are mentioned. Some of the most important recent empirical studies are mentioned briefly to pique a reader's interest in examining the originals. Conclusions and recommendations are provided.

THE EVOLUTION OF INSTITUTIONAL AND MANAGERIAL GOALS

Prior to World War I, physicians treated affluent family members in their homes. Hospital facilities in the United States were for "poor people who had nowhere else to go" (Vladeck, 1985, p. 116). Hospital revenues came from charity, direct public subsidies, and patient fees, although fees represented a small amount. "Voluntary hospitals were formed with the mission of taking care of the members of a religious, ethnic, rural, or small suburban community to the extent allowed by their own ability to raise revenues" (Webb, 1989a, p. 52). During World War II, physicians became increasingly dependent upon hospitals for their practices, and patient fees increased to the extent that they provided more than half of a hospital's revenues.

Early hospitals have been characterized as benevolent institutions devoted to providing health care to as many patients as resources allowed. Hospital administration and management in the past was not the specialized job it is now. More likely, practitioners (doctors and nurses) gave the orders and did the paperwork themselves in their spare time, or gave direction to assistants. As the simple model shown graphically in Figure 1 illustrates, hospital services were provided at the break-even level, Q_4, where total revenues (TR) equal total costs (TC) and profits (P) are zero.

Hospitals as places of business rather than of benevolent services developed under the influence of government subsidies, tax exemptions, Hill-Burton program grants and loans, and explosions in private insurance and medical technology. Medicare and Medicaid were begun in 1965 to encourage hospitals to extend higher levels of medical care to the aged and indigent with the assurance that government would pay the bills. The promise of increased money flows encouraged the expansion of hospitals and gave birth to the health care industry. Along with the growth in the size and scope of hospitals and other health care facilities grew the need for the specialized skills of hospital administrators and managers. Entrepreneurs

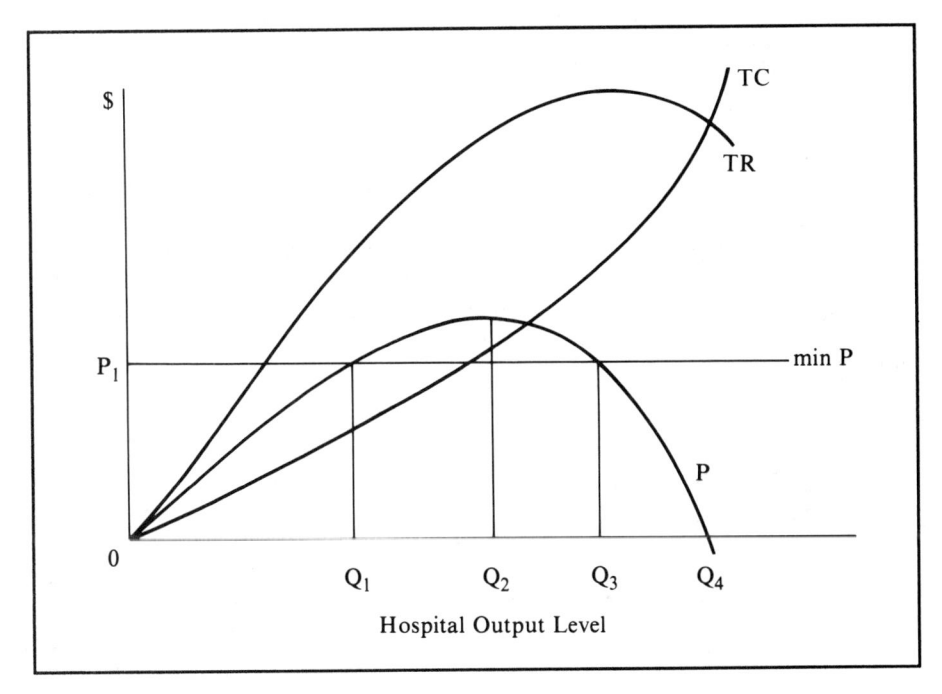

Figure 1 *The Basic Hospital Model*

among physicians, administrators, insurers, suppliers, and others were drawn to the industry by the promise of profits and personal wealth. Today, both movements — the rush for corporate and private gain and the transformation of health care delivery — remain in process.

In terms of Figure 1, the pure profit-maximizing corporation chooses hospital output level Q_2, which corresponds with the peak of the total profit (P) curve. (The P curve is derived as the vertical distance between the TR and TC curves.) There is no assurance that the profit curve will be above the horizontal axis. Many hospitals, both for-profit and not-for-profit types, strive continuously to obtain some minimum acceptable positive surplus of revenues over costs in order to ensure their survival.

The affluent hospital corporation, which has the luxury of targeting a profit level below its potential maximum, for example P_1, may pick any output level in the range Q_1 to Q_3. Hospital managers (who may include physicians, nurses, and others) have discretion over the resources that may be allocated to achieving additional goals. These goals may include building additions; branching into new areas; purchasing more advanced equipment; funding research, education, higher salaries, perquisites, or lobbying; or developing a particular image. Service level Q_3 is consistent with William J. Baumol's famous sales-maximization hypothesis, which holds that large U.S. corporations maximize sales subject to a minimum profit constraint that keeps investors satisfied (Baumol, 1967). Level Q_1 is for the corporation with managers who seek leisure, that is a more relaxed work environment designed to minimize stress among hospital staff and perhaps among patients as well.

Both for-profit and not-for-profit hospitals can pursue a variety of institutional and discretionary goals. In fact, it is the diversity of goals and performance criteria that cloud the issue of which organizational form is superior for serving society (Webb, 1989b). The study of hospitals is complicated by the existence of different features, which in some ways makes each individual hospital unique. Each of the features in a set of hospital characteristics interact with each other in various degrees, similar to the overlapping penumbrae of circles that make different shaded areas (Georgescu-Roegen, 1971; and Webb, 1976). Hospital types are distinguishable by their individual, unique managements, employees, institutional settings, stated missions and goals, demographic characteristics of patients served, hospital treatment specialties, and a host of personal agendas held by managers, staff, and interested third parties. It is little wonder that researchers have trouble making meaningful generalizations concerning hospital organizations that can be supported by empirical studies.

REVIEW OF SELECTED NONPROFIT AND HEALTH CARE LITERATURE

The recent literature of both nonprofit firms and health care economics warns that the more efficient corporate hospital structure does not always serve society best. A review of some of the most important contributions to this literature is quite enlightening.

A two-year comprehensive study by the Institute of Medicine found insufficient evidence that investor-owned hospitals are best for society (Gray, 1986). A study committee composed of theoreticians and practitioners found that such hospitals have:

1. Increased health care costs.
2. Tended to serve relatively fewer people who are unable to pay.
3. Not provided superior quality of health care.
4. Had little to do with professional education and unsponsored research.

On the other hand, for-profit hospitals are able to raise capital independent of government subsidy, provide more and better services by way of acquisitions and construction, and develop innovative and diverse ways of serving patients more efficiently (Gray, 1986).

In his review of the literature devoted to modelling and empirical research on nonprofit enterprises, A. G. Holtmann provides an excellent summary of both early and recent work. He explains that two conflicting general views are emerging: "non-profit firms are inefficient and wasteful" and "non-profit firms are a response to market failure, and thus, may actually improve efficiency." (Holtmann, 1988, p. 30) In the latter vein, Holtmann notes that Burton Weisbrod provided the first model designed to explain the existence and operation of nonprofit enterprises. Weisbrod (1975) sees nonprofit firms emerging to provide services with attributes of public goods (goods available to all without direct cost, such as public roads, parks, education, and health programs) that would not be provided by for-profit firms. Henry Hansmann (1980) suggests that nonprofit organizations may be better able to keep health care providers from gaining opportunistically from exploitation of market imperfections, such as transactions costs, uncertainty, and asymmetrical information, than for-profit organizations. Holtmann's conclusion from his review of the literature gives only qualified support to for-profit hospitals: "Non-profit care seems to be more expensive than for-profit care, but the hypothesis that outputs differ in kind or quality or organizational type cannot be ruled out." (Holtmann, 1988, p. 41) Certainly, outputs differ in kind, quality, and organizational type.

A useful summary of nine recent empirical studies is provided by Charles A. Register, Ansel M. Sharp, and Lonnie K. Stevans (1988) from which they conclude:

> First, the question of the relative performance of for-profit and nonprofit hospitals is far from answered. Second, there exists relatively little evidence from nationwide studies based on samples large enough to avoid questions of conclusion generalization. (p. 27)

The authors, finding published evidence indecisive, proceed to make their own analysis using extensive data obtained from the annual hospital survey of the American Hospital Association. They found: "Nonprofit hospitals tend to be larger, offer more extensive outpatient services [an important efficiency indicator], and treat a relatively more sophisticated mix of cases than their for-profit counterparts." (p. 27) The performance of nonprofit and for-profit hospitals was found to be similar if the difference in case mixes is ignored. When case mixes were taken into account, "for-profit hospitals are economically inferior to the nonprofits" (Register, Sharp, and Stevans, 1988, p. 36).

Edwin G. West (1989) reviews many different hypothesized characteristics of nonprofit organizations that can be mentioned only briefly in this essay. A common argument is that those who control not-for-profit organizations are barred from distributing net earnings or proceeds from asset liquidation among themselves. Such organizations exist to meet "the problem of 'contract failure' that arises where a consumer is incapable of accurately evaluating the goods promised or delivered by for-profit firms." (West, 1989, p. 165) Thus, the uncertain consumer would prefer to deal with a nonprofit firm, which does not have an incentive to take advantage of him or her (Hansmann, 1980; Arrow, 1963). Consumers may also prefer the nonprofit firm over the for-profit firm because of the legal protection provided by restrictive operational constraints and because of their greater trust that some dimension of quality in care of which he or she is ignorant will be delivered with greater certainty (Hansmann, 1980; Pauly, 1987). West concludes that there is a need for more empirical inquiries as to the social value of nonprofit versus for-profit firms. Perhaps the type of studies West has in mind is represented by the work of Anne E. Preston (1988).

Preston's empirical study is based upon a theoretical model of monopolistic competition and supports the notion that the presence of nonprofit firms in an industry populated by for-profit firms will generate social benefits. She builds upon a model by Michael Spence (1976), specifying that goods are differentiated according to both product attribute and degree of public benefits, where "social benefits are defined as social externalities, benefits enjoyed by parties external to the transaction, or more specifically by society as a whole" (Preston, p. 494). Technically, she assumes that "social benefits are linearly related to private benefits" and that nonprofit firms tend to receive more donations than for-profit firms because "tax laws make it less expensive for a donor to give money to a nonprofit firm than to a for-profit firm" (Preston, p. 495-496). She concludes from an analysis too involved to cover here that

> products with a high ratio of revenue to consumer benefits will be privately consumed goods. They may be produced by either for-profit or nonprofit firms . . . . On the other hand, goods with a low ratio of revenue to private benefits, goods which can loosely be defined as specialty goods, can only be maintained in the marketplace if they have a large public benefit component. These types of products will be produced by nonprofit firms, and a majority of their funding will come from donative income. (Preston, p. 498)

Thus, in theory, there is a potential for nonprofit firms to direct donated resources to specialty products (those with low ratios of revenue to private benefits) that have a high public benefit component. Examples of such specialty products in the health care industry could include medical treatment of the indigent and day care services for the mentally retarded and developmentally disabled.

CONCLUSIONS AND RECOMMENDATIONS

Adherents to the property rights tradition of thought hold that decision makers in nonprofit hospitals lack the necessary incentive to enforce efficient behavior because their individual compensations are not tied to the hospital's performance (De Alessi, 1980; Clarkson, 1972). In contrast, decision makers in for-profit hospitals are motivated to operate efficiently by promise of being able to share in any hospital surplus revenues they help to produce. For-profit hospitals are supposed to be more efficient, but much of the empirical research says they are not. An explanation of why the theory is not supported by research is that the theory is flawed. First, the managers of nonprofit hospitals, especially staff physicians, are able to share in the fruits of hospital surplus revenues in many ways, including higher incomes, better equipment, more pleasing work environment, and enhanced prestige (Register, Sharp, and Stevans, 1988). This is in accord with the physician control model of Pauly and Redisch (1973). Second, if for-profit hospitals are controlled by the hospital's investors who are also residual claimants to the hospital's assets upon sale or dissolution, then lower-level decision makers (that is, administrators, staff physicians, and so forth) have only indirect control of operations (Register, Sharp, and Stevans, 1988). Perhaps efficient behavior incentives are actually greater among operational decision makers in not-for-profit hospitals than in for-profit hospitals. If nonprofit hospitals are maximizing net revenues to the same extent that for-profit hospitals are maximizing profits, then one type is not likely to be more efficient than the other. This would help to explain why researchers frequently find nonprofit hospitals to be more efficient than for-profit hospitals. All of this is consistent with the simple Baumol model mentioned earlier.

The agenda for future research on hospitals and the health care industry should evolve and move away from ideological lines stressing the differences between competing for-profit and not-for-profit hospitals. New research should move toward an examination of additional important institutional characteristics of health care facilities and their related public policy issues. Research is essential in important health areas such as the economic effects of laws, managerial modes, malpractice, rationing of medical services, and promotion of specialization among individual hospitals in a given region in order to reduce the potentially devastating continuous escalation of health care costs.

REFERENCES

Arrow, Kenneth J. 1963. "Uncertainty and the Welfare Economics of Medical Care." *American Economic Review*, 53(5): 941-973.

Baumol, William J. 1967. *Business Behavior, Value, and Growth*, rev. ed. New York: Harcourt, Brace & World.

Clarkson, Kenneth W. 1972. "Some Implications of Property Rights in Hospital Management." *Journal of Law and Economics*, 15(2): 363-384.

De Alessi, Louis. 1980. "The Economics of Property Rights: A Review of the Evidence." *Research in Law and Economics*, 2(1): 1-47.

Georgescu-Roegen, Nicolas. 1971. *The Entropy Law and the Economic Process.* Cambridge, MA: Harvard University Press.

Gray, Bradford H. 1986. *For-Profit Enterprise in Health Care.* Washington, D.C.: National Academy Press.

Hansmann, Henry B. 1980. "The Role of Non-Profit Enterprise." *Yale Law Journal*, 89(5): 835-901.

Holtmann, A. G. 1988. "Theories of Non-Profit Institutions." *Journal of Economic Surveys*, 2(1): 29-45.

Pauly, Mark V. 1987. "Nonprofit Firms in Medical Markets." *American Economic Review*, 77(2): 257-262.

Pauly, Mark V., and Michael Redisch. 1973. "The Not-For-Profit Hospital as a Physicians' Cooperative." *American Economic Review*, 63(1): 87-99.

Preston, Anne E. 1988. "The Nonprofit Firm: A Potential Solution to Inherent Market Failures." *Economic Inquiry*, 26(3): 493-506.

Register, Charles A., Ansel M. Sharp, and Lonnie K. Stevans. 1988. "Profit Incentives and the Hospital Industry: New Evidence." *Atlantic Economic Journal*, 16(1): 25-38.

Spence, Michael. 1976. "Product Selection, Fixed Costs, and Monopolistic Competition." *Review of Economic Studies*, 43(2): 217-235.

Vladeck, Bruce C. 1985. "The Dilemma Between Competition and Community Service." *Inquiry*, 22(2): 115-121.

Webb, Samuel C. 1989a. "A Brief Theoretical Discussion of Hospital Goals, Constraints and Cost Control." *American Business Review*, 7(1): 50-57.

Webb, Samuel C. 1989b. "Physician Goals and Hospital Performance." *Health Care Management Review*, 14(1): 81-89.

Webb, Samuel C. 1976. *Managerial Economics.* Boston: Houghton Mifflin Company.

Weisbrod, B. A. 1975. "Toward a Theory of the Voluntary Non-Profit Sector in a Three Sector Economy." In Edmund Phelps, ed. *Altruism, Morality, and Economic Theory.* New York: Russell Sage Foundation, pp. 171-195.

West, Edwin G. 1989. "Nonprofit Organizations: Revised Theory and New Evidence." *Public Choice*, 63(2): 165-179.

ADDITIONAL REFERENCES

Easley, D., and M. O'Hara. 1983. "The Economic Role of the Nonprofit Firm." *Bell Journal of Economics,* 14(2): 531-538.

Hansmann, Henry B. 1987. "The Effects of Tax Exemption and Other Factors on the Market Share of Nonprofit Versus For-Profit Firms." *National Tax Journal,* 40(1): 71-82.

Newhouse, Joseph P. 1970. "Toward a Theory of Nonprofit Institutions: An Economic Model of a Hospital." *American Economic Review,* 60(1): 64-74.

Rose-Ackerman, Susan, ed. 1986. *The Economics of Nonprofit Institutions — Studies in Structure and Policy.* New York: Oxford University Press.

Sloan, A. F. 1988. "Property Rights in the Hospital Industry." In H. E. Frech, ed., *Health Care in America.* San Francisco: Pacific Research Institute for Public Policy.

Tuckman, Howard P., and Cyril F. Chang. 1988. "Cost Convergence Between For-Profit and Not-For-Profit Nursing Homes: Does Competition Matter?" *Quarterly Review of Economics and Business,* 28(4): 50-65.

Weisbrod, B. A., and N. Dominguez. 1986. "Demand for Collective Goods in Private Non-Profit Markets: Can Fundraising Help Overcome Free-Rider Behavior?" *Journal of Public Economics,* 30(6): 83-96.

> **ISSUE FOUR**
>
> *The extension of prospective payment systems to all health care providers will stimulate efficiency in the delivery of health care services and prove to be an effective means of cost control.*

The primary argument underlying the legislation that created a prospective payment system (PPS) for Medicare patients in 1983 was that hospitals had no incentive to control costs with cost-based reimbursement. Few decisions in recent times have been so widely discussed as PPS. Some observers have hailed PPS as the key to cost containment; others have criticized it as unfair and ineffective. Whether proponent or opponent, all admit that the reality of hospital administration and health services financing have radically changed since the creation of PPS and are not likely to ever be the same.

In 1967, Medicare expenditures for inpatient services were $3 billion. By 1983, the figure had increased to $30 billion (Joy and Yurt, 1990). Prospective reimbursement, according to the theory underlying the legislation, would slow this high rate of increase in expenditures by providing economic incentives for cost-conscious behavior while ensuring the maintenance of high-quality care (Davis and Rhodes, 1988). Advocates of prospective payment systems point out that the rate of increase in inpatient expenses did actually slow down somewhat after the introduction of PPS and did not substantially affect the margins for most hospitals (Cromwell and Puskin, 1989; Menke, 1990). It would be inappropriate, however, to attribute all cost efficiencies since 1983 to PPS because other changes, such as the oversupply of physicians and the increased competitiveness of the health care industry, have taken place during this time and may have contributed to the reduction in hospital costs.

As far as quality is concerned, advocates of the prospective payment system suggest that quality may have actually improved since 1983. They contend that the cost constraints imposed by PPS have forced the concentration of more complicated procedures at those facilities where they can be done most effectively and efficiently. If PPS were used throughout the health care system, is it possible that the positive benefits obtained by controlling hospital costs could be extended to other providers, such as physicians, health maintenance organizations, and nursing homes?

Opponents of PPS are not willing to admit this form of reimbursement has solved more problems than it has created. Many, for example, believe that the manner in which payments are computed is not fair. They contend that hospitals are not adequately compensated for the severity of illness of patients and rural hospitals are not adequately compensated for the high number of Medicare patients they have (Henikoff, 1990; Horn and Backofen, 1987; Gianfrancesco, 1990). The issue of fairness becomes particularly critical if, in fact, PPS works a special hardship on a hospital because of its location or mission.

Other opponents of PPS are concerned about the quality of patient care. One of the major ways costs have been reduced under PPS is by decreasing the average length of stay in a hospital. This, according to some, has resulted in incomplete convalescence, causing patients to leave the hospital "quicker and sicker" than before the introduction of PPS (Fisher, 1989).

The future of PPS is of critical concern to health care providers and patients. Experts agree that PPS is here to stay and the days of cost plus medicine are gone forever. Is PPS the only alternative? More importantly, are there significant improvements that could be made in PPS, and how can we begin making them? Is there any inherent reason why other health care providers (long-term care facilities, for example) could not use the guidelines applied to PPS? In the discussion that follows, E. Greer Gay and Richard E. Nordquist, both of the University of Arkansas at Little Rock, argue that PPS should be extended to all providers. They focus on the need to develop reimbursement systems that provide incentives for desired outcomes rather than simply micromanaging through regulations with the hope that no unanticipated consequences develop. Robert W. Broyles, of the University of Oklahoma, offers some cautions about the extension of PPS. Professor Broyles is not convinced that PPS will contain costs, particularly the costs of physician services and long-term care.

REFERENCES

Cromwell, Jerry, and Dena Puskin. 1989. "Hospital Productivity and Intensity Trends: 1980-1987." *Inquiry*, 26(3): 366-380.

Davis, Carolyn K., and Deborah J. Rhodes. 1988. "The Impact of DRGs on the Cost and Quality of Health Care in the United States." *Health Policy*, 9(2): 117-131.

Fisher, Lucy R. 1989. "Quicker and Sicker: How Changes in Medicare Affect the Elderly and Their Families." *Journal of Geriatric Psychiatry*, 22(2): 163-191.

Gianfrancesco, Frank D. 1990. "The Fairness of the PPS Reimbursement Methodology." *Health Services Research*, 25(1): 1-23.

Henikoff, Leo M. 1990. "PPS Operating Margins: The Flip Side." *Health Affairs*, 9(2): 238-239.

Horn, Susan D., and Joanne E. Backofen. 1987. "Ethical Issues in the Use of a Prospective Payment System: The Issue of a Severity of Illness Adjustment." *Journal of Medicine and Philosophy*, 12(2): 145-153.

Joy, Sharon A., and Roger W. Yurt. 1990. "An All-Payor Prospective Payment System (PPS) Based on Diagnosis-Related-Groups (DRG): Financial Impact on Reimbursement for Trauma Care and Approaches to Minimizing Loss." *Journal of Trauma*, 30(7): 866-873.

Menke, Terri. 1990. "Impacts of PPS on Medicare Part B Expenditures and Utilization for Hospital Episodes of Care." *Inquiry*, 27(2): 114-126.

> **POINT**
>
> *The extension of prospective payment systems to all health care providers will stimulate efficiency in the delivery of health care services and prove to be an effective means of cost control.*

E. GREER GAY
The University of Arkansas at Little Rock

E. Greer Gay teaches health administration, health policy, international health, and management of long-term care facilities to graduate students in health services sdministration. She received her Ph.D. in health services administration from the University of South Carolina after completing her master's degrees in nursing from Emory University and public health from the Univer-sity of South Carolina. She received a bachelor of science degree in nursing from Emory University. Dr. Gay's research focuses on appraisals of health service organizational response to changes in regulations and the concomitant impact on health care delivery systems. She has published articles in *Social Science and Medicine, New England Journal of Medicine, Journal of Health and Social Behavior, Nursing Economics,* and *Journal of Women and Aging.* At present, Gay is working with researchers at the medical school to appraise the financial impact of treating cancer patients at home and how that cost compares with costs for treating a matched sample of hospitalized patients. She is a faculty sponsor for student chapters of the American College of Health Administration and Sigma Iota Epsilon.

RICHARD H. NORDQUIST
The University of Arkansas at Little Rock

Richard H. Nordquist is a research associate in a joint appointment at the Health Department of Arkansas and the Department of Health Administration at the University of Arkansas at Little Rock. He received a master's of science in industrial engineering at the University of Oklahoma. Nordquist is currently performing research in the areas of accident prevention and chronic disease. He has served as a guest lecturer on reimbursement systems for nursing homes and is teaching decision analysis in the university's graduate program in health services administration. Prior to his university work, he was associate director of a grant to formulate a prospective-payment reimbursement system for Virginia's nursing homes. The results of this work have been published in *Medical Care* and *Health Services Research*. Nordquist is working on his dissertation, "The Impact of Nursing Home Ownership upon Efficiency," in Health Services Administration at the Medical College of Virginia.

BACKGROUND

Retrospective cost-based and fee-for-service physician reimbursement systems are becoming extinct as government and other third-party payers attempt to contain spiraling health care costs in the United States (Cohodes, 1987). In 1988, national health care costs were an exorbitant $540 billion, 89 percent of which was spent on personal health care (Office of National Cost Estimates, 1990). This amount is far greater in terms of absolute dollars and in percentage (now 12.2 percent) of GNP than it is in any other major industrial country, even though the United States has fewer hospital beds per unit population, about the same physician-to-population ratio, and one of the lowest use rates with regard to physician visits, hospitalizations, and length-of-hospital stay (LOS) among industrialized Western nations. The gap between the United States and Canada, which is second only to the United States in expenditures for health care, widens each year (Schieber and Poullier, 1990).

Many factors can be blamed for these costs. Physician training, clinical inclination, and institutional willingness to expand and utilize expensive technology have contributed to cost escalation. Malpractice litigation has led to unnecessary diagnostic services. However, the root cause of inflation in the health care system is a flawed reimbursement system.

Reimbursement policies based on the traditional cost-based approach for hospitals' and physicians' "usual customary and reasonable" fee structure have inflated health care expenses far more than is justified on the basis of outcome. Among the 24 countries belonging to the Organization of Economic Cooperation and Development (OECD), which includes predominantly Western-industrialized countries, the United States ranks eighth in crude mortality rates, seventeenth in infant mortality rates, and ninth in male-life-expectancy at birth (Poullier, 1990).

It is a given that organizations and individuals can be expected to act in their own best interests. The first and most natural priority of any organization is survival. In that context, regardless of altruistic affiliations (i.e., religious or nonprofit sponsorship), hospitals (especially for-profit hospitals) will attempt either to maximize revenue or, in the case of nonprofit hospitals, to increase size and/or scope of services (Palmer and Vogel, 1985).

Given that every increase in cost brings a concomitant increase in revenue, the primary financial incentive of a cost-based system is for the organization to increase costs. A strong negative incentive exists for increasing efficiency because each increase in efficiency results in decreased revenue. Thus, for example, we find each hospital in a given area acquiring one of each type of expensive diagnostic/treatment machines available, regardless of the number of patients that may benefit from them. The result is per patient costs that far exceed an appropriate level. Although exotic services, such as heart transplants, are offered, they are rarely utilized. Many horror stories exist of hospitals investing in the necessary equipment for such services and then rarely making use of it. Not only does this result in exorbitant costs, it also puts the occasional patient at risk because of the staff's lack of experience.

Efforts have been made, and progress achieved, toward elimination of cost-based reimbursement. Unfortunately, the shift to the diagnostic-related-group (DRG) prospective payment system for Medicare reimbursement, coupled with efforts by major insurers to obtain discounts, has muddied the waters and stimulated the ingenuity of hospital financial managers. Their response has been to implement a many-tiered charge system wherein costs are shifted to those insurers who still pay charges. Charge figures, not to mention price and costs figures, in hospitals these days have little relation to comparable figures in the real world. They are the result of some of the highest forms of creative accounting extant, conducted with the sole intent of maximizing revenue.

The other major area of health care cost is physician reimbursement. Uwe Reinhardt, the noted health economist, has asserted that physicians are but "piece rate workers" who get paid per service provided with no control other than self-control on how much service is appropriate (Relman and Reinhardt, 1986). Reinhardt (1985) also has pointed out that between 1980 and 1982, as total health care costs rose 12.7 percent, Medicare physician costs rose 30.9 percent. He states that we have granted physicians "a license to take from our collective insurance treasuries virtually as they pleased . . ." He does present the bright side of the picture, however, conjecturing that ". . . certain ethical constraints (possibly) have induced the providers from taking less than they might have" (Reinhardt, 1985, p. 108). He wonders, in a thankful manner, what investment bankers and lawyers might have done with such license.

Given the minimum influence that a hospital has over this private entrepreneur, who can always take his or her business elsewhere, it is not surprising that the cost containment approaches we have tried have had little impact on physician behavior. This behavior should not be surprising. Again, we all act on the basis of enlightened self-interest. It should be noted in passing, however, that health maintenance organizations (HMOs), where they have achieved some market penetration, have had a somewhat modifying effect on physician reimbursement in that physicians are usually recompensed on a salary (or prepaid amount per encounter) approach, which may be augmented by a share of HMO profits.

In short, the well-meaning efforts (Medicaid, Medicare) of the federal government to provide better health care to those in need (the elderly and indigent) have been poorly implemented with regard to reimbursement aspects. The agreements that had to be reached with the individuals involved to obtain passage of enabling legislation prevented any major reworking of the overall reimbursement structure. It would appear that the trust placed in the private sector and in care providers to make the system work turned out to be misplaced. A great number of unintended consequences resulted. Today, we have a health care system that provides undistinguished service, on a relative basis, at an outlandish cost.

Clearly, some rather drastic change is required to bring health care costs under control, though a loud outcry from several publics may be needed to elevate the issue on the public agenda.. The new system that must eventually evolve before we go broke, must take into consideration the normal behavior of those involved and must be so designed that such behavior will not enrich providers at the expense of the public good in terms of the level and quality of care and the cost of care. It must also provide a level of reimbursement that is fair to the providers to ensure their participation.

The insurance industry, which is composed of a mixture of nonprofit and for-profit organizations, is another major force in the health care arena. These organizations, together with the government agencies that pay for health care expenditures, are loosely referred to as third-party payers. An understanding of the motives and incentive structures of insurance organizations and their customers is required in order to understand how the health care market works.

Regardless of the assertions of those classically trained economists who refuse to believe that the free market is not a universal phenomenon, individuals do not make rational choices with respect to health care and particularly health insurance. Most people looking at home or automobile insurance want coverage for high-cost, low probability of occurrence events with some form of copayment or deductible to minimize the cost of the insurance.

Health insurance is quite a different case. Many plans offer first dollar coverage, and individuals invariably opt for the most comprehensive plan available when offered alternatives. The market for supplemental plans is flourishing as many individuals purchase second and third levels of coverage to cover the deductible and copayment costs of the basic plan and to provide a per-diem payment for hospitalized periods. In this country we don't fool around when it comes to health care insurance. We tend to want the most and best, and we (those who are lucky enough to be in such a position) expect our employers to provide it as an employment perquisite. The overinsured status of many quite naturally leads to a high incidence of individuals taking advantage of the system — a condition termed *moral hazard.*

In those instances where individuals do make decisions based on cost, for example, between hospitals that have different cost levels, they often pick the most expensive under the presumption that if it costs more it must be better. The free market, the laws of supply and demand, rational man, the informed consumer, and other myths promoted by economists do not exist in the health care world. Indeed, Vladeck (1981) suggests that "it may not even be desirable to encourage people to behave more like a rational 'economic man' " (p. 217). To expect price sensitivity from individuals in the need of care for life-threatening maladies is unreasonable. This fact must be thoroughly understood by all concerned with control over health care costs.

Our system of free competition in the health insurance market and fee-for-service reimbursement for physicians is rooted in the free enterprise system, which is basic to our culture. There is still a strong presumption that free-market forces will operate to drive out the inefficient producer. Except for Medicare, Medicaid, and indigent care, virtually all health care is paid for by those for-profit and nonprofit insurance entities that compete for insurance accounts. In the majority of cases, this competition takes the form of insurers negotiating with employers to obtain the right to insure all or some portion of the work force. The size of the work force will directly influence the cost per worker. The insurer may arrange a private fee schedule with a hospital or a group of hospitals and may also negotiate separate fee schedules with a physician group. The so-called Blues (Blue Cross and Blue Shield) have been quite successful in obtaining substantial discounts from both hospitals and physician groups because of the large number of individuals enrolled in their plans. The ability of insurers to negotiate favorable fee schedules is also a function of the total number of subscribers. Small insurers have little clout and are often forced to pay higher charges than large insurers.

The result of this marketplace activity is a bewildering array of hospital fees and insurance pricing plans. The large employer obtains a more favorable price than does the small employer because of the larger number of workers (customers). A given insurer charges each employer a different rate. Hospitals receive a different level of payment for a given procedure from each insurer. The burden of simply keeping up with the mix of payment schedules is, in itself, a significant administrative cost escalator.

Contrast this approach with the approach used in most European industrialized countries that have national insurance plans. In these countries, sick funds, the equivalent of third-party payers, cooperate, either voluntarily or by regulation, to work in the best interest of all insured individuals. Government assumes the role of referee to assure a fair rate for all parties (Glaser, 1983). In Canada, national insurance plan fee schedules are negotiated at the provincial level.

Our system is patently unfair, particularly given that it is based on employment status. In effect, the unemployed, and in many cases even those employed (particularly in service industries such as food chains or department stores), cannot obtain insurance. Costs are prohibitive for the individual who wishes to obtain insurance on his or her own. Insurers are afraid that such individuals may be bad risks and thus greatly overcharge for individual policies. Small businesses face a similar problem when attempting to obtain a plan for employees. Insurance firms are not interested in insuring small groups with an unknown risk potential.

The final area of interest in this look at health care markets is long-term care, which has experienced a rapidly escalating level of cost that is expected to continue to increase as the baby-boom generation ages. The major expenditure item in long-term care is nursing home cost. At present state Medicaid programs are the major funding agencies for nursing home residents unable to afford nursing home expenses. Each state has different rules, conditions, and reimbursement plans for such residents. Until the last decade, the most common reimbursement plan used a retrospective cost-based approach. Under such plans, different providers often received greatly differing levels of reimbursement for essentially the same service. Recently, there has been a shift toward prospective cost-based systems with a maximum per diem payment, based on some function of average cost of all nursing homes. Such systems in the past have reimbursed at a flat rate per resident without differentiating between differing needs for care. However, care requirements for individuals in nursing homes have been shown to vary by 400 percent (Arling, Nordquist, Brant, and Capitman, 1987). This situation has caused an equity problem that has resulted in those most in need of care finding great difficulty in obtaining admittance. Given a shortage of beds in most states, providers will naturally admit those who require the least amount of care whenever possible. This equity issue is perhaps the most serious reimbursement problem in long-term care (except, naturally, the overall shortage of funds) and has led to various schemes for making patient need for care a factor in reimbursement.

PROPOSED SOLUTION(S)

To restrain growth in health care costs and to promote efficiency and effectiveness in the U.S. health care system, we must simplify the financial incentive structure and impose an all-payer, prospective payment system for both individuals and institutional entities in the acute care market. Such a system will ensure that providers are fairly reimbursed for services rendered at a going rate that is the same for all patients after taking into account cost differences on a regional or type-of-provider basis. The system must be designed with the understanding that all regulated entities will try their best to "game" the system. To the maximum extent possible, the incentives should be structured so that gaming efforts will enhance, not detract from, the public good. The efficient producer should be rewarded; the inefficient, penalized.

Physician reimbursement policies should be reworked to embody the principles of a resource-based relative value system that determines fees based on two cost elements: relative physician work and practice costs. The challenges of implementing such a politically difficult system will be faced as of January 1, 1992. Finally, long-term care reimbursement plans should be required to include patient severity components and enhanced allowances for home-based or community-based care for those with marginal needs for service.

PROSPECTIVE PAYMENT ARGUMENT

Prospective payment systems (PPS) originated in response to the bias and perverse incentives inherent in cost-based systems. A cost-based system encourages expansion of services because the more services offered, the more a provider is reimbursed. PPS rates, on the other hand, are based on some empirical sample of costs or charges deemed to be at least in the ballpark as appropriate for the family of services involved. Such rates usually are adjusted for factors thought to be relevant (e.g., location, teaching/nonteaching, and so forth). Under a prospective payment system, hospitals receive a fixed payment for the service/case/days provided. The actual cost to the hospital for the incident of care is not considered. If the hospital treats the patient at a lower cost than the reimbursement rate, it may keep the difference; if the case cost is higher, the hospital makes up the difference. The DRG system implemented in 1983 is a PPS approach and is presently the basis of reimbursement for all Medicare patients.

State governments began experimenting with PPS in the 1970s. Maryland began setting rates for all hospitals on a per service basis in 1974. In 1976, Maryland adopted the first case-based system (the guaranteed inpatient revenue or GIR, program) for almost half of the state's hospitals. The system implemented a per case rate that served as a binder on reimbursement. Researchers found that changes in medical practice patterns would occur only under stringent per case payment limits (Salkever, Steinwachs, and Rupp, 1986).

Another state to experiment with PPS was New Jersey. Between 1978 and 1980, New Jersey experimented with a PPS system known as the Standard Hospital Accounting and Rate Evaluation (SHARE). This program, however, applied only to Blue Cross and Medicaid patients. The program (paid on a per diem basis) was unpopular, inefficient in that length of stay (LOS) increased rather substantially, and had only qualified success in containing costs (Rosko, 1989).

In 1981, New Jersey switched to an all-payer, all-service, case-based system with rates based on data from a sample of New Jersey hospitals. Analysis demonstrated that an all-payer system controlled costs most effectively than did a partial-payer system (Rosko, 1989). Cost-shifting, and hence artificial inflation of charges, is discouraged because all payers are under the same system.

The success of the New Jersey program led the federal government to adopt a PPS system (implemented in 1983) for Medicare reimbursement. The DRG algorithm used for patient classification was developed by a team of Yale researchers headed by Robert Fetter. Data used for actual rate setting were taken from a national sample of hospitals (public hospitals were excluded). There has been a great deal of criticism of the DRG method of patient classification, much of which is concerned with either the small percentage of variation explained in patient need for care or the lack of consideration of severity of illness. A paraphrase of Churchill's description of democracy may well serve as a descriptor of the DRG methodology: It is the worst possible approach, except for every other one we have ever tried.

One important fact must be emphasized. This is not an all-payer approach. It applies only to Medicare patients and therefore invites hospitals to take an innovative accounting approach to shift costs to other payers. This situation negates much of the positive effect on efficiency that might have otherwise been expected.

Hospitals and physicians responded quickly to the DRG program. Efficiency increased as patient records became more complete. Unnecessary surgery and unnecessary hospitalization were discouraged because the federal DRG system implemented statewide peer review organizations (PROs) to monitor admission practices (Gay, et al., 1989; and Mickel, 1984). Length of stay, total overall services, and readmissions (a general indicator of appropriateness of care) declined (ProPAC, 1989). In so doing, the rate of inpatient hospital expenditures under PPS slowed. Prospective payments are not short-run gimmicks. On average, mature mandatory prospective payment programs can reduce hospital costs between 3 to 4 percent per annum and still ensure a profit for providers (Sloan, 1981).

However, cost-shifting and cream-skimming are significant problems that will continue to occur as long as the motivation (enlightened self-interest) and opportunity (multipayers in the market) exist. Hospitals raised prices for outpatient hospital and physician services [reimbursement in these areas remain on a cost-based payment system (ProPAC, 1989)], cut-back services considered 'losers,' and expanded those assumed to be 'winners.' For example, surgical cases are generally winners; medical cases more often are losers. It has been shown that intensive care unit usage (surgical) has increased while critical care unit usage (medical) has declined (Gay, et al., 1989). Many hospitals have moved from the inner city with its preponderance of charity or Medicaid patients to the suburbs where the clientele has better insurance.

Reported inpatient charges are considerably higher since the implementation of PPS (ProPAC, 1989). Because each payer establishes its own payment rules either unilaterally or on a basis of market principle, hospitals do not have to act as price-takers with commercial insurers. Therefore, charges continue to grow so that marginal revenue equals marginal cost. In these situations, hospitals act as revenue-maximizers in a monopolistic market. Hospitals are shifting costs to those insurers for which they do not have to be a "price taker." Commercial insurers who do not have a sufficiently large market share are forced to pay charges. Hospital administrators and financial officers often readily admit to playing this cost-shifting game and are quite frank about the specific tactics used (Gay, et al., 1989).

The ability to shift costs is patently inequitable. Hospitals that have 50 percent or more government-sponsored or indigent patients have a difficult time raising prices to cover losses. If they do so, they may find commercial insurers less willing to use their facilities. This situation is a major, unintended consequence of the manner in which the DRG system was implemented, i.e., not an all-payer system.

An all-payer system that reimburses all clients under the same guidelines (i.e., no payment differentials among payers) could alleviate both cost-shifting and cream-skimming. No longer would Medicaid patients, the group most often cited as underinsured or inadequately insured, be considered pariahs. Payment would be on the same basis as private insurance. In an all-payer system, each payer pays the same rate for the same treatment. In a multipayer environment, found in the United States, a free-for-all occurs. Each payer establishes its own payment rules either unilaterally or on a market principle basis. The hospital is forced to become a price-taker for the regulated or more powerful insurer in an attempt to make up the difference from other classes of payers.

With regards to equity (restricting output), hospitals have been reluctant to take their fair share of poor and uninsured patients. Public hospitals have had to bear the brunt of care for the poor. Fewer than 9 percent of the nation's hospitals delivered 40 percent of the care provided to poor, Medicaid, and underinsured patients (Feder, Hadley, and Mullner, 1984).

Wasserman (1986) reported that after the passage of an all-payer system in New Jersey, there occurred a "rather substantial increase in the number of self-pay discharges" (p. 643). Wasserman concluded that this finding "should be considered an important benefit in evaluating New Jersey's all-payers system's approach . . . [an inference] not necessarily related to New Jersey's uncompensated care," but rather to increased willingness on the part of hospitals to accept uninsured patients (p. 643).

We are not focussing on the all-important issue of who pays for the non- or underinsured population, considering it beyond the scope of this essay. However, even a shift to an all-payer system among those who do presently pay would have salutary effects on efficiency and serve to positively impact the rising cost of health care.

Physician reimbursement for that major segment of physicians who operate in private practice on a fee-for-service basis is indeed a sticky wicket. Given the political clout of physicians, it is unrealistic to expect to obtain passage of a sweeping overhaul of the reimbursement approach. Total revamping will only occur when public opinion is totally mobilized in agreement that the time has come. Nevertheless, there are approaches that will work. Perhaps the most promising is one proposed in 1988 by the Physician Payment Review Commission, which was created by Congress in 1986. Research on the mechanics of this resource-based relative value system has been conducted by W. C. Hsiao at Harvard University for the last several years. The system would establish physician fees based on two elements: relative physician work (based on complexity of task and time spent) and practice costs. A scale would indicate the value of each service/procedure relative to other services/procedures. A conversion factor, which would be updated yearly would translate the relative value scale (RVS) into dollar fees for each service. A geographic multiplier would be used to account for geographic differences. This approach, scheduled for partial implementation in 1992, appears most promising, particularly given its source of recommendation and endorsement by numbers of respected physicians.

The fix that appears most needed in long-term care is a mandated patient classification system included in the reimbursement formula (Arling, et al., 1987; and New York State Department of Health, 1984). Such systems have already been implemented in a number of states (New York, Maryland, Illinois, and Minnesota among others), and the federal government is currently running pilot programs in several states, perhaps as precursors to defining a national policy. The approach increases access to those most afflicted and therefore most in need of nursing-home care. Without a concomitant increase in total beds, however, present residents will be less able to obtain space. Some, however, may be more appropriate candidates for alternative care systems in the community at a lower cost. This category must then receive additional funding.

SUMMARY

It is indeed difficult to define the necessary methodology to cure the nation's health care cost problems in such limited space. It is also somewhat arrogant. We obviously have neglected many areas and concepts that should be included. Some omissions were deliberate; some were oversights. Many caveats appropriate to scholarly literature are omitted. However, the basic mission of this essay is to stimulate controversy and thought on a series of problems important to the future well being of the health care industry. We hope that the arguments and viewpoints presented here will serve that purpose.

One concept that was deliberately emphasized was the basic necessity to understand the motivations of regulated institutions and the nature of incentives implicit in regulations. It is strongly felt that too high a percentage of rules and regulations are naively published without such understanding — inevitably this leads to serious, unintended consequences. Regulations should not micromanage. Regulations should be aimed at the end, not the means, and allow some freedom to define the means appropriate for each setting. If this appreciation of the nature of regulations is communicated, then future efforts will be more effective.

REFERENCES

Arling, G., R. H. Nordquist, B. A. Brant, and J. A. Capitman. 1987. "Nursing Home Case Mix: Patient Classifcation by Nursing Resource Use." *Medical Care,* 25(1): 9-19.

Cohodes, D. S. 1987. "The Loss of Innocence: Health Care Under Siege." In C. J. Schramm, ed., *Health Care and Its Costs: Can the U.S. Afford Adequate Health Care?* New York: W.W. Norton & Company, pp. 64-104.

Feder, J., J. Hadley, and R. Mullner. 1984. "Falling Through the Cracks: Poverty, Insurance Coverage, and Hospital Care for the Poor, 1980 and 1982." *Milbank Memorial Fund Quarterly/Health and Society,* 62(4): 544-566.

Gay, E. G., J. J. Kronenfeld, S. L. Baker, and R. L. Amidon. 1989. "An Appraisal of Organizational Response to Fiscally Constraining Regulation: The Case of Hospitals and DRGs." *Journal of Health and Social Behavior,* 30(1): 41-55.

Glaser, W. A. 1983. "Paying the Hospital: Foreign Lessons for the United States." *Health Care Financing Review,* 4(4): 99-109.

Mickel, C. 1984. "PRO Contracts Aim to Cut Medicare Admissions." *Hospital Week,* 26(1): 10.

New York State Department of Health. 1984. "New York State Long-Term Care Case Mix Reimbursement Project." *Executive Summary: Derivation of RUG-II.* Albany, NY: New York State Department of Health.

Office of National Cost Estimates. 1990. "National Health Expenditures, 1988." *Health Care Financing Review,* 11(4): 1-41.

Palmer, H. C., and R. J. Vogel. 1985. "Models of the Nursing Home." In R.J. Vogel and H.C. Palmer, eds., *Long-Term Care: Perspectives from Research and Demonstrations*. Rockville, MD: Aspen Publishers, Inc.

Poullier, J. P. 1989. "Compendium: Health Care Expenditure and Other Data." *Health Care Financing Review.* Annual Supplement, pp. 111-194.

ProPAC. 1989. *Medicare Prospective Payment and the American Health Care System: Report to the Congress.* Washington, D.C.: U.S. Government Printing Office.

Reinhardt, U. E. 1985. "Impact on Beneficiaries." *Health Care Financing Review.* Annual Supplement, pp. 105-111.

Relman, A. S., and Uwe Reinhardt. 1986. "An Exchange on For-Profit Health Care." In B. H. Gray, ed., *For-Profit Enterprise in Health Care.* Washington, D.C.: National Academy Press, pp. 209-223.

Rosko, M. D. 1989. "A Comparison of Hospital Performance Under the Partial-Payer Medicare PPS and State All-Payer Rate-Setting Systems." *Inquiry,* 26(1): 48-61.

Salkever, D. S., D. M. Steinwachs, and A. Rupp. 1986. "Hospital Cost and Efficiency Under Per Service and Per Case Payment in Maryland: A Tale of the Carrot and the Stick." *Inquiry,* 23(1): 56-66.

Schieber, G. J., and J. P. Poullier. 1990. "Health Expenditures in Major Industrialized Countries, 1960-87." *Health Care Financing Review,* 11(4): 159-167.

Sloan, F. A. 1981. "Regulation and the Rising Cost of Hospital Care." *The Review of Economics and Statistics,* 63(4): 479-487.

Vladeck, B. C. 1981. "The Market vs. Regulation: The Case for Regulation." *Milbank Memorial Fund Quarterly/Health and Society,* 59(2): 209-223.

Wasserman, J. 1986. "The New Jersey DRG System and Uncompensated Care: Some Empirical Results." *Bulletin: New York Academy of Medicine,* 62(6): 638-645.

COUNTERPOINT

*The extension of prospective payment systems to all health care providers will **not** stimulate efficiency in the delivery of health care services nor will it prove to be an effective means of cost control.*

ROBERT W. BROYLES
University of Oklahoma

Robert W. Broyles is a professor in the Department of Health Administration and Policy, College of Public Health, University of Oklahoma Health Sciences Center in Oklahoma City. He received a Master of Arts in economics from the University of Nebraska and a Ph.D. in economics from the University of Michigan. Dr. Broyles has taught at the University of Ottawa in Ontario, Widener University, and the Medical University of South Carolina before joining the University of Oklahoma. He is the author or coauthor of eleven books and monographs in the field of health administration. His articles have been published in the *Journal of Health Politics, Policy and Law, Medical Care, Medical Care Review, Inquiry,* and *Healthcare Management Review* among others. His continuing research interests include health finance, access, and distributional equity.

Predicated on the proposition that the method of financing health care should control inflationary pressures and reduce or eliminate inequities in the use of service, the purpose of this analysis is twofold. The first is to examine the features of prospective payment systems (PPS) that reduce the potential for rate regulation to control spending on hospital care and to ensure that the use of service is determined by the medical needs of the patient. Based on the assessment of PPS to finance the use of hospital care, the second objective is to examine the potential outcomes that might result from a reliance on rate regulation to compensate providers of physician and long-term care.

For purposes of presentation, expenditures will be distinguished from costs or expenses. The term *expenditure* will refer to actual or anticipated payments from patients and public or private insurers to providers of care. *Costs* or *expenses* will refer to the monetary value of direct resources, which are comprised primarily of the labor and consumable supplies that are used to provide patient care or, in the case of hospitals and long-term care facilities, general support services. Accordingly, the analysis excludes the costs associated with the capital assets of the provider and focuses on the effects of rate regulation on the volume of care, the efficiency of resource use, and factor prices, components that determine the direct costs of care.

CONTROLLING INFLATION IN THE HOSPITAL INDUSTRY

The implementation of the Diagnostic-Related-Group system as a price mechanism ushered in an era of increased reliance on rate regulation as a means of financing hospital care. The proliferation of prospective payment mechanisms has resulted in a plethora of pricing systems that employ different methods of establishing rates, controlling use, and adjusting prices. However, among the features that characterize prospective payment mechanisms, the scope of regulatory authority and the unit of payment exert the most influence on spending and the distribution of hospital services.

Most policy analysts recognize that a partial application of a prospective payment motivates hospitals to transfer costs from regulated sources of funding to other patients or insurers. Others have already demonstrated that costs, charges, and profitability differ among multiple sources of funding (Danzon, 1982; Sloan and Becker, 1984; and Eby and Cohodes, 1985). Although contradictory results have been reported, the weight of evidence suggests that the concurrent dependence on multiple payers and financial arrangements induces hospitals to charge differential prices and to transfer costs from regulated sources of funding to other groups of patients or insurers, thus avoiding the fiscal pressure to control operating expenses.

The relative effects of partial and universal applications of prospective payment systems have been explored previously. Recent results suggest that a universal application of PPS reduces or eliminates the ability of hospitals to engage in differential pricing practices and exerts uncompromised fiscal pressure on hospitals to control expenses. For example, compared to the rate of inflation that would occur in the absence of prospective payment, Hadley and Swartz (1989) concluded that a universal application of rate regulation lowered costs by 13 to 15 percent while a partial application reduced expenses by 11 percent. Results reported by Broyles (1990) and by Rosko and Broyles (1986, 1987) indicate that a universal application of prospective payment exerts greater fiscal pressure to control costs than a partial extension of regulatory authority. That a universal application of prospective payment reduces price differentials and thereby increases the imperative to control costs has also been documented by Rosko (1989), Thorpe (1987), and Blair (1987). Obviously, the failure to extend the scope of regulatory authority to all sources of funding mitigates the effectiveness of prospective payment to control costs in the hospital industry.

The unit of payment also reduces the potential of rate regulation to control costs and may exacerbate inequities in the distribution of care. The most prominent payment units are the day of care, ancillary services, and the discharge (grouped by diagnostic nomenclature). Most analysts recognize that the regulation of per diem rates, charges, and the price per discharge induces hospitals to improve the efficiency of operations or to acquire resources at lower prices and that these outcomes do control the cost per day, the cost per service, and the cost per case.

Unfortunately, the savings attributable to the regulation of per diem rates and the decline in the cost per day are offset by incentives to stimulate revenues, improve profitability, and increase expenditures by extending the length of stay and providing additional days of care. Usually the costs per day are higher during the early phase of hospitalization than during the later phases prior to discharge. Because a regulated per diem rate is constant, hospitals are encouraged to extend the length of stay and the provision of stay-specific services. The net surplus earned during the latter phase of hospitalization is used to subsidize losses incurred during the earlier stage. This outcome may contribute to inflationary pressures in the hospital industry.

In much the same way, the regulation of charges, or the price per discharge, induces hospitals to increase the volume of care or admissions and thereby stimulates expenditures. An increase in the number of units to which fixed costs are assigned lowers the expense per unit and, holding price constant, improves profitability or reduces net losses. Rosko and Broyles (1987) and Salkever, Steinwachs, and Rupp (1986) have documented that a reduction in the cost per service or case is offset by an increase in volume. They suggest that the savings associated with decline in the cost per case are attenuated by an increase in admissions.

It is also possible that the mix of admissions, costs, and expenditures are influenced by the net surplus, or loss per case. If rates of payment, for example, include a uniform profit margin per patient, hospitals are induced to improve their fiscal performance by stimulating the admission of patients assigned to all diagnostic categories. Although this results in an improvement in access, it also increases both costs and expenditures. On the other hand, differences in the profit margin per case encourage hospitals to reduce their dependence on medical need for admission by increasing that portion of the patient population for which a relatively high net surplus is anticipated and reducing the number of cases that are expected to yield a low net surplus or result in a net loss. The adoption of a stringent set of prices reduces not only admissions, costs, and expenditures but also access to inpatient care.

The regulation of the price per case also induces hospitals to improve fiscal performance and to avoid fiscal pressure to control costs by altering case severity and the method of assigning patients to one of several diagnostic categories. The use of the patient and diagnostic condition as the unit of payment may cause hospitals to admit patients with less severe conditions that require less intensive or costly treatments. This practice may control expenses and improve profitability, but it has little, if any, influence on expenditures. A reliance on case mix to establish prospective prices encourages hospitals to assign patients to those diagnostic categories associated with higher payment rates — a practice that relaxes revenue constraints and reduces the fiscal imperative to control costs.

As this discussion suggests, the concurrent dependence on multiple sources of funding and payment systems prevents a coordinated effort to stimulate efficiency, control costs, and reduce expenditures in the hospital industry. The partial application of regulatory authority and reliance on several units of payment not only fragments responsibility for reducing inflationary pressures but also exacerbates inequities in the distribution of services.

CONTROLLING EXPENDITURES IN PHYSICIAN CARE

The problem of controlling expenditures in physician care is perhaps the most difficult issue confronting the policy analyst. The potential effectiveness of proposals to rely on mechanisms similar to PPS to reduce physician care expenditures depends on the scope of regulatory authority and the unit of payment. For reasons cited previously, a universal rather than a partial application of rate regulation enhances the potential for controlling inflationary pressures on physician services. However, a dependence on fees, capitation rates, or salaries to compensate physicians is likely to exert differential effects on expenditures, productivity, and the prescribing patterns of the physician.

It is well known that relying on fees to compensate physicians has several serious deficiencies. First, the fee-for-service mechanism encourages physicians to augment their professional incomes by prescribing additional units of service (Langwell and Nelson, 1986; Wilensky and Rossiter, 1986). Further, because profit margins differ among components of physician care, the physician may be tempted to prescribe those services for which the net surplus is greatest. This, of course, would distort the course of treatment in relation to the medical needs of the patient.

Recent policy deliberations have resulted in a proposal to reduce the inflationary tendencies that are inherent in the fee-for-service mechanism by adopting the principles of prospective payment to finance physician care and relying on a relative value scale to establish charges. Among the various approaches to the problem of developing a relative value scale, the most prominent are proposals to rely on prevailing charges or the resource consumption associated with each component of care. Results reported in recent studies reveal that most of the variation in Medicare prices is attributable to practice costs and the time requirements and complexity of each procedure. This implies that the charges adopted by the Medicare program reflect the resource consumption associated with various components of care (Cromwell, et al., 1989; McMenamin, 1990). It is possible, however, that the insurance mechanism and imperfect market conditions distort the relative charges that prevail in other markets for physician services (Juba, 1979). Therefore, a reliance on prevailing prices to establish the relative value scale as well as prospective prices may perpetuate differential profit margins and the incentive to augment income or expenditures by prescribing additional units of service.

The recommendation to employ time requirements, complexity, and practice costs to develop a relative value scale may establish a congruence between the cost per unit of service and the corresponding fee. As a consequence, the adoption of resource costs as the basis for establishing prospective fees may reduce or eliminate the dependence of prescribing patterns on differential profit margins and redress inequities in the charges for cognitive and technical procedures (Hsiao, et al., 1988). However, the adoption of a prospective fee schedule based on the consumption of resources fails to sever the dependence of professional income on the quantity of service provided by the physician. In the absence of limitations imposed on expenditures or volume, the adoption of a prospective fee schedule that is characterized by a uniform profit margin per service, like a reliance on prevailing prices, may encourage physicians to augment professional incomes and increase expenditures by prescribing additional units of care.

There are several advantages to the use of per capita rates to compensate physicians. First, depending on the method of adjusting payment rates, capitation systems may reduce the financial incentive to increase the volume of service. If adjustments in the rate of compensation are independent of previous prescribing patterns, the physician may reduce the amount of care per case. Although this practice reduces costs, it exacerbates inequities in the distribution of care and exerts little, if any, effect on expenditures in the short term. A reliance on capitation also transfers fiscal risk from the insurer to the provider, which increases the requirement to improve the efficiency of operations, acquire resources at lower prices, and control costs of medical practice.

These advantages, however, may be overshadowed by several undesirable outcomes that are the result of a reliance on a system of capitation. In the absence of provisions that reduce or eliminate the effects of selection bias, physicians may augment their net incomes by only enrolling patients who require relatively few diagnostic and therapeutic services. If adjustments to the payment per patient reflects prior prescribing patterns, physicians may prescribe additional units to increase the capitation rate in a future period. This will result in inflationary pressures similar to those stimulated by the reliance on costs to compensate hospitals. In addition to the potentially perverse effects on spending, capitation systems seem to reduce the productivity of the physician, the amount of time committed to market activity, and the provision of patient care (Rosko and Broyles, 1988).

The use of annual salaries to compensate physicians severs the dependence of professional income not only on the volume of care prescribed but also on the case load of the physician. These features are more likely to restrict spending than those associated with capitation methods or fee-for-service mechanisms. On the other hand, annual salaries may encourage physicians to restrict their case loads, to commit less time to market activity, and to lower the volume of service per hour or per patient. In addition to these potentially adverse effects on quality, access, and productivity, a reliance on salaries is complicated by the problem of establishing an income structure that depicts the relative value of the services provided by various specialties. In addition, the salary structure would need to reflect differences in a variety of factors, including not only the risks of malpractice litigation but also the location, training, and experience of the physician.

The potential application of prospective payment to compensate physicians is also complicated by political considerations. Recognizing the inevitable opposition of the medical community to alternate payment mechanisms, the adoption of capitation systems or salaries to compensate physicians is unlikely. Unfortunately, the most viable option of regulating charges, modified to reflect resource consumption, will probably fail to control inflationary pressures.

CONTROLLING INFLATIONARY PRESSURES IN THE LONG-TERM CARE INDUSTRY

Most policy analysts recognize that the dependence on two payment mechanisms and two sources of financing long-term care vitiates the potential of rate regulation to control costs and expenditures, exacerbates the problem of distributional equity, and compromises the quality of service. Although the partial application of prospective payment to establish per diem rates has lowered the growth in expenditures by state Medicaid programs, during the past twenty-five years spending on long-term care has increased more rapidly than any other component of service (Office of National Cost Estimates, 1990).

Furthermore, efforts to improve the efficiency of resource use by establishing stringent rates of payment exacerbate the difference between prevailing market prices and the regulated per diem rate. This outcome may reduce the access of Medicaid recipients to long-term care and may mitigate the effects of the prospective pricing system on inflationary pressures. The behavioral model developed by Scanlon (1980) suggests that if the market price exceeds the regulated per diem rate, the facility is motivated to improve profitability by increasing the proportion of capacity that is allocated to private patients. If other factors remain constant, an increase in the proportion of capacity allocated to private patients not only reduces the access of Medicaid or Medicare beneficiaries to service but also reduces the dependence of providers on regulated sources of funding. As Holahan and Cohen (1987) have demonstrated, a reduction in the percentage of revenue derived from regulated sources of funding lessens the fiscal pressure to control costs. The decline in the proportion of revenue derived from Medicaid — from approximately 49 percent in 1975 to 44 percent in 1988 — reduced the potential of prospective payment to control costs and expenditures (Office of National Cost Estimates, 1990). An institution that derives little or no revenue from regulated sources is virtually unaffected by the adoption of prospective payment.

Recently, policy deliberations have focused on the adoption of case-mix standards to establish rates of payment that are equitable, improve the access of recipients requiring extensive care, stimulate efficiency, and motivate providers to control costs. Designed to identify iso-resource groups, a plethora of case-mix systems have been recommended for establishing prospective rates of compensation. Among the most frequently cited are the management minute system, three resource utilization group approaches (RUG-I, RUG-II, and RUG-T18), the Minnesota case-mix system, and the Maryland case-mix system.

The management minute system constructs an index that reflects the cumulative amount of time devoted to the provision of the mix of care required by the patient. Based on expert opinion rather than a statistical analysis, the system assembles the time value associated with a set of routine services, represented by 18 items; a set of skilled procedures, comprised of 22 items; restorative nursing care; and special attention precipitated by obesity, rigidity, or the need to isolate the patient.

Similar to the management minute system, the RUGs and state mechanisms rely on the mix of service and the level of physical functioning, as indicated by the patient's ability to perform activities of daily living, to classify patients. The RUGs and state systems share several common features. In particular, the systems are designed to ensure that the patient categories are statistically stable, clinically meaningful, limited in number, and sufficiently general to cover a broad spectrum of long-term care facilities.

As suggested by the discussion of the Medicare pricing systems, the classification scheme should result in patient groups that are homogeneous with respect to resource use. This type of homogeneity should reduce not only the incentive to implement a selective admission policy but also the differences in fiscal performance that are attributable to variation in case mix. However, recent evidence reported by Fries (1990) indicates that the RUGs and state systems explain approximately 50 percent of the variation in resource use. Because most states specify a minimum mix of staff and service availability, the variation in resource use and costs are constrained by external regulations, which suggests that the explanatory ability of the case-mix system is overstated. Accordingly, if a case-mix system is adopted as the basis for establishing rates of compensation, the heterogeneity in the use of resources by patients assigned to the categories would result in incentives to retain or implement policies that may limit the access of recipients who require costly and intensive treatment.

It is also possible that the adoption of proposals to rely on a case-mix system and the composition of required care will stimulate costs and expenditures. To prevent manipulation through the assignment of patients to categories that result in higher rates of compensation and expenditure, the classification system must be based on objective information. Unfortunately, an evaluation of a patient's ability to perform activities of daily living is determined largely by subjective judgement. Accordingly, providers are induced to exercise discretion in the classification of patients and to augment revenue by understating the independence of residents. This outcome stimulates expenditures on long-term care.

In addition to the discretion that might be exercised when evaluating dependence, several other factors enable the facility to alter the mix of required care and thereby augment income. Smits (1984), for example, suggests that a urinary catheter is a convenient device for dealing with chronic incontinence. However, the decision to use a catheter for this purpose is based on subjective criteria. In the same way, although a number of patients may be hand-fed with patience, tube-feeding is necessary for others. This distinction, however, again involves a subjective evaluation.

Although physicians are required to prescribe a course of treatment for a patient, services are normally provided by employees of the facility. In particular, the nursing staff is responsible for care during the prolonged periods in which the physician is absent. Hence, the physician is dependent in varying degrees on employees of long-term care facilities for recommendations concerning a course of treatment. When combined with the discretionary determination of service mix, the subjective assessment of the resident's dependence on assistance enables the facility to alter the classification of patients, increase the rate of compensation, and thereby augment income. This outcome also stimulates expenditures and reduces the fiscal imperative to control costs.

A reliance on service mix to classify patients also encourages providers to maximize the number of days requiring extensive resource consumption, thus increasing revenues and expenditures. If the provision of identifiable components of care generates higher levels of income, the incentives to rehabilitate the patient are reduced, an outcome that is undesirable for several reasons. First, failure to rehabilitate the resident prevents an improvement in the quality of life. Second, providers are motivated to avoid the decline in short-term profitability that reflects the large outlays required to rehabilitate the patient. Unfortunately, the reluctance to provide necessary care also prevents the realization of cost savings that result from rehabilitation and occur after the passage of time.

CONCLUSIONS

This analysis suggests that the potential of prospective payment to control inflationary pressures in the hospital sector is mitigated by the scope of regulatory authority and the adoption of multiple units to express rates of compensation. The universal application of rate regulation to compensate providers of physician and long-term care is also an unresolved and contentious issue. The reliance on modified charges and the per diem rate, adjusted to reflect case mix or the composition of care, is unlikely to control spending on physician services and long-term care. Accordingly, in the absence of dramatic changes in the financial environment, inflationary pressures in the American health industry will continue without abatement.

REFERENCES

Blair, G. 1987. "Maryland Hospital Financial Trends: 1977 Through 1986." Baltimore: Maryland Chapter of the Hospital Financial Association.

Broyles, R. 1990. "Efficiency, Costs, and Quality: The New Jersey Experience Revisited." *Inquiry*, 27(1): 86-96.

Cromwell, J., J. Mitchell, M. Rosenbach, W. Statson, and S. Hurdle. 1989. "Using Physician Time and Complexity to Identify Mispriced Procedures." *Inquiry*, 26(1): 7-23.

Danzon, P. 1982. "Hospital Profits: The Effects of Reimbursement Policy." *Journal of Health Economics*, 1: 29-45.

Eby, C., and D. Cohodes. 1985. "What Do We Know About Rate Setting?" *Journal of Health Politics, Policy, and Law*, 10(2): 299-327.

Fries, B. 1990. "Comparing Case-Mix Systems for Nursing Home Payment." *Health Care Financing Review*, 11(4): 103-119.

Hadley, J., and K. Swartz. 1989. "The Impacts on Hospital Costs Between 1980 and 1984 of Hospital Rate Regulation Competition and Changes in Health Insurance Coverage." *Inquiry*, 26(1): 35-47.

Holahan, J., and J. Cohen. 1987. "Nursing Home Reimbursement: Implications for Cost Containment, Access, and Quality." *The Milbank Quarterly*, 65(1): 112-147.

Hsiao, W. C., P. Braun, D. Ynetna, and E. R. Becker. 1988. "Estimating Physician Work for a Resource-Based Relative Value Scale." *New England Journal of Medicine*, 319(13): 835-841.

Juba, D. 1979. "Price Setting in the Market for Physicians' Services: A Review of the Literature." Pennsylvania Blue Shield, HCFA contract no. 600-76-0149. Washington, D.C.: Health Care Financing Administration.

Langwell, K., and L. Nelson. 1986. "Physician Payment Systems: A Review of History, Alternatives and Evidence." *Medical Care*, 43(1): 5-58.

McMenamin, P. 1990. "What Price Medicare? Geographic Variability in Medicare Payment Levels." *Inquiry*, 27(2): 138-150.

Office of National Cost Estimates. 1990. "National Health Expenditures, 1988." *Health Care Financing Review*, 11(4): 1-44.

Rosko, M. 1989. "A Comparison of Hospital Performance Under the Partial Medicare PPS and State All-Payer Rate Setting Systems." *Inquiry*, 26(1): 48-61.

Rosko, M., and R. Broyles. 1986. "Impact of the New Jersey All-Payer DRG System." *Inquiry*, 23(1): 67-75.

Rosko, M., and R. Broyles. 1987. "Short-Term Responses to the DRG Prospective Pricing Mechanism in New Jersey." *Medical Care*, 25(2): 88-99.

Rosko, M., and R. Broyles. 1988. *The Economics of Health Care: A Reference Handbook*. Westport, CT: Greenwood Press.

Salkever, D. S., D. M. Steinwachs, and A Rupp. 1986. "Hospital Cost and Efficiency Under Per Service and Per Case Payment in Maryland: A Tale of the Carrot and the Stick." *Inquiry*, 23(1): 56-66.

Scanlon, W. 1989. "A Theory of the Nursing Home Market." *Inquiry*, 17(1): 25-41.

Sloan, F. A., and E. R. Becker. 1984. "Cross Subsidies and Payment for Hospital Care." *Journal of Health Politics, Policy, and Law*, 8(4): 660-685.

Smits, H. 1984. "Incentives in Case-Mix Measures for Long-Term Care." *Health Care Financing Review*, 6(2): 53-59.

Thorpe, K. 1987. "Does All-Payer Rate Setting Work? The Case of the New York Prospective Hospital Reimbursement Methodology." *Journal of Health Politics, Policy, and Law*, 12(3): 391-408.

Wilensky, G., and L. Rossiter. 1986. "Alternative Units of Payment for Physician Services." *Medical Care Review*, 43(1): 133-156.

ISSUE FIVE

Vertical integration is a useful strategy that allows health care organizations to control patient flow, enter fast-growing markets, and better acquire the returns necessary to survive in competitive environments.

Adoption of vertical integration strategies by health care organizations is proceeding at an increasing rate (Mick and Conrad, 1988). Similar to diversification, vertical integration strategies result from increased pressures on operating margins. Much of this pressure has come from the growing intensity of competition within the industry. In addition, health care providers face more knowledgeable and aggressive purchasers of health services. Vertical integration strategies have been pursued in order to provide a full range of health care and therefore control the flow of patients through a system. By keeping patients within the system, vertical integration strategies may provide a competitive advantage.

A vertical integration strategy is a decision to grow along the channel of distribution of the core operation. In the case of health care organizations this involves providing a continuum of health care services. Thus, a health care organization may grow toward suppliers (upstream) or toward patients (downstream). As a result of vertical integration, primary, secondary, tertiary, rehabilitative, custodial, and other care modalities may be available within one system. A fully integrated health care system is capable of providing all services to patients who present themselves for care.

As W. L. Fox (1989) has pointed out, there are critical distinctions between the health care industry's vertical integration and its diversification strategies. Diversification is aimed at moving away from the core operation (in this case, health care) to focus on the attractiveness or growth potential of new markets. The rationale underlying vertical integration is the desire to support the core business. Therefore, a close fit with the core business is paramount. In addition, vertical integration need not always involve complete ownership. It may be accomplished through joint ventures, licensing, and in some cases, contractual arrangements such as alliances, cooperatives, and networks.

Vertical integration strategies have been the basis for creating local and regional health care systems and linking health care institutions. Such systems help to assure adequate patient volume moving from one segment of the system to the next. For the most part, vertical integration has been limited to local and regional systems because of the service area limitations imposed by the nature of health care delivery.

Vertically integrated local and regional health care systems continue to be formed. Have these systems lived up to their promise? Has the total cost of health care really been reduced? Have vertically integrated systems created an unfair competitive advantage that has weakened independent health care institutions? Are there ethical problems associated with controlling patient flow? Are the providers within the system always the best source of patient referral?

In exploring the issue of vertical integration, Douglas A. Conrad, of the University of Washington, provides evidence that vertical integration has been a successful strategy, is a critically important strategic alternative for health care organizations, and offers the best structural model for effective health care. On the other hand, Jan P. Clement, of Virginia Commonwealth University, points out the problems with vertical integration and indicates that the strategy provides only a limited ability to increase returns or control patient flow.

REFERENCES

Fox, Wende L.   1989.   "Vertical Integration Strategies: More Promising than Diversification."   *Health Care Management Review,* 14(3):   49-56.

Mick, Stephen S., and Douglas A. Conrad.   1988.   "The Decision to Integrate Vertically in Health Care Organizations."   *Hospital & Health Services Administration,* 33(3):   345-360.

POINT

Vertical integration is a useful strategy that allows health care organizations to control patient flow, enter fast-growing markets, and better acquire the returns necessary to survive in competitive environments.

DOUGLAS A. CONRAD
University of Washington

Douglas A. Conrad is a professor in the Department of Health Services and the Department of Dental Public Health Sciences, as well as an adjunct professor in the Department of Finance and Business Economics. He received a Ph.D. in economics and finance from the University of Chicago. Conrad's current research involves the economics of vertical integration and managed-care in health services, cost modelling of cancer prevention programs, and methodologies for assessing economic outcomes of alternative medical treatment modalities in health services. He has served on the university's Solid Waste Management Task Force (1990) and in the Graduate School Program Review Committee for the School of Business Administration. Currently he is the editor of *Frontiers of Health Services Management* and is completing five years of service on the Accrediting Commission on Education for Health Services Administration, most recently as Chair (1990-1991).

The fundamental premise of this essay is that vertical integration — properly conceived, implemented, and managed — not only is, but must be, an important element in the core strategy of health care organizations in the future. In this paper, I will define the concept of vertical integration, articulate its different forms, state its benefits, and describe how the risks and costs of vertical integration can be minimized. As Robert Montgomery (1991) has so aptly stated in discussing strategic alliances in health care, vertical linkages are "no substitute for an organization's core strategy" (p. 26). My aim is to show that vertical integration should be a key component in that core strategy.

VERTICAL INTEGRATION: A DEFINITION

A vertically integrated health care arrangement aligns a broad array of patient care and support services in an administratively and clinically unified manner. To fit this definition, the vertical linkage(s) must be effected at the local and/or regional level where health care is delivered.

Thus, true vertical integration is not necessarily the same as diversification by hospitals or other health care organizations into new services or products. The litmus test for vertical integration is the connection of different points of service for individual patients (and patient populations) within an administratively and clinically coherent structure. Accordingly, an entity (e.g., an HMO) offering comprehensive wellness services, primary care services, hospital inpatient services, and long-term care to individual patients within the framework of a single organization or interorganizational network that has identifiable managerial accountability for all points of service in the continuum of care does exemplify vertical integration. In constrast, a hospital providing wellness services to patients who do not use its inpatient or ambulatory care services is diversifying, rather than integrating, its service mix. Although an HMO integrates both the delivery and financing of health care, the organization may choose to vertically integrate the delivery spectrum only. For example, a hospital that acquires a physician group practice or a long-term care facility may only intend to use the physicians or the long-term care capacity in coordinating the care of hospital inpatients.

DIFFERENT FORMS OF VERTICAL INTEGRATION

In other articles, my colleagues and I have elucidated the various forms that vertically integrated arrangements may take (Conrad and Dowling, 1990; Conrad, et al., 1988; and Mick and Conrad, 1988), so here I will just sketch the broad array of possible vertical structures to develop my point.

First, vertical integration does not require single (common) ownership of all the stages in the health care production process. Although a singly owned, prepaid group practice model HMO (of the "group" or "staff" type) is the quintessential vertically integrated health care organization, preferred provider networks (PPOs) with joint ownership structures and unified management control represent another viable form of vertical integration. Vertical integration occurs along a spectrum of vertical control, which can be achieved by a number of means: internal development of a new service, interorganizational agreements or affliliations, mergers or acquisitions, joint ventures, or franchises.

The organization entering a vertically integrated arrangement needs to strike what Bill Dowling and I have termed "the integrative balance" between strategic flexibility and production and transaction cost efficiency (Conrad and Dowling, 1990). Different organizational forms will present different trade-offs between these ends. An integrated hospital — a multispecialty group practice, for example — would provide strong potential for transaction cost savings and production efficiency within a unified medical organizational structure but would forego the strategic flexibility of contracting with the full array of medical specialists in the community. In principle, an equal degree of vertical integration can be achieved by common ownership or contract.

BENEFITS OF VERTICAL INTEGRATION

The benefits of vertical integration can be summed up in two words: effectiveness and efficiency. Because true vertical integration involves coordinated care across different points of service for a given patient, it offers the strong prospect of better continuity of care over time and more effective patient care at each stage in the process. By substituting the one-time costs of arranging a coordinated continuum of care (either within a single organization or across the elements in an interorganizational network) for the repeated costs of arranging individual transactions at each point of service, vertically integrated health care organizations also economize on the administrative and transaction costs of health care.

Furthermore, by unifying the patient care process, the vertically integrated organization gains economies of scope from sharing common inputs (e.g., clinician time, physical plant, medical technology, and information systems) among different health services. Vertically organized systems also are more capable of concentrating their bargaining power with the providers they hire or whom they choose to contract, thus allowing such systems to realize savings in the costs of their productive inputs.

Notice that the primary benefits of vertical integration — enhanced effectiveness in patient care and increased production, plus transaction cost efficiency — are social benefits that accrue to individual patients and defined population groups, regardless of whether the integrated health care organization captures additional market shares or other direct, private competitive advantages from the vertical integration.

What then are the *private* benefits for the health care organization contemplating vertical integration as an element of the firm's core business strategy? The sources of private competitive advantage flow naturally from the social benefits previously outlined. They include:

- Improved control of patient inflows to each strategic business unit involved in patient care within the organization.
- Coordinated patient outflows from one patient care unit to another that are more appropriate.
- Reduced total business risk for the integrated organization compared to the sum of the individual business risks of the (otherwise unintegrated) discrete levels of patient care.

- Reduced transaction costs and improved efficiency through better terms for large employer groups and insurers seeking managed care contracts with provider organizations.
- Heightened "strategic speed," i.e., the capacity to tap new markets and adopt new patient care and informational technologies as a result of knowledge acquired through real-time, continuous observation of the patient care process across several levels (inpatient, outpatient, rehabilitation, wellness) in the continuum of services.
- Increased returns to the vertically integrated organization from short-run competitive advantages, which stem from reduced transaction costs and decreased production costs.

Increased patient inflows do not arise automatically from an organization's (for example, the hospital's) integration with a vertically related stage in the patient care process (for example, the acquisition of a medical group practice through a long-term contract or other agreement). To realize new market share, the organization must offer physicians, patients, and organized payer and consumer (employer) groups better, more coordinated, and/or less expensive health care. In a competitive marketplace, each of these constituencies has alternatives to the proposed vertically integrated organization, so the prospective vertical firm will have to demonstrate improved continuity, quality, and efficiency over time in order to sustain increased patient inflows. Nonetheless, by deliberately integrating "upstream" toward the original source of patients (primary-care physicians, satellite clinics, health promotion programs), the organization certainly increases the probability of securing new patients.

Improved coordination of care among services designed to offer health promotion, primary care, hospital acute inpatient care, services for chronic illness and continuing rehabilitation is the fundamental source of all other gains from vertical integration. The strongest incentive for comprehensively coordinated care (managerially and clinically) emerges when the organization is paid by capitation for a range of vertically related services (that is, along the care continuum). Under capitation, all savings in administrative, transaction, and production costs (both in terms of inputs per unit of service and number of services required to produce a given level of health and consumer satisfaction) flow directly to the organization's bottom line. It is possible, in principle, to coordinate the overall care process under carefully managed fee-for-service arrangements, but the providers' interests in doing so are certainly diffused and attenuated.

The long-term benefit of better continuity and coordination of patient care (and its management) is that it creates a feedback loop for the organization: Patients who are treated better in the handoff from one point of service to another (e.g., from the hospital to the rehabilitation unit) are more likely to return to the appropriate "upstream" services (e.g., health promotion and primary care) of the organization. As these consumers are educated to use the integrated system more appropriately, further economies in transaction and administrative costs (e.g., reduced paperwork, fewer delays, and less rework) are achieved.

Closer coupling of the stages in the continuum of care can reduce the organization's total business risk. Business risk does not refer to the randomness of outcomes in different health care activities but rather to the systematic covariance between the revenues and costs of a particular service (e.g., hospital acute inpatient care) and the overall demand for health care in a local or regional market. By consciously matching the resource requirements of adjacent stages in the patient care production process (e.g., hospitalization and subsequent long-term care), the vertically integrated organization actually takes control of this systematic risk and actively minimizes it. Moreover, the vertical patient care linkages require, and thus encourage, the creation of an integrated information system across all levels in the spectrum of health services. The vertically connected information system in turn serves to reduce business risk. By producing coordinated data for the vertical stages of production, the integrated data base helps resolve the uncertainty that is at the heart of business risk.

There is a cascade of organizational benefits from the increased patient inflows, improved coordination of patient outflows (exchange of patient services between one stage and another), and the reduced business risk discussed above. Unlike freestanding organizations in which any such gains are unbundled and diffuse, the integrated organization can package these benefits to insurers, large employer groups, and other consumer organizations. Either in the fees for service charged to such consumer groups, negotiated capitation, or in the form of increased demand for its package of services, the vertical organization can capture in its bottom line the full benefits of this cascade of advantages.

The concept of strategic speed is crucial to the long-run viability of vertically integrated health care organizations. A vertically aligned health care firm will be more able to respond to strategic opportunities in new markets. Having created a series of core competencies across several vertically related stages in health care production, the organization is poised to move more quickly and with great precision into new opportunities. With linked services at several levels of health care (acute, chronic, wellness, rehabilitation), the vertical organization can spread the fixed costs of new technology over a larger volume of distinct, but logically related, patient care outputs. These economies of scope not only enhance efficiency but also promote organizational learning in a variety of areas.

Increased returns to the vertically integrated health care organization are best demonstrated by the rapid growth of HMOs and PPOs in the last decade, particularly since the introduction of Medicare prospective payment for hospital inpatient care. On the survivorship principle articulated by Stigler (1958), the increasing market penetration of these organizational models is evidence of their superior returns. Though the greatest relative growth in recent times has been among the IPA and network model HMOs, I would predict a rise in the market share of prepaid group practice HMOs over the next decade. My thesis is that the challenges of the 1990s will reward greater effectiveness and efficiency (that is, closer coordination) even more handsomely than strategic flexibility. Organizations that can afford to offer improved access through increased efficiency and more integrated patient care will command a premium in the marketplace. The vertical organization is better equipped to deal with the pressures of uncompensated care and the continuing rise of health care costs.

MINIMIZING RISKS AND COSTS OF VERTICAL INTEGRATION

The sole significant risk of vertical integration is, in my judgment, the potential creation of excess capacity. For example, a hospital that has newly developed long-term care services and primary-care satellite clinics may have overestimated the demand for these services. To reduce this risk, it is better to "grow" the vertically integrated structure by contracting and early experimentation rather than by immediately acquiring and owning all the assets of the care continuum. In short, incremental make vs. buy decisions at each stage in the health care production process provide a means of managing the risk of surplus capacity.

The prime costs of vertical integration are the opportunities foregone from specializing at one point in the health care continuum. However, I would argue that the market forces of prospective payment and the increasing cost sensitivity of employer groups and third-party payers have combined to raise dramatically the degree of interdependence between different links in the chain of health care delivery. Given this heightened interdependency between hospitals and physicians, providers and payers, primary-care physicians and specialists, health care organizations simply cannot afford *not* to incur the opportunity costs of vertical integration. Unless one manages these interdependencies through some mixture of contract and ownership, the costs of system errors, lack of coordination in patient care, and missed opportunities for new ways of serving the population will overwhelm the health care organization of the future.

CONCLUSION

On balance, then, I conclude that vertical integration is a viable and critically important strategy for health care organizations. The vertical organization not only responds best to the efficiency challenges of the future, in my judgment, but also offers the best structural model for effective health care. Essentially, vertical integration proactively tackles the fundamental epidemiological problem in health services: definition of a population and assumption of organizational responsibility for a broad range, if not all, of its health care needs. At the same time, such vertical systems are designed in ways that manage and minimize the costs of achieving health. This is, after all, the ultimate aim of the health services organization.

REFERENCES

Conrad, D. A., S. S. Mick, C. W. Madden, and G. Hoare. 1988. "Vertical Structures and Control in Health Care Markets: A Conceptual Framework and Empirical Review." *Medical Care Review*, 45(1): 49-101.

Conrad, D. A., and W. L. Dowling. 1990. "Vertical Integration in Health Services: Theory and Managerial Implications." *Healthcare Management Review*, 15(4): 9-22.

Mick, S. S., and D. A. Conrad. 1988. "The Decision to Integrate Vertically in Health Care Organizations." *Hospital & Health Services Administration,* 33(3): 345-360.

Montgomery, Robert. 1991. "Alliances: No Substitute for Core Strategy." *Frontiers of Health Services Management,* 7(3): 25-28.

Stigler, George S. 1958. "The Economics of Scale." *Journal of Law and Economics,* 1(1): 54-71.

COUNTERPOINT

*Vertical integration is **not** a useful strategy because it does not allow health care organizations to control patient flow, enter fast-growing markets, or better acquire the returns necessary to survive in competitive environments.*

JAN P. CLEMENT
Virginia Commonwealth University

Jan P. Clement is an assistant professor in the Department of Health Administration at the Medical College of Virginia campus of Virginia Commonwealth University. Previously, Dr. Clement was on the faculty of the University of Michigan at Ann Arbor and the University of Texas at Austin. She received a Ph.D. from the University of North Carolina-Chapel Hill in health administration and policy, specializing in business finance. She has published in the areas of financial strategy, interactions of financing and investment, investment decision making, and case-teaching. Her current research focuses on financial decision making by not-for-profit hospitals and the effects of diversification and vertical integration by acute care hospitals.

Vertical integration, the integration of successive stages of production into one firm, has been a characteristic of most health care organizations for many years. As S. S. Mick and D. A. Conrad have noted, all organizations consist of production units that are technologically separable and can be "unbundled" from the firm (Mick and Conrad, 1988). Although we often think of vertical integration in static terms (e.g., whether a firm really is vertically integrated or the degree of vertical integration within a firm), vertical integration is actually a fluid process of integration and de-integration. Over time, various vertical combinations become norms in an industry (Mick and Conrad, 1988).

During the last decade, vertical integration in the health care industry has attracted attention because many health care firms, especially acute care hospitals, have deviated from earlier industry norms by increasing their vertical integration.

Sometimes their changes in service mix have also involved organizational restructuring and partial ownership arrangements. Some hospitals, for example, have formed subsidiaries to deliver new services or have formed joint ventures with other firms.

Among the benefits that health care firms have expected from these changes are improved control of patient flow, entry into fast-growing markets, and financial returns. Problems in achieving these benefits from vertical integration are related to both vertical integration itself and the organizational and ownership arrangements used to pursue the strategy. Because the difficulties in realizing the three benefits overlap, I shall discuss the first two in the context of the third, financial returns. Although the discussion concentrates on increases in vertical integration (even when the word "increases" is omitted), I purposely make no effort to specify concretely the normal pattern of vertical integration in the health care industry or to delineate which services are to be added as a part of vertical integration. There are two reasons for this. First, the norm differs for each type of firm. Second, although there are unique challenges associated with every service added, there are some common problems associated with any increases in vertical integration.

FINANCIAL RETURNS

Firms contemplating increased vertical integration are interested in more than the ability of the services added to earn returns by themselves. Of greater importance is their ability to increase the firm's overall returns when compared to those that would have been earned in the absence of vertical integration.

What would have been earned in the absence of vertical integration, however, depends in part upon the actions of competitors. Sometimes vertical integration may be a strategic move to prevent the diversion of clients to competitors, which could lower returns. Although the myriad possible actions of competitors precludes a thorough discussion of improvement in returns through vertical integration, the arguments presented below are also relevant to strategically motivated vertical integration decisions.

Failure to earn better returns following vertical integration may be the result of low revenues, high expenses, or both. Even if revenues are low, a firm may be able to improve returns if it can realize some economies in expenses. If expenses are high, the firm may be able to earn higher returns if it can capture additional revenues. Although firms must consider revenues and expenses simultaneously, to permit a thorough discussion of the reasons why vertical integration may not improve revenue prospects and costs may not be lowered, revenue and cost issues will be considered separately.

A complete discussion would also include ethical or legal problems with vertical changes and associated organizational restructurings. Instead, a brief caution is extended here regarding potentially costly antitrust violations (Sneed and Marx, 1990), misuse of Medicare or tax-exempt bond funds (Mancino, 1991), competition that is perceived to be unfair by competitors, and lack of attention to community and social goals.

Increased Revenue

If a firm cannot increase the volume of services delivered or cannot receive more revenue per unit of output, it will not be able to improve its overall revenues through vertical integration. Among the cited means of realizing volume or price benefits are improved control of patient flows; entry into fast-growing markets; and the capture of the benefits of market imperfections in price competition. The limitations of each in improving the firm's overall revenues are discussed in turn.

Improved Control of Patient Flows. Improved patient flows and consequent increases in the volume of a firm's services are the expected result of funneling patients to services provided by the firm rather than by others. There are, however, at least four reasons why increases in volume or revenue over that expected without further vertical integration may not result.

First, because of the uncertainty about any client's needs during an episode of illness (or wellness), production chains of unequal length and nonlinear patient flows through the stages of health care services are common (Clement, 1988; and Conrad, et al., 1988). One client, for example, may purchase outpatient, ancillary, intensive, and home health services during an episode of illness. Another may only use ancillary and secondary inpatient care services. Consequently, it is difficult to construct a vertical structure with enough breadth and number of stages to appeal to the diversity of clients or to avoid having to refer clients to other providers. In this discussion, I am using K. R. Harrigan's definition of *stage* as a successive production unit in a firm and *breadth* as the range of services at one stage of production (Harrigan, 1984).

Using vertical integration to differentiate the firm's products is likely to fail because the ultimate consumer, the patient, typically lacks the sophistication necessary to understand the relevance of particular vertical arrangements. Consequently, the patient is unlikely to be more attracted to a hospital outpatient clinic than to a private physician's office, for example. Under these circumstances, differentiation achieved through vertical integration is more likely to be successful with physicians and third-party payers. However, these agents for the consumer have varying service-mix preferences that may be challenging to satisfy. Furthermore, they may require price concessions that offset any volume increases. Hospital firms, for example, may have to offer price discounts to attract new PPO or HMO contracts.

Second, most health care firms also face competition in the services they add, which makes improving volume more difficult. There may be existing providers for the vertically integrated services or other firms in the market may add the same services. To increase revenues, the firm may be faced with changing longstanding consumer provider selections and practitioner referral networks. When competitors add services, vertical integration as a strategy for maintaining the client base may be unsuccessful unless the appropriate mix and quality of services are implemented. Also, if there is price competition in the market, the price for each service may be lower.

Third, even if vertical integration changes do result in higher client volumes, revenues may not increase because of the substitution of new services for existing (or other new) services. If the price of the new service is much lower than the price of the replaced service, a large increase in volume will be required to offset the price effects. For example, lower priced ambulatory services may be substituted for inpatient hospital care.

Finally, volume increases may be threatened if the new services do not fit with the mission of the firm as it is perceived by its customers or employees (Conrad and Dowling, 1990). Customers may be more comfortable with the image of a community hospital as a small, friendly, service-oriented organization than as a part of a health care conglomerate with goals that appear to be primarily financial. This impression may become even stronger if a nonprofit firm restructures with for-profit subsidiaries. The effect for the firm may be the loss of some customers.

Alternatively, the goals of the various units in a vertically integrated firm may conflict. A clear example of this occurs when insurance and inpatient hospital care are integrated (Conrad and Dowling, 1990). Although the goals of the hospital part of the firm must include utilization of capacity (i.e., high occupancy) the goals of the insurance portion include decreasing utilization.

Entry into Fast-Growing Markets. Entry into fast-growing markets has the potential for increasing a firm's revenues over the amount expected without further vertical integration if at least one of the following three conditions is met. First, the markets entered really are fast growing. Second, the entry is early. Third, the entry is of sufficient scale. In evaluating markets for potential entry, the health care firm must recognize that the market for each service may be different and thus requires separate analysis. The market for a hospital's tertiary care services, for example, is likely to be different geographically from its market for outpatient care services.

Not all health care markets are expected to grow rapidly. Market growth may be measured either in terms of volume of output or in terms of revenues, and the two measures are not always positively correlated. For example, although an aging population signals an increase in patient volume for nursing-home services, market growth in revenue terms may not be fast because Medicaid, which typically pays a low price, is a major payer for such services. Some health care markets are not expected to grow rapidly in either volume or revenue measures. These include the markets for some inpatient care services.

Although a market may be growing rapidly, its growth may not be sustainable. Product life-cycle curves usually depict an early upsurge in volume that is followed by leveling off and then decline. Even if the vertically integrating firm has been able to forecast short-term and long-term growth accurately, it may still be unable to divest itself later of the new services because of exit barriers. Exit barriers include management's emotional barriers, governmental and social restrictions, strategic interrelationships, ownership of specialized assets, and costs, such as labor agreements, that remain even after exit. These barriers are discussed fully in Porter (1980).

When markets for new services are growing rapidly, pursuing the "follow-the-leader" behavior that is prevalent in the health care industry now is likely to result in wasted resources. If a firm waits until a competitor has established a foothold, customers may be lost permanently to the competitor, and entry barriers may rise. Furthermore, unless a firm enters a market on a relatively large scale, it will not capture the growth in demand and achieve the market share necessary to improve the firm's overall revenues (Biggadike, 1979).

Market Imperfections. Increases in revenues may be possible if the vertically integrating firm can exploit market imperfections in pricing and competition. Because many of the prices for health care services are regulated or are set by buyers with market power, the firm could choose to integrate those services that are relatively overpriced. However, this strategy is likely to be successful only in the short-run if the price-setters adjust prices when they receive information regarding the imperfection. Recent examples include Medicare prices for cataract surgery and Medicare's identification of overpriced physician services. Even if regulators are coopted by regulated firms into keeping prices high, a vertically integrating firm should not count on this phenomenon persisting. The sophistication of regulators, consumers, and business purchasers has increased during the last decade and should be expected to continue to increase.

Imperfections in competition can occur either because of regulation or because there are too few providers in the market. Higher prices and higher volume may be a consequence of such market structures. Certificate of need (CON) laws, for example, may erect entry barriers for competitors. Vertical integration in itself, however, may contribute to reducing competition in a market by increasing the overall economic strength of existing firms through the consolidation of services. Although hospital mergers have been the focus of most prosecution, vertical consolidations have been challenged in other industries. The long-term persistence of these market imperfections is uncertain. They may become more pronounced as vertical integration continues, or they may be eliminated. Therefore, it is dangerous to base vertical integration decisions on this type of existing condition.

Decrease in Costs

Even if increases in vertical integration do not increase the firm's overall revenues, the firm's returns can improve if it is able to realize economies in production or transaction costs. Realizing such economies, however, is difficult.

Production Efficiencies. Production efficiencies may result from sharing resources, such as labor and fixed assets, across the stages of production or within the same stage of production, or they may result from otherwise reducing the inputs necessary to achieve a level of output. The difficulty in achieving such economies results from problems in producing sufficient volume of output at each stage, transferring sufficient volume from stage to stage, decreasing the variance of demand, and managing start-up and learning costs.

Because the production chain for many health care services is nonlinear and of unequal length for different clients, it is important to examine the ability to achieve economies of scale or scope at any single stage of production. Resources within any stage may be shared if enough similarities in the services exist. Typically, however, there are important differences in the inputs required to produce most health care services. For example, even though a variety of intensive care services are usually grouped in the same stage of production, staff and equipment may not be easily transferrable among them because of differing skills and equipment. Furthermore, the equipment required may be stationary, or equipment and staff flexibility may be limited if they are required to respond to emergencies (demand fluctuations).

In addition, even where such technologically substitutable inputs exist, in order to minimize its production costs at any single stage of production, a firm must produce a critical amount of output. Some research has indicated that economies of scale may not exist for all health care services (Grannemann, Brown, and Pauly, 1986).

Productivity improvements in providing health care services have only become a concern recently. Since we know little about how to produce the current mix of services well, vertically integrating firms should not be expected to produce additional services efficiently either alone or in combination with existing services.

According to some observers, however, "the key to production cost savings does not seem to be at the unit-cost level, but rather in relation to the utilization of inputs between different stages in health care delivery" (Conrad and Dowling, 1990, p. 13). This may be true for societal health care costs, as Conrad and Dowling intimate. Unfortunately, exactly which production inputs can be shared within a firm is seldom specified. Indeed, some episodes of medical care in vertically integrated firms can require greater inputs at various stages of production. The presence of an emergency room, for example, may attract more complex inpatient cases that require more equipment and care (Grannemann, et al., 1986).

Even when shareable inputs can be readily identified, sharing resources across stages appears to be plagued by the same problems as sharing resources within stages. There may not be a critical mass of transfer from stage to stage to achieve economies because of the nonlinearity and unequal length of the production chain. Without sufficient volume, firms will be unable to exert buyer power to lower the cost of some inputs, such as supplies. The sharing of resources will also be difficult if there is a geographical separation between stages of production. Since a service is produced and consumed at the same time, geographical proximity is necessary to share resources.

One production input that can be shared between stages is information regarding patient condition. This information is derived from diagnostic tests during an episode of illness (or wellness). Economies may not often occur, however, because the value of such inputs expires relatively rapidly for many conditions. Diagnostic tests, for example, may have to be repeated if there is a long time gap between when the patient uses the service at one stage and the next stage. Thus, economies in costs are limited by the technological process of care delivery.

Economies in costs are also unlikely to result from a reduction in demand uncertainty, or variance, which is a second definition of improved control of patient flows (Mick, 1990). The benefits of achieving such a reduction include less need for stand-by capacity. Because the variability of demand for health care services is primarily a function of the health of the population, genetic differences, and uncontrollable environmental events, vertical integration will do little, if anything, to change the variability of when clients present themselves to the health care firm. For the same reasons, the variation of clients' consumption of services within the firm will remain variable.

In discussions of the benefits of vertical integration, start-up and learning costs are frequently ignored. Start-up costs include the costs of fixed assets as well as the costs of overcoming entry barriers, differentiating the firm's product from those of the competitors, and marketing. All of these costs can be high for a health care service added to a firm. Firms are unlikely to avoid some of the start-up costs even if they purchase businesses from others rather than develop the service or business in-house. The market price of a purchased business is likely to reflect the previous owner's start up costs. Furthermore, once the assets are purchased, costs may be incurred because of lost flexibility (Harrigan, 1984; and Mills and Schumann, 1985).

The costs of learning how to provide the added services should not be underestimated. There are many ways in which services may differ from each other that lead to learning costs when new services are added. Chase and Tansik (1983), for example, distinguish services that require high- and low-customer contact. If, for example, an insurance firm used to relatively low-customer contact adds medical care services that require high-customer contact, significant learning will be required. To keep pace with the growth in fast-growing markets, even higher learning costs will be paid over time. Although learning costs will probably diminish gradually, the pace of change in health care services suggests that learning costs will remain, to some extent, for each new service added, even in the long run.

Transaction Cost Efficiencies. The transaction costs that may be reduced through vertical integration are the costs of finding firms that produce or supply the firm's inputs or distribute the firm's outputs and negotiating, monitoring, and enforcing contracts for supplies, clients, or other items with external parties (Mick and Conrad, 1988). When more stages of production are integrated into a firm, the firm is expected to benefit because it purportedly can make decisions sequentially (plan better), coordinate its production activities better, settle disputes more easily, and align the goals of subgroups with those of the firm (Mick, 1990).

Although transaction cost theory is intellectually appealing, it is of limited use in predicting the return effects of vertical integration because transaction costs are difficult to measure. Even though some transaction costs may be eliminated by vertical integration, others will be created, because both the number and type of transactions will change as the firm integrates more.

As the length and breadth of the vertical chain increase, more transactions will be required. More, not less, communication will be required to coordinate patient/client care activities. The integrating firm will face managing even more of the types of transactions most health care service firms have not yet mastered. Cost, clinical, and management information systems are weak in many health care delivery organizations as well as in some financing organizations. It is therefore hard to believe that health care firms will be able to lower transaction costs by managing an increased number of transactions more efficiently.

In addition to facing an increased number of transactions, the integrating firm will also be challenged by transactions of a different type than those with which it has had experience. Managing these transactions will be more complicated if the firm adds services with which it has little experience or are new to the market. Purchasing an existing business, entering a rapidly expanding market, or creating subsidiaries will also add new types of transactions.

In contrast to the prediction of transaction cost theory, goal conflicts may be more numerous, not less. These conflicts may be more difficult when formerly independent professionals join the firm, when partial ownership arrangements exist, or when for-profit subsidiaries of nonprofit firms are created. The list of potentially new or aggravated transaction costs could be lengthy. Conrad and Dowling (1990) are instructive in the volume of managerial tasks they list for vertically integrating firms.

SUMMARY

Although each firm finds itself in a unique position with respect to its competitors, clients, and existing service mix, vertical integration must be viewed as a strategy with limited ability to increase a health care firm's revenues or decrease its expenses relative to those generated in the absence of changes in vertical integration. When revenues and expenses are considered together, there is reason to believe that the strategy will not lead to higher returns for the firm. The contribution of vertical integration to improving control of patient flows or entry into rapidly growing markets should not be overestimated.

Many of the difficulties in realizing benefits from vertical integration are not problems that can be readily solved with the passage of time. They are related to fundamental problems in combining services for which the environment is constantly changing, demand is uncertain, and production processes are specialized but variable and hard to standardize.

REFERENCES

Biggadike, E. R. 1979. *Corporate Diversification.* Cambridge, MA: Harvard University Press.

Chase, R. B., and D. A. Tansik. 1983. "The Customer Contact Model for Organization Design." *Management Science,* 29(9): 1037-1050.

Clement, J. P. 1988. "Vertical Integration and Diversification of Acute Care Hospitals: Conceptual Definitions." *Hospital & Health Services Administration,* 33(1), 99-110.

Conrad, D. A., S. S. Mick, C. W. Madden, and G. Hoare. 1988. "Vertical Structures and Control in Health Care Markets: A Conceptual Framework and Empirical Review." *Medical Care Review,* 45(1): 49-100.

Conrad, D. A., and W. L. Dowling. 1990. "Vertical Integration in Health Services: Theory and Managerial Implications." *Health Care Management Review,* 15(4): 9-22.

Grannemann, T. W., R. S. Brown, and M. V. Pauly. 1986. "Estimating Hospital Costs." *Journal of Health Economics,* 5(2): 107-127.

Harrigan, K. R. 1984. "Formulating Vertical Integration Strategies." *Academy of Management Review,* 9(4): 638-652.

Mancino, D. M. 1991. "Nonexempt Uses of Tax-Exempt Hospital Bonds." *Journal of Health and Hospital Law,* 24(3): 73-87.

Mick, S. 1990. "Explaining Vertical Integration in Health Care: An Analysis and Synthesis of Transaction-Cost Economics and Strategic-Management Theory." In S. Mick and Associates, eds. *Innovations in Health Care Delivery.* San Francisco: Jossey-Bass, 1990, pp. 207-240.

Mick, S. S., and D. A. Conrad. 1988. "The Decision to Integrate Vertically in Health Care Organizations." *Hospital & Health Services Administration,* 33(3): 345-360.

Mills, D. E., and L. Schumann. 1985. "Industry Structure With Fluctuating Demand." *American Economic Review,* 75(3): 758-767.

Porter, M. E. 1980. *Competitive Strategy.* New York: The Free Press, 1980.

Sneed, J. H., and D. Marx, Jr. 1990. *Antitrust: Challenge of the Health Care Field.* Washington, D.C.: The National Health Lawyers Association.

> **ISSUE SIX**
>
> *Employers should be required to provide health insurance for employees as a means of ensuring that all citizens have access to health care.*

It can be argued that the United States has both the best health care system in the world and the worst system in the world. The Nobel prize for physiology and medicine, first awarded in 1901, has been presented eighty-one times. Americans have won the award outright or shared it thirty-nine times (World Almanac, 1990). Yet, the United States has an infant mortality rate higher than other industrialized nations even though over 12 percent of our gross national product (GNP) is spent on health care. The Health Care Financing Administration (HCFA) estimates that health care will account for 15 percent of the GNP by the year 2000 (Enthoven and Kronick, 1989). Despite these enormous expenditures on health care, the needs of many of our nation's poor are not being met.

Providing equitable access to quality health care has been an issue in this country for many years. Increasing costs, brought about in part by new, life-extending technologies, such as open heart surgery and bone marrow and organ transplants, are focusing even more attention on the need for reforms. Many in the health care system are feeling the burden of paying the costs for the uninsured and underinsured. Over 37 million U.S. citizens have no health insurance and another 15 million are underinsured (Updata, 1991). Over half of the uninsured adults in the United States are classified as "working poor." Although they are employed, their incomes are too high to qualify for Medicaid but too low to afford insurance coverage (Strasser, 1990).

Those without health insurance seldom receive preventative care and, as a result, have more emergency situations. Treatment needs are greater in emergency situations, and consequently, the cost of providing care becomes higher. Prior to prospective payment systems (PPS), hospitals were able to provide medical care for uninsured patients by shifting the costs to those individuals who had private insurance coverage. PPS, however, reimburses providers on the basis of diagnostic-related-groups (DRGs), and the costs are frequently higher than the reimbursements. Because of their location (ghetto, urban, and rural) or specialty (obstetrics and emergency), some providers face a disproportionate share of indigent care. They may not be able to survive without a change in the health care system.

The major stakeholders in developing a system that ensures health care for all citizens include politicians, who ultimately have the responsibility to provide for the public good, insurers who want to remain in business, physicians who want to maintain their standards of living and desire freedom from controls, providers who want reasonable (or at least adequate) reimbursement rates, members of business and labor who do not want to assume the burden of the nation's health, and consumers who desire quality care at reasonable prices. The key concerns with any plan seem to be access to care, quality of care, and cost.

The most frequently cited options include national health insurance administered by the federal government or some combination of federal and state government, a revamping of the Medicaid/Medicare system, or legislation that requires employers to provide health insurance for working persons. In 1988, Congress created a bipartisan commission (known as the Pepper Commission for Claude Pepper, Florida Democrat and the oldest member of Congress at the time) to investigate comprehensive health care in the United States. The Pepper Commission report recommended health coverage for everyone. The coverage would be paid for by requiring employers to provide insurance coverage for their employees or, in the case of small businesses, pay a tax that would finance a public fund to cover uninsured employees. The federal government would develop a list of the minimal benefits that employers would have to provide. These would probably include primary, preventive, and some catastrophic care. The commission recommended insurance reform to provide predictable rates and uniform coverage. In addition, the government would provide a new federal program that would become a safety net for the poor and unemployed (Rockefeller, 1990).

The results of a nationwide survey, published in *Hospitals*, indicated that 75 percent of all Americans feel that employers should be required to provide health benefits (Schaffer, 1988). Requiring employers to insure employees may not be the answer, however. There are questions about the number of workers who would be displaced because employers find it easier and less expensive to layoff employees than to pay the higher cost of health care if such a requirement were approved. Additional questions concern the effect the requirement would have on consumer prices and worldwide competitiveness. Furthermore, although people would have greater financial access to care, would they have physical access? And what result would the waiting time for care have on the quality of care?

Two colleagues from the University of Alabama at Birmingham eloquently present opposing views concerning mandatory employer-financed health insurance for American workers. Myron D. Fottler argues that employers should provide health insurance for all employees, and Michael A. Morrisey argues against that position.

REFERENCES

Enthoven, A., and R. Kronick. 1989. "A Consumer-Choice Health Plan for the 1990s." *The New England Journal of Medicine,* 320(2): 94-101.

Rockefeller, J. 1990. "The Pepper Commission Report on Comprehensive Health Care." *The New England Journal of Medicine,* 322(14): 1005-1007.

Schaffer, M. 1988. "Social Issues." *Hospitals,* 67(17): 110.

Strasser, A. 1990. "Would Universal Health Insurance Undermine the Quality of Health Care?" *Occupational Health and Safety,* 59(1): 52.

Updata. 1991. *Healthcare Financial Management,* 2: 6.

World Almanac and Book of Facts. 1990. New York: St. Martin's Press.

> **POINT**
>
> *Employers should be required to provide health insurance for employees as a means of ensuring that all citizens have access to health care.*

MYRON D. FOTTLER
University of Alabama at Birmingham

Myron D. Fottler is professor of management and director of the Ph.D. Program in Administration-Health Services with joint appointments in the School of Business and the Department of Health Services Administration in the School of Health Related Professions at the University of Alabama at Birmingham. He has an MBA from Boston University and a Ph.D. in business from Columbia University. Prior to joining the faculty at UAB, he taught at the University of Iowa and the State University of New York at Buffalo. His current interests include health care cost containment, job design, managed care, and the strategic management of human resources and other stakeholders. Dr. Fottler has published extensively in most of the major health care and management journals and has been active in the Academy of Management and in the Association of University Programs in Health Administration. His coauthored books include *Prospective Payment* (1985), *Strategic Management of Human Resources in Health Services Organizations* (1988), *Challenges in Health Care Management* (1990), and *Applications in Human Resource Management* (1992). He has served as a reviewer for many academic journals and currently serves on the editorial review boards of *Health Care Management Review* and *Journal of Behavioral Economics*.

The author would like to thank John Hyde, a Ph.D. candidate in administration-health services at the University of Alabama at Birmingham, for his research assistance in the preparation of this essay.

THE PROBLEM

The American health care system is approaching a breaking point. It has consumed more than $600 billion or 11.3 percent of all the goods and services produced in the United States in 1990. Yet even with this vast expenditure, access to the U.S. health care system is limited.

One of the most compelling health policy issues in the 1990s is the growing number and proportion of the population that has no health coverage — no private health insurance, no Medicare or Medicaid coverage, and no coverage through any other public or private program. Those without any coverage for health care expenses have become known as "the uninsured."

The uninsured increased from 27 million, or 13 percent of the U.S. population, in 1977 to 37 million, or 16 percent of the population in 1987 (Kasper, Walden, and Wilensky, 1978; and Short, Monheit, and Beauregard, 1988). From 1980 to 1990, the proportion of uninsured has increased approximately 20 percent. This significant growth in the uninsured population has reversed the trend that had lasted for more than half a century (Brown, 1989). Part of the decrease in the proportion of the employed population who receive employment-based insurance coverage was due to an increase in the share of total employment in the retail and service sectors of the economy (Congressional Research Service, 1988).

The uninsured represent 15.6 percent of the total population and 17.5 percent of those under age 65 (Congressional Research Service, 1988). Some people are uninsured part of the year, and others are uninsured over the entire year. Monheit and Schur (1988) found that a total of 30 percent of the nonelderly population they surveyed were without health insurance at some time during the thirty-two-month period of the survey and that 22 percent of those who were privately insured lost their coverage at some time during the survey.

Anyone can become uninsured regardless of age, income, or employment status. However, the uninsured are more likely to be attached to the work force in low-wage jobs, young, members of families headed by a single parent, poor or near poor, and members of minority groups (Brown, 1989; Moyer, 1989; Pepper Commission, 1990). Workers and their families comprise more than three-quarters of the uninsured population (Monheit, et al., 1985; Moyer, 1989). More than half of all uninsured people are working. Industries with high percentages of uninsured include agriculture, construction, personal services, and entertainment.

Employers of all sizes have uninsured workers, but small employers are less likely to insure their workers than are large employers. In 1987, among all workers whose employers did not offer health benefits, 65 percent worked in firms with fewer than twenty-five employees (Employees Benefits Research Institute, 1987; ICF, 1987). Although many small employers provide insurance for their workers, large numbers cannot afford the high cost. Because they have fewer employees among whom to spread administrative costs and any losses for extremely costly enrollees, small employers must pay more for insurance than large ones.

Among firms that do not sponsor employee health plans, the most common reason given by small firms (fewer than 100 employees) was insufficient profits (67 percent) and the high cost of insurance (62 percent). The major factor that contributes to the high cost of health insurance in small firms is experience rating, which has isolated smaller risk groups and exposed them to ever escalating rates

(Brown, 1988). Small firms in industries thought to present high risks pay extremely high health insurance rates or are forced to exclude certain classes of employees or certain conditions. Sometimes they are unable to obtain coverage at any price.

Significance of the Problem

Access to health insurance is an important issue for at least three reasons:

1. Health insurance coverage is a determinant of access to health services.
2. The lack of adequate health insurance puts individuals and families at risk for significant economic losses from medical expenses.
3. Providers and others end up paying for uncompensated care provided to uninsured persons.

First, the uninsured have less access to necessary health services than do the insured. Davis and Rowland (1983) found that insured persons under age 65 averaged 3.7 physician visits per year. This is 54 percent more than the average of 2.4 visits per year for the uninsured. Freeman (1987) found that uninsured persons are less likely than the insured to see a physician in a twelve-month period (59 percent vs. 68 percent); less likely to get their young children adequately immunized (81 percent vs. 94 percent); less likely to have their blood pressure checked (50 percent vs. 60 percent); and less likely to see a physician within 30 days of serious symptoms (32 percent vs. 61 percent). The uninsured are also more likely to receive their care in institutional settings such as hospital emergency rooms and outpatient clinics than the insured (Congressional Research Service, 1988). Furthermore, there is evidence that access to health services for the uninsured declined during the 1980s (Freeman, et al., 1987).

Second, although private health insurance has successfully spread the financial risks for the majority of the population, lack of sufficient coverage leaves many people (the insured as well as the uninsured) open to extraordinary consumption of their family's financial resources in the event of large medical bills. In most cases, it is inadequate coverage or no coverage at all that results in these relatively catastrophic expenses (Berki, 1986).

Third, despite their lower rate of health services utilization, the uninsured do obtain care when they feel they cannot postpone or forgo it. In these circumstances, however, because their care is uncompensated, they are more likely to incur excessive out-of-pocket expenses and to place financial burdens on health care providers, government, and third-party payers. Historically, hospitals have rationed uncompensated care by discouraging use by the uninsured or by reducing the services heavily used by the uninsured (Feder, Hadley, and Mullner, 1984). They have also shifted much of the cost of providing uncompensated care to privately insured patients and their employers. Because "cost-shifting" has become more difficult in the last few years, access to care for the uninsured has become even more restricted.

The Current Crisis

U.S. health care costs continued to escalate at a rate of 12 to 14 percent per year from 1988 to 1990. Health benefit costs for employers increased an average of 20 percent per year over the same period. By the end of this century (the year 2000), it has been projected that the United States will spend $1.5 trillion, or 15 percent of GNP on health care.

Rapidly rising health care costs are increasing the numbers of people without health insurance and straining the system's capacity to provide care for those who cannot pay (Pepper Commission, 1990). The cost escalation is not only reducing access to the U.S. health care system but also affecting the quality of the service. Most employers have responded to rising health insurance costs by restricting health care coverage, shifting greater portions of the cost to employees, placing restrictions on policies, and specifying which health care providers the patient may use. These policies have not only failed to stabilize health care costs but have resulted in less access to the system.

The gap is widening between the majority of insured Americans, who can take advantage of the best medical services in the world, and the uninsured, who find it hard to obtain even basic, needed care. As this gap increases, the burden of financing care for those without adequate coverage is undermining the stability of our health institutions. Even for the insured majority, the unchecked growth in health care costs is steadily eroding the private insurance system. This further undermines the insured population's defense against financial risk in case of illness.

The type of health insurance that is available in the United States is part of the problem. Insurance policies emphasizing front-end coverage pay for routine services or the initial costs of a service but not the later, heavier expenses. Unfortunately, those who are poorly served by front-end coverage are those who need help the most when faced with unexpectedly serious illnesses leading to very high medical bills. By leaving policyholders vulnerable to catastrophic losses while covering inexpensive routine costs, front-end insurance operates contrary to all other forms of insurance in this country (Butler and Haislmaier, 1989).

Moreover, these types of policies reward physicians for prescribing more treatments. The more treatment a doctor provides, the more money he or she receives. Doctors are encouraged to prescribe additional treatments up to the limit of the patient's insurance coverage even if these treatments may contribute only marginal improvements in the patient's health or well-being.

The equivalent of front-end, acute care health insurance is an automobile insurance policy that pays the first $500 annually for labor and replacement parts due to accidents or mechanical breakdown. Under this type of policy, the average car owner would have most repairs paid for in return for a (employer-provided) premium, and the auto mechanic is allowed to determine what work should be done. The car owner would have little incentive to question the costs of minor repairs or to spend money on proper preventive maintenance. Ultimately, the effect would be the same kind of cost and insurance crisis we now see in health care.

Although few Americans would purchase this type of insurance policy for their automobiles, millions are encouraged by the tax code to purchase such policies for their health care. Because the money an employer spends on furnishing health insurance for a worker may be excluded from taxable income without limit, the worker tends to view health insurance plans as tax-free compensation. The result is insurance that is no longer used to spread risks but to avoid taxes on income for routine, minor medical costs.

With patients no longer paying directly for the more common services, normal incentives to question the cost and quality of these services diminishes. Instead, patients have an incentive to demand more services and more expensive services. At the same time, physicians and hospitals have incentives to increase the price and quantity of their services. This situation is exacerbated by legislation in most states, which mandates that all health insurance companies offering insurance within the state must offer coverage for numerous specific services.

All of these factors in combination have created a crisis. A Harris poll, taken in February 1989, found that 89 percent of the American public are dissatisfied with the nation's health care system and only 10 percent think it is working "pretty well." More than 60 percent of the American people are ready and eager for a fundamental change in the way health care is financed in this country (Blendon and Taylor, 1989). They are not critical of the basic delivery system per se but rather experience financial insecurity due to inadequate coverage.

A MANDATED BENEFITS PROPOSAL

The federal government should require all employers either to provide a minimum health insurance package for all employees working 15 or more hours a week or to contribute to an assigned-risk plan for those employees not covered by health insurance.

This mandated benefit proposal would have the following characteristics:

1. All employers would be required to offer employees a basic package of health insurance benefits or to contribute to an assigned-risk pool. The minimum benefit package would not include routine health services and would contain significant consumer cost-sharing, based on ability to pay and an out-of-pocket maximum. The federally specific minimum benefit package would include all physician and hospital care once a threshold level (perhaps 2 percent of gross income) of health expenditures for the individual had been reached. State laws that require particular minimum benefits would be preempted.
2. Experience rating and preexisting condition exclusions would be prohibited. Special rules would be established for marketing to small groups. Insurers offering managed-care to large employers would be required to extend the option to small employers as well. The underwriting, rating, and marketing practices that are unraveling private insurance protection for small employers would be ended.
3. Small businesses would be encouraged through tax credits/subsidies to provide coverage for their employees until the changes specified above had been fully implemented. Larger businesses that did not provide coverage would be required to contribute to an assigned risk plan without subsidy.

4. Employers who are not providing health insurance after a phase-in period, would be required to contribute to a federal assigned-risk program on the basis of a fixed share of their payroll expense.
5. All employed individuals and their dependents would be required to obtain health insurance either from their employer or from the assigned-risk program.
6. All health insurers would be required to offer incentives in the form of rebates to insured consumers who did not overutilize services and to providers who operated in a cost-efficient manner.

Economic Feasibility

Among all the proposals to expand health insurance coverage, short of national health insurance, this proposal would cover the largest subset of the uninsured and their dependents. Coverage would be extended to about 28 million people, accounting for 12 percent of the population and 75 percent of the uninsured. While national health insurance could theoretically cover 100 percent of the population, it is not economically or politically feasible in the near future.

Costs for the proposed program would be relatively light and would be borne outside the federal budget. The Pepper Commission (1990) recommended mandated employer health insurance and an expansion of the Medicaid program for those who are not employed. The estimated net cost for both programs was only $12 billion dollars for 1990. This is less than 2 percent more than the nation now spends for health care. This $12 billion would have raised health care expenditures from $647 billion to $659 billion in 1990. The mandated benefits program alone probably would have cost only $6 billion to $7 billion, or about 1 percent of our current health care expenditures.

The Pepper Commission (1990) calculated that the costs of subsidizing small employers and the assigned-risk pool in the mandated benefit program would increase federal spending about $18.0 billion. In addition, employers who do not now insure their employees would spend $27.5 billion for employee insurance. However, the total $45.5 billion in new expenditures would be partly offset by reductions of $7.4 billion in state and local spending, $12.8 billion for employers who now insure, and $19.3 billion in household expenditures by health care consumers. The net total cost of the mandated program then would be about $6 billion. The expansion of the Medicare Program would also cost about $6 billion.

It has been projected that employers presently offering health insurance to their workers and dependents would save almost $13 billion because they would no longer have to pay for uncompensated care provided to the uninsured. Individuals and families would save over $19 billion as employers and government share their health care costs. State and local governments would save more than $7 billion in payments now made for the uninsured.

The federal government and those employers who do not now provide health insurance for their workers would share the new costs. The $27.5 billion in increased payroll costs for health insurance accounts for less than 4 percent of payroll expenses after taxes. For a single employer, however, the increase could not exceed a specified percentage of payroll. This provision, as well as the phase-in period, should cushion the cost impact for employers not previously offering health insurance. The proposal would also contribute to a "level playing field," i.e., an employer offering health insurance to his employees would not be forced to indirectly subsidize the costs of health care for a competitor choosing not to offer insurance.

What economic impact would the mandated benefits proposal have on the country? Several studies considering the jobs that would be gained in the health care sector found no net job loss, and some found a small increase in employment over a three-year period (U.S. Congress, Committee on Labor and Human Resources, 1989). More importantly, the costs of a mandated program must be compared to the far greater human and economic costs of continuing to deny millions of Americans access to health insurance.

A lean and basic insurance package focusing on major health expenditures is only one of the keys to cost containment. The other key is a strong system of provider and consumer incentives (Fottler and Lanning, 1986). Employers would have an incentive to provide a basic health insurance package because the alternative would be to contribute to an assigned-risk program. Federal subsidies would only be available to pay for the basic plan, not a more comprehensive alternative.

Consumers would have strong incentives to be cost-effective purchasers of health services. The routine, less-expensive services would not be covered at all. Services that would be covered would have significant deductibles and cost sharing. Rebates would be offered to consumers who did not file a claim in a given year. Because health insurance would no longer be a tax-free employee benefit, consumers would have a strong incentive to shop for the best overall insurance package, considering price, coverage, and quality of service. Insurance companies would therefore have an incentive to offer new and innovative products. In the long run, all of these incentives would result in a more cost-effective health care system with greater access and more options for consumers.

Political Feasibility

The idea of requiring employers to offer health insurance coverage enjoys extraordinarily broad public support. Two recent polls found that approximately three out of every four Americans felt that employers should be required to provide health insurance (U.S. Congress, Committee on Labor and Human Resources, 1989). This level of support is found in all regions of the country and among all political ideologies. The American Hospital Association, various medical associations, and a variety of other organizations that represent health providers, business, consumers, and labor have endorsed this approach as part of a comprehensive strategy to expand access.

Obviously, health care providers will be better off financially once the burden of uncompensated care is reduced. Those employers and consumers who are well insured presently should see the costs of their health insurance increase more slowly because the proposal would significantly reduce cost-shifting. Employers offering health insurance would no longer be required to bear the health costs for employees of less responsible competitors who do not provide health insurance. Organized labor would also benefit because each employer would be required to provide a basic health insurance package.

There is some controversy over who ultimately bears the cost of that portion of health insurance paid by the employer. Is it the employer (through lower profits), the employee (through lower direct wages), or the consumer (through higher prices)? Although evidence on this subject is not currently available, the most likely answer is "all of the above." It would depend on the nature of the product and labor markets for each employer. Because small employers typically operate in more competitive product and labor markets with more elastic demand curves in each, the possibility of passing on higher health insurance costs to the consumer or employee is less likely than in the case of large employers.

Not surprisingly, most of the opposition to employer mandates have come from small businesses that are concerned about the impact of the new requirement on their economic viability. However, the plan proposed here would eliminate or mitigate most of these concerns. By mandating a true insurance program with an emphasis on major expenses, offering an alternative risk pool to minimize administrative expenses, providing a federal subsidy for cases in which health insurance premiums exceed a certain percentage of payroll, reforming the market for health insurance, preempting state laws that mandate minimum benefits, and allowing for an appropriate phase in of the requirements, small business opposition should be muted.

Some have criticized mandated health insurance benefits because they do not offer a comprehensive solution to the health care access problem now faced. Those who are not employed (or employed less than 15 hours per week) and their dependents are not covered. There is no question that mandated benefits offer an incremental or partial solution to the problems identified earlier in this paper. Perhaps a more realistic question is whether or not the mandated insurance approach should be part of an incremental approach that will eventually result in comprehensive coverage for all citizens? The answer is an unequivocal yes. It is the only approach that is likely to be economically and politically feasible during the 1990s. A rejection of mandated insurance will result in a worsening of the present crisis and a breakdown in our health care system to the detriment of all of us. Mandated health insurance is necessary and the time to act is now!

REFERENCES

Berki, S. E. 1986. "A Look at Catastrophic Medical Expenses and the Poor." *Health Affairs,* 5(4): 138-145.

Blendon, R. J., and H. Taylor. 1989. "Views on Health Care: Public Opinion in Three Nations." *Health Affairs,* 8(1): 149-157.

Brown, E. R. 1988. "Principles for a National Health Program: A Framework for Analysis." *Milbank Quarterly,* 66(4): 573-617.

Brown, E. R. 1989. "Access to Health Insurance in the United States." *Medical Care Review,* 46(4): 349-385.

Butler, S. M., and E. F. Haislmaier. 1989. *Critical Issues: A National Health System for America.* Washington, D.C.: The Heritage Foundation.

Congressional Research Service. 1988. *Health Insurance and the Uninsured: Background Data and Analysis.* Washington, D.C.: U.S. Government Printing Office.

Davis, K., and D. Rowland. 1983. "Uninsured and Underserved: Inequities in Health Care in the United States." *Milbank Memorial Fund Quarterly,* 61(2): 149-176.

Employee Benefits Research Institute. 1987. "A Profile of the Nonelderly Population Without Health Insurance." Issue Brief Number 66. Washington, D.C.: Employee Benefits Research Institute.

Feder, J., J. Hadley, and R. Mullner. 1984. "Falling Through the Cracks: Poverty, Insurance Coverage, and Hospital Care for the Poor." *Milbank Memorial Fund Quarterly,* 62(4): 544-566.

Fottler, M. D., and J. A. Lanning. 1986. "A Comprehensive Incentive Approach to Employer Health Care Cost Containment." *California Management Review,* 29(1): 75-94.

Freeman, H. E. 1987. *Americans Report on Their Access to Health Care: The 1986 Robert Wood Johnson Foundation Survey.* Los Angeles: Institute for Social Science Research.

Freeman, H. E., R. J. Blendon, L. H. Aiken, S. Sudman, C. F. Mullnix, and C. R. Corey. 1987. "Americans Report on Their Access to Health Care." *Health Affairs,* 6(1): 6-18.

ICF, Inc. 1987. *Health Care Coverage and Costs in Small and Large Businesses.* Final Report for the U.S. Small Business Administration. Washington, D.C.: ICF Publishers.

Kasper, J., D. C. Walden, and G. R. Wilensky. 1978. "Who Are the Uninsured?" *National Health Care Expenditures Study.* Hyattsville, MD: National Center for Health Services Research.

Monheit, A. C., M. M. Hogen, M. L. Beck, and P. J. Farley. 1985. "The Employed Uninsured and the Role of Public Policy." *Inquiry,* 22(4): 348-364.

Monheit, A. C., and C. L. Schur. 1988. "The Dynamics of Health Insurance Loss: A Tale of Two Cohorts." *Inquiry,* 25(3): 315-327.

Moyer, M. E., 1989. "A Revised Look at the Number of Uninsured Americans." *Health Affairs,* 8(2): 102-110.

Pepper Commission (U.S. Bipartisan Commission on Comprehensive Health Care). 1990. *A Call for Action: Executive Summary.* Washington, D.C.: U.S. Government Printing Office.

Short, P. F., A. Monheit, and K. Beauregard. 1988. *Uninsured Americans: A 1987 Profile.* National Center for Health Services Research and Technology Assessment, U.S. Department of Health and Human Services.

U.S. Congress. Committee on Labor and Human Resources. 1989. *Background Information on the Basic Health Benefits for All Americans Act of 1989.* 101st Congress, 1st session.

COUNTERPOINT

*Employers should **not** be required to provide health insurance for employees as a means of ensuring that all citizens have access to health care.*

MICHAEL A. MORRISEY
University of Alabama at Birmingham

Michael A. Morrisey is an economist and health services researcher. Before joining the faculty of the University of Alabama at Birmingham, he was senior economist and assistant director of the Hospital Research and Educational Trust, the research affiliate of the American Hospital Association. Morrisey received his Ph.D. in economics from the University of Washington. His research activity has included studies of health maintenance organizations, state regulation of hospitals, multihospital systems, hospital capital finance and an evaluation of the Medicare prospective payment system. His current research focuses on rural health care delivery, the regulation of insurance markets, and employer sponsored health insurance. He also teaches courses in health economics and health insurance and is deputy editor of *Medical Care*. He has served as a consultant to the Health Insurance Association of America, the Employee Benefits Research Institute, and the Federation of American Health Systems as well as numerous federal and state agencies.

In 1987, there were approximately 30 million uninsured Americans (Moyer, 1989). Some two-thirds of these were employed or living in households in which there was one working adult (Thorpe, 1989). It would seem that a straightforward way to eliminate a large portion of the uninsured problem would be to require employers to provide health insurance for all their workers and dependents. Things are not always as straightforward as they seem. In this case, the key issue is: Who pays for the newly mandated health insurance?

I will argue that approximately three-quarters of the costs of these benefits would be borne by low-income workers. Taxpayers would pay about one-quarter. Under the plan, small firms would be disadvantaged compared to larger ones, and there would be some modest unemployment effects. Once these points are established, it is easy to show that as a matter of economic reasoning, most workers would correctly perceive themselves as worse off under an employer mandated health insurance plan than they are currently.

A GENERIC EMPLOYER MANDATE

The states of Hawaii and Massachusetts have enacted legislation that mandates employer provision of health insurance for most workers. The Kennedy-Waxman bill proposes such a law for the entire country. Employer mandates are also part of the Pepper Commission recommendations. A generic employer mandate requires employers to provide at least a minimum benefit package for their employees. Embellishments include the definition of covered workers (the distinction between full-time and part-time workers), the required coverage of spouses and dependents, and the extent to which employers and employees share the premium. Elements of the Kennedy-Waxman bill, for example, require coverage for all those employed 17.5 hours per week or more. Dependents must be covered unless they are covered by another employer plan, and 80 percent of the premium is to be paid by the employer unless the worker earns less than 125 percent of the minimum wage. The plan covers medically necessary inpatient and outpatient care to a $3,000 stop-loss (Kennedy, 1989). These features have been the subject of several simulations that are summarized in the next section.

COSTS AND COVERAGE UNDER A MANDATE

Before proceeding further, it will be instructive to consider the estimates of the number of people covered under an employer mandate and the costs of such a program. Morrisey (1991) provides a detailed summary of alternative estimates. Surprisingly, four groups of people are affected by this straightforward employer mandate proposal. The first group are the currently uninsured. Roughly 24 to 25 million uninsured persons would have coverage under a mandate.

The second group are those who currently have public coverage: Medicaid, Medicare, or CHAMPUS (Civilian Health and Medical Program of the Uniformed Services) for example. Although estimates vary, it is thought that between 5.3 and 9.5 million people who currently have public coverage would switch to private coverage under an employer mandate. Most mandate provisions require private coverage to pay before a public plan is liable.

The third group affected by an employer mandate are those who currently hold private individual or private group policies. It is generally acknowledged that holders of individual coverage would drop it in the face of an employer mandate. Thorpe (1989) estimates that there are approximately 10.3 million of these persons. Group switchers are usually those who move from one employer plan to another. A typical example of a group switcher is a wife employed outside the home and covered under her husband's plan who then switches to her own group plan. Private switchers are generally estimated as a group; the simulations suggest some 50 million persons are affected.

A final group of affected persons are those who currently have employer-sponsored health insurance and benefits that do not meet the minimum coverage provisions of the legislation. Needleman, et al (1990) estimated that there are nearly 26 million of these people.

Ignoring the costs of the last group, the costs of an employer mandate are on the order of $21 to $32 billion (Morrisey, 1991). There are, however, public program savings of approximately $5 to $8 billion and savings from cost shifting of $3 billion.[1] To see who pays these costs, it is necessary to understand the nature of worker compensation and employer-sponsored health insurance.

ECONOMICS OF EMPLOYER SPONSORED HEALTH INSURANCE

The theory of labor compensation has a long history in economics. Rigorous study of employer-sponsored health insurance in the context of labor market theory, however, is relatively recent, appearing in the work of Goldstein and Pauly (1976), Jensen (1986), and Danzon (1989). Firms hire workers and, at the margin, pay them what they are worth. Worth is defined as the amount of extra revenue that the firm gets from the efforts of the last worker in each job class. Of course, the firm would like to pay less, but if it did, workers would tend to work for other employers.

Why would an employer ever offer health insurance in this simple world? The answer is equally simple: It costs less to do so. Because workers place some value on health insurance, they are willing to accept compensation bundles that include health insurance and somewhat lower wages rather than wages alone. If a firm finds that it can get health insurance at a price lower than what the worker is willing to give up in wages, the worker is happy with the new insurance-wage bundle, and the firm has lowered its labor costs.

In fact, health insurance tends to be less expensive when purchased through an employer. There are three reasons for this. The first reason has to do with insurance underwriting. Employed people tend to be healthier on average than unemployed people. Thus, employment serves as a good signal of lower expected claims costs, and an employer group can purchase coverage at lower cost than can an individual.

The second reason has to do with the nature of existing tax laws. Health insurance is not taxed as federal or state income, nor is it subject to FICA taxes. Thus, if an employee were to value a dollar of health insurance as equivalent to a dollar of take home pay, then an employer needs to spend only a dollar on health insurance rather than a dollar plus tax on take-home pay.

Third, there are economies in the marketing and administration of employer-group plans when compared to individually purchased insurance. The personnel

---

[1] The cost-shifted savings are questionable, however (Morrisey, 1991).

department of a firm keeps track of who is employed, when they are absent, and other related facts. Many of these statistics are necessary to administer a health plan, and there are some economies in doing these things only once.

From the worker's perspective, wages would be adjusted to reflect the change in the new form of compensation. Other things being equal, more health insurance means lower wages. Any attempt to reduce health insurance through the use of increased deductibles, for example, requires workers to be compensated in some other way. This concept of compensating differentials is key to understanding insurance in the employment setting.

Compensating differentials imply that large firms providing dependent health insurance, for example, do not subsidize the labor costs of smaller firms that do not offer health insurance. Instead, workers in both sets of firms are paid what they are worth. Those in the larger firm take their compensation in the form of lower wages and more health insurance. Workers in the smaller firm take higher wages and little or no health insurance.

If health insurance lowers labor costs, why don't all firms offer health insurance? The answer is twofold. First, all firms do not face the same costs of offering health insurance. Firms with high turnover face higher administrative costs, and small firms have higher administrative costs per worker. Furthermore, as Chollet (1988) notes, small firms are particularly prone to adverse selection, including the employment of family members for the explicit purpose of insuring anticipated future medical expenses.[2] Second, firms may be willing to offer health insurance but minimum wage statutes prevent the compensating differential from taking place.[3]

If some firms have lower labor compensation costs because they can offer health insurance more cheaply than others, why don't these lower-cost firms drive the others out of business? The answer is that different workers place different values on health insurance. There are several reasons for this. First, some workers prefer to spend their limited income on food and shelter rather than on health insurance, even given the lower price of insurance available through an employer plan. Second, some workers are less likely to become ill than are others. If they don't expect to use the benefit, it is of little value to them. Third, some workers may be covered under their spouse's or parent's plan. For them, insurance is largely redundant. Finally, the income and assets of some workers may be near the Medicaid eligibility threshold in their state. A good Medicaid program would then substitute for private coverage.

---

[2] It has been argued that the law of large numbers works against small employers because the coverage of a smaller number of persons is always relatively more risky than the coverage of a larger number. While this is true, if the underlying expected loss and its variance are equal across small groups, an insurer (or a cooperative of small employers) could pool these groups and reduce the risk to that comparable to a single large group. Either the administrative costs of such pooling are prohibitive or the expected losses and variances of losses are not the same. The problem appears to be differences in risk, not small size per se.

[3] There is also a potentially severe adverse selection problem if a firm offers only health insurance. The firm should expect to attract disproportionately more workers who expect to use health insurance. Its claims experience is unlikely to be the same as a firm that offers health insurance as a small portion of a larger compensation bundle. Consequently, the small firm's insurance premium would be higher than that of a firm not subject to adverse selection.

Thus, the theory argues that those firms that have low costs of providing health insurance will tend to attract those persons who have stronger preferences for health insurance. Those firms with higher costs of providing health insurance will attract workers who value insurance less intensely.[4]

The theory of compensating differentials has several implications for any policy mandating employer-sponsored health insurance. It argues that forcing an employer to provide health insurance means that the wages or other benefits of those workers without health insurance will fall. These workers will pay the bulk of the price of mandated benefits.

In addition it implies that federal and state income taxpayers will shoulder a significant share of the cost. If a worker faces a 15 percent federal income tax rate, a 3 percent state tax rate and a 14.9 percent (combined) FICA tax rate, taxpayers as a group will pay roughly 33 percent of the so-called employer-paid mandated benefit cost in the form of tax revenue losses. In most proposals there is some form of "premium sharing." If the employer-paid portion is 80 percent of the premium, taxpayers will pay about 25 percent (0.33 × 0.8) of the full cost. Obviously, the taxpayer share depends upon the relevant marginal tax rates.

Using the theory of compensating differentials, it is clear that the predominant effect of introducing premium sharing between the employer and employee is the reduction of lost tax revenue. If the "employer pays," the worker actually pays with pre-tax dollars. If the employee pays, the worker pays with post-tax dollars.[5]

Firms forced to offer health insurance will be worse off financially. They did not offer health insurance initially because it was more costly than offering wages only. Because insurance is more costly to them, after the mandate they will have to reduce wages more than other firms if they are to have no change in labor costs. However, because their workers value health benefits less intensely, the wage decrease cannot be too great. Indeed, the wage reduction must be less than the cost of the benefits if their workers are to believe that they are as well off as before the mandate. As a consequence, these firms will face higher labor costs. They will hire somewhat fewer workers. Some of the displaced workers will migrate to other, most likely larger, firms. Others will become unemployed.

The presence of a minimum wage constraint further complicates the story. A worker earning the minimum wage is unable to absorb the compensating differential of a newly required health insurance mandate. Some of these people will lose their jobs, or they will begin working in positions offering too few hours to qualify for the mandate.

---

[4] Goldstein and Pauly (1976) were the first to develop this theory of a "separating equilibrium." The theory can be expanded to deal with firms offering multiple insurance options within a single firm (Jensen, 1986). This problem becomes complex because the firm must trade-off attracting workers with differing insurance tastes while it faces internal problems of adverse selection among the plans offered.

[5] This result will not hold precisely if currently uninsured employees have other forms of untaxed benefits that could be adjusted. However, those without health insurance also tend to lack other forms of health benefits. Furthermore, if flexible spending accounts continue to be available and widely used, the "who pays the premium" issue becomes moot. The flexible spending account effectively takes what would be post-tax income spent on health insurance and converts it into pre-tax income.

EVIDENCE THAT WORKERS PAY

Simulations have suggested that the cost of a generic employer mandate would be approximately $30 billion. Because of the tax shield that is brought about by the way in which the federal and state income tax laws are written, currently uninsured workers would pay approximately three-quarters of this amount — $22.5 billion. Federal and state taxpayers would pay for the other quarter in the form of reductions in tax revenues. This will amount to approximately $7.5 billion annually.

A number of economic analysts have long supported the view that workers would pay for insurance mandates. When a mandate proposal was advanced in the late 1970s as a national health insurance scheme, Phelps (1980) argued that workers would pay and demonstrated that given the inflation of the time, a single year without raises would allow real wages to decline sufficiently to pay fully for mandated benefits. More recently, the analysis by the Congressional Budget Office (CBO) of the Kennedy-Waxman bill explicitly broke with policy to show the effects of an employer mandate. CBO routinely presents its findings in a static world. For example, in estimating the effects of a change in tax law, for example, CBO would not estimate the effects that incentives to save more would have on economic activity and ultimately on tax revenues. In its analysis of the Kennedy-Waxman bill, however, CBO explicitly considered the shifting of the costs of mandated health insurance to workers and estimated the tax revenue effects based upon the assumption that the costs were borne by workers (Gramlich, 1987).

Given this firmly held belief, what evidence is there to show that health benefit costs actually would be paid by workers? Direct empirical studies are rare because of the difficulty in getting suitable data sets that include wage, health insurance, and worker and firm characteristics and still allow the analyst to control for relevant state laws. Nonetheless, there are three careful studies that shed light on the issue.

First, Woodbury (1983) examined the degree to which wage and nonwage benefits, including health insurance, were substitutes. He found that the elasticity of substitution was 1.6, which indicates that these forms of compensation are commonly substituted for each other.[6] Thus, one would expect that increasing one form of compensation, such as health insurance, would result in at least partial reductions in other forms, such as money wages.

Second, Sloan and Adamache (1986) examined the tendency to substitute nonwage for wage compensation when tax rates change. They found that the proportion of compensation received as health and life insurance increases when tax rates are higher. (The proportion received as pension benefits is even more responsive to tax law changes.) These findings are consistent with the view that workers and their employers trade off forms of compensation to account for changes in regulatory/tax provisions.

Finally, recent work by Gruber and Krueger (1990) sought to examine the extent to which worker wages declined in order to pay for state-mandated increases in the level of workers' compensation insurance. They examined individual level data from

---

[6] It is difficult to put an elasticity of substitution into policy relevant terms. Elasticity of substitution is defined as the percentage change in the ratio of the shares of wage and nonwage compensation divided by the percentage change in the ratio of the relative prices of the two forms of compensation.

1979 through 1988 using the current population survey and other data. They concluded that 86 percent of the cost of workers' compensation premiums were paid by workers in the form of lower wages. Thus, the empirical literature is consistent with a view that workers pay.

UNEMPLOYMENT CONSEQUENCES

If a health insurance mandate were to be enacted with the existing minimum wage, the wages for some workers could not adjust to reflect the newly imposed health benefits. Many of these workers would lose their jobs or see the nature of their positions redefined to less than 17.5 hours. Gramlich (1987) estimated that 6 million workers who earned less than $4.00 per hour might face layoffs or reductions in hours. Most other estimates of the unemployment effect come up with estimates of 100,000 to 250,000 jobs lost. These estimates focus on the low elasticity of demand for labor. (See Brown [1988] for an excellent review of the analogous effects of minimum wages on employment.) They do agree, however, that most of the effect will be among part-time workers and teenagers because these are the easiest jobs and workers to convert to 17 hour employment. I suspect that the unemployment effects would be minimal, but there would be far more teenagers with two very part-time jobs!

CONCLUSION

Mandated health insurance coverage for all workers and their dependents is a bad idea. The problems are twofold. First, the bulk of the program's costs are paid for by low-income workers. Second, the program is politically dishonest; a quarter of the costs are paid for by taxpayers in the off-budget form of tax revenue reductions.

The irony of the mandated benefit plan is that those who are supposed to benefit from it are made worse off. This is easy to see. Economists usually assume that employment and consumption decisions are based on people's desire to make themselves as well off as possible. In the labor market today, people can choose to work for firms that provide compensation in the form of wages and health insurances, or they can choose firms that provide only money wages.

Maximizing calculus lead some to work for firms not offering health insurance but offering higher wages. These are the workers who would be most affected by an employer mandate. If most workers are right in their choice, then the insurance mandate will give them a less desirable compensation package. By definition they are worse off.

Mandated health insurance coverage is pretty straightforward after all. It is an attempt to replace individual decisions about the optimal compensation bundle with a governmental decision. Because workers generally don't gain under this plan, the relevant question is: Who does?

REFERENCES

Brown, C. 1988. "Minimum Wage Laws: Are They Over-Rated?" *Journal of Economic Perspectives,* 2(3): 133-146.

Chollet, D. J. 1988. "Uninsured Workers: Sources and Dimensions of the Problem." Paper presented at the annual meeting of the Allied Social Sciences Association.

Danzon, P. M. 1989. "Mandated Employer-Based Health Insurance: Incidence and Efficiency Effects." Discussion paper 66, Leonard Davis Institute, University of Pennsylvania.

Goldstein, G. S., and M. V. Pauly. 1976. "Group Health Insurance as a Local Public Good." In R. Rosett, ed., *The Role of Health Insurance in the Health Services Sector,* Chicago: University of Chicago Press, pp. 73-109.

Gramlich, E. M. 1987. "Statement of Edward M. Gramlich, Acting Director, Congressional Budget Office." U.S. Senate, Committee on Labor and Human Resources, 100th Congress, 1st session.

Gruber, J., and A. B. Krueger. 1990. "The Incidence of Mandated Employer-Provided Insurance: Lessons from Workers' Compensation Insurance." Working paper 3557, National Bureau of Economic Research, New York.

Jensen, G. A. 1986. "Employer Choice of Wage Supplements." Working paper, School of Public Health, University of Illinois at Chicago.

Kennedy, E. 1989. *Minimum Health Benefits for All Workers Act of 1988: Report Together with Additional and Minority Views.* Washington, D.C.: Superintendent of Documents, U.S. Government Printing Office Report, 100-360.

Morrisey, M. A. 1991. "Health Care Reform: A Review of Five Generic Proposals." In W. Custer, ed., *Winners and Losers in Reforming the U.S. Health Care System.* Washington, D.C.: Employee Benefits Research Institute.

Moyer, M. E. 1989. "A Revised Look at the Number of Uninsured Americans." *Health Affairs,* 8(2): 102-110.

Needleman, J., J. Arnold, J. Sheils, and L. S. Lewin. 1990. *The Health Care Financing System and the Uninsured.* Washington, D.C.: Lewin/ICF.

Phelps, C. E. 1980. "National Health Insurance by Regulation: Mandated Employee Benefits." In M. V. Pauly, ed., *National Health Insurance: What Now, What Later, What Never?* Washington, D.C.: American Enterprise Institute.

Sloan, F. A., and K. W. Adamache. 1986. "Taxation and the Growth of Nonwage Compensation." *Public Finance Quarterly,* 14(2): 115-137.

Thorpe, K. E. 1989. "Costs and Distributional Impacts of Employer Health Insurance Mandates and Medicaid Expansion." *Inquiry,* 26(3): 335-344.

Woodbury, S. A. 1983. "Substitution Between Wage and Nonwage Benefits." *American Economic Review,* 73(1): 166-182.

> **ISSUE SEVEN**
>
> *Certificates of need and other regulations are necessary to limit the number of competitors and facilities in a market so that existing organizations can achieve sufficient economic returns to ensure survival.*

For over three decades, health care organizations have had to deal with an increasing number of alternative care facilities and expensive technologies. Some view growth optimistically and believe that the competition among different health care organizations ultimately will benefit patients by ensuring lower prices and easier access. Others are more pessimistic. To them, the rate of increase in the number of health care facilities, especially those desiring to purchase expensive technologies, is alarming and can only lead to lower quality as facilities are forced to reduce prices in order to survive.

Traditionally, the health care industry has attempted to handle the increase in the number of hospital beds, the acquisition of expensive technologies, and so on with a variety of regulations. One of the most familiar has been the certificate of need (CON).

The basic structure for administering CON requirements was built around a network of planning organizations called Health Systems Agencies (HSA). Established by the federal government, these organizations were charged with ensuring that health facilities, equipment, and services did not exceed the needs of the community (Ashby, 1984). HSAs, however, have had problems from the beginning. First, because there is general disagreement over the appropriate goals of health planning, the presence of multiple goals has made cost containment difficult. Second, the agencies have had little direct power to enforce their recommendations (Altman and Rodwin, 1988).

Ultimately, much of the controversy surrounding CONs is a reflection of the enduring argument in the health care industry between centralized government regulation and relatively free competition. In the former, the government, acting through an appropriate agency, defines the standards for health systems, monitors performance, rewards those organizations that play according to the rules, and punishes those that do not. The assumption is that society's health needs can best be formulated and pursued with the aid of governmental control.

The opposite approach is the competitive model. In health care, as in other industries, providers are expected to act in their own self-interest, and patients are expected to do the same. Both groups pursuing self-interest in the presence of competition results in lower costs and more relevant services (Bradbury, 1987). CONs are dominant in the regulatory role and almost nonexistent in the competitive model.

More recently, a form of managed competition has been suggested (Enthoven, 1988). Under managed competition, two important ideas are merged. The first idea is that there is a need for a network of competitive medical plans that operate under economic incentives to encourage efficiency. The second is that there should be a regulatory framework that ensures the competitive plans operate in ways that best respond to the needs of the community and the larger society (Hill-Chinn, 1987).

To what extent is competition good for health care? Does the patient really benefit from fierce competition, or does it encourage providers to reduce quality in order to meet the prices of other organizations? Has CON regulation accomplished what it was originally intended to do? Are the benefits gained from centralized planning worth the cost involved in protecting existing facilities from competition? Can government regulate health care better than the free market?

Questions of this nature will be addressed by Howard L. Smith, of the University of New Mexico, and Neill F. Piland, of the Lovelace Medical Foundation. They will argue that regulations like CON have accomplished a number of positive outcomes and the need for such regulations has not been negated by prospective payment systems. John D. Blair, of Texas Tech University, and Susan M. Long, of the Methodist Hospital in Lubbock, Texas, present the case for less regulation. They argue that CON, which in their words is "one of the most widely used and abused types of regulations," is not fair and has not accomplished the intended results.

REFERENCES

Altman, Stuart H., and Marc A. Rodwin. 1988. "Halfway Competitive Markets and Ineffective Regulation: The American Health Care System," *Journal of Health Politics, Policy, and Law,* 13(2): 323-338.

Ashby, John L., Jr. 1984. "The Impact of Hospital Regulatory Programs on Per Capita Costs, Utilization, and Capital Investment." *Inquiry,* 21(1): 45-59.

Bradbury, Robert C. 1987. "A Community Approach to Health Care Competition." *Inquiry,* 24(3): 253-265.

Enthoven, A. C. 1988. "Managed Competition: An Agenda for Action." *Health Affairs,* 7(3): 25-47.

Hill-Chinn, Linda. 1987. "Add Cooperation to Regulation and Competition." *Hospitals,* 61(23): 88-89.

> **POINT**
>
> *Certificates of need and other regulations are necessary to limit the number of competitors and facilities in a market so that existing organizations can achieve economic returns to ensure survival.*

HOWARD L. SMITH
University of New Mexico

Howard L. Smith is associate dean and professor in the Anderson School of Management at the University of New Mexico, where he teaches strategic management and health services administration. Dr. Smith received a Ph.D. in administrative theory and organizational behavior from the University of Washington. Prior to joining the faculty at New Mexico, he taught at the University of Alabama and the Medical College of Virginia. Dr. Smith's research interests include strategic management and rural health delivery issues, and he is a research scientist with the Lovelace Medical Foundation in Albuquerque, New Mexico. He has published and consulted extensively in the areas of strategic management and rural health care. His publications have appeared in a wide variety of journals, including *Health Services Research, New England Journal of Medicine, Journal of the American Medical Association, Academy of Management Journal, Journal of Rural Health, Nursing Research, Health Care Management Review, Decision Sciences, Interfaces,* and other scholarly journals.

NEILL F. PILAND
Lovelace Medical Foundation

Neill F. Piland earned the Doctor of Public Health degree from UCLA and is currently director of the Center for Health and Population Research at the Lovelace Medical Foundation in Albuquerque, New Mexico. Prior to Lovelace, he was at the Stanford Research Institute. He is the principal investigator on a number of health services research projects involving quality care assessment, smoking cessation, and efficacious health delivery among rural and minority populations. Dr. Piland has published widely on health services topics. His articles have appeared in the *Journal of the American Medical Association, Health Services Research, Journal of Rural Health, Nursing Research,* and *Health Care Management Review.*

One key, unresolved strategic issue that faces the health care industry in the 1990s is the prognosis for regulatory efforts that have been designed to achieve cost containment, quality of care, and accessibility. Regulations can be designed to accomplish rather broad and diverse purposes. Among other things, they can be used to address inefficiencies in:

1. the demand for quality medical care (e.g., patients' lack of information about appropriate treatment required for specific illnesses),
2. the supply of services (e.g., monopoly of specialized services),
3. the governmental expenditures on medical care, and
4. the access to care (e.g., market forces might limit services in rural areas) (Feldstein, 1979).

In other words, regulation within the health care industry is designed to accomplish more than just control of acute care institutions. It applies to the entire health care system with its diverse facilities, institutions, providers, suppliers, administrators, owners, and clients.

It is appropriate to question whether or not regulation is essential to ensure that health care organizations achieve economic returns needed for financial survival. Will nursing homes, hospitals, multispecialty group-practice clinics, ambulatory surgery centers, and other health care organizations benefit financially from regulation? One way to answer this question is to examine the consequences of a specific regulatory policy — certificates of need (CON). Did CON help health care organizations overcome market dysfunctions caused by health insurance, physician supply, provider distribution, and consumer choice? Did health care organizations benefit financially from CON regulations? Should policymakers encourage regulations like CON in the 1990s to promote the economic welfare of health care organizations?

BACKGROUND ON CON PROGRAMS

Comprehensive health planning was the federal government's initial attempt to control health care expenditures and to establish order in a system gone awry in the late 1960s and early 1970s. The health planning function evolved into an infrastructure of health systems agencies at local and state levels. Although experiences varied considerably, for the most part, these agencies lacked sufficient clout to affect the forces driving up health costs. In 1972, Section 1122 of the Social Security amendments was passed, which enabled states to review proposed hospital capital expenditures. Section 1122 essentially created the CON concept and process. Subsequently, the National Health Planning and Resources Development Act of 1974 authorized funding for state and local health planning agencies to undertake CON programs.

At least two trends from CON's evolution are important for developing conclusions about the efficacy of regulation for the financial well-being of health care organizations. First, it is clear that CON regulation has required years to develop and fine-tune. Effective regulation of a complex system does not happen suddenly. It entails careful forethought, critical ongoing analysis, and the ability to institute supporting legislation. Second, CON programs have expanded the scope of their reviews. Initially, CON was designed to control costs. Over time, CON has not only acted as a substitute for market forces involving capital expenditures, but in some states it has also incorporated considerations of indigence issues, the quality of care, and the geographic distribution of that care.

THE CON SCORECARD

To gain insight on CON's ability to support economic survival of health care organizations, we need to consider what CON offers: a substitute for weak market restraints; an incentive for rational planning and efficient management; the development of health systems; and the promotion of competition. Admittedly, CON is not without its limitations. It took years to formulate the underlying policies, procedures, standards, and criteria through which CON has reached successful implementation. In many cases, the organizations benefitting from CON programs have encountered significant short-run costs as they cope with regulatory compliance (Burda, 1990; Cherskov, 1986; Horty, 1986). Nonetheless, these short-run costs appear to be outweighed by the long-run benefits that have acrrued to providers and the public.

Substitution For Weak Market Restraints

During the early stages of CON's development, theoretical and empirical evidence pointed to its impending failure. Seminal work by Salkever and Bice (1979) concluded that CON obstructed free-market forces from taking their due course and awarded existing providers a form of franchise or monopoly. Various authorities supported the contention that CON programs encountered significant implementation problems (Abernathy and Pearson, 1979; Carpenter and Paul-Shakeen, 1984). Others pointed to the gradual termination of CON programs in several states during the early years of Medicare's prospective payment system (Brown and Saltman, 1985).

Although open to speculation, it is possible that initial experiences with CON generated support for a free-market or competitive perspective among policymakers (Rossiter, 1982). Leading researchers (Enthoven, 1978; Luft, 1978; Pauly, 1980) advocated a return to a competitive, rather than regulation-based, health system. This stance was supported by other research findings (Langwell and Moore, 1982). In fact, there is a long line of research implying that regulation is less effective in controlling utilization and costs than competition (Robinson, Garnick, and McPhee, 1987). From a public policy perspective, however, it is not a simple choice of regulation or competition. Implementation of a competitive health system model may be inexorably linked with the development of various regulations designed to maintain competition (Bovjberg, 1980).

A major problem in dismissing CON as ineffective is the growing number of studies that have documented CON's benefits. Howell (1984) noted that many critics of CON fail to acknowledge the cross-sectional nature of their research and analysis. Using a longitudinal data base of Massachusetts hospitals, Howell found that hospital construction occurs in fourteen-year cycles. The short time frame of previous CON studies (a five-year period in the Salkever and Bice study) prevented them from measuring these cycles. Howell concluded that CON leads to meaningful restraint on unnecessary expenditures.

Another problem with previous CON studies has been the tendency to focus only on hospital regulation (Moyer and Calabria, 1988). CON appears to have worked more effectively in the nursing home sector than in the acute care sector (Feder and Scanlon, 1980). Opponents of CON may have been too optimistic in dismissing benefits of regulation having overfocused on hospital experiences. A broader perspective on CON is deserved. Verifiable results from limiting capital expenditures cannot be measured precisely over a few years. Similarly, CON's effects on hospitals do not necessarily apply to the entire health system.

Perhaps the acid test of CON's efficacy is to observe market forces at work once regulation is lifted. After Utah removed its CON program, hospital construction permits increased 80 percent, and Arizona observed a 30 percent increase in permits after terminating CON (Burda, 1987). The construction of psychiatric inpatient facilities has been especially volatile (Larkin, 1987). Arizona, California, Kansas, New Mexico, Texas, and Utah all witnessed planning for or the construction of psychiatric facilities once CON was removed (Fine and Super, 1986). These events raise serious doubts about the contention that CON does not work.

Additional evidence of CON's capabilities is seen in the purchase of costly medical equipment. Steinberg, Sisk, and Locke (1985) concluded that magnetic resonance imagers (MRIs) were acquired more slowly in the health system than computed tomography (CT) scanners because of CON. Hillman and Schwartz (1985) supported this contention. It appears that nonhospital organizations, such as outpatient facilities or physician offices, increased their purchases of MRI systems because ambulatory clinics often fall outside of CON regulations. In other words, CON regulations appear to control investments in capital-intensive equipment that has the potential to raise health costs.

Incentive for Rational Planning and Efficient Management

CON can be credited with developing the sophisticated planning methods now used by health care organizations and planners. Better planning should lead to better financial performance by organizations and improved cost control in the public sector (Rhyne, 1986). Neumann and Kim (1985) have proposed that health planners use cost prediction simulation models during the CON review. They contend that simulation models can clarify the ratio of operating costs to capital costs. Unless health providers manage capital assets efficiently, operating costs can escalate. This in turn raises total health care costs. Neumann and Kim argue for a financial penalty or tax on providers who exceed operating cost targets after receiving CON approval on major buildings or equipment.

CON has stimulated still other advances in health planning capability. A major concern among CON applicants is the methodology used in assigning priority to capital investment proposals. Some CON programs have considered setting specific limits on total capital investments. In order to implement such a policy, there must be some sound methodology for distinguishing among the merits of specific proposals. As Hannan, Rouse, Barnett, and Uppal (1987) have underscored, many factors must be considered in prioritizing relative need. It is the articulation of these factors, their measures, and the process for evaluation that lend rigor to the CON system and confidence in the resulting decisions. In this sense, CON has provided an incentive for planners to upgrade the art and science of health planning.

CON has also encouraged hospital providers to examine admission and discharge policies, which may help to control unnecessary use (Restuccia, et al., 1987). In essence, the application process can serve as a quasi-form of external review and oversight. CON reviewers are able to provide alternative perspectives that may not have been clearly understood or perceived by the applicants. The review process raises new interpretations of data, perhaps additional data, and alternative premises upon which planning can be undertaken. In this way, CON enhances the applicant's understanding of the proposed project.

Health System Development

CON can be credited with promoting the development of health systems. Kornblatt (1985) has observed that through the CON process, many health agencies have acquired enough expertise and planning mechanisms to bring about meaningful change in the health system. Funding threats and rescission of regulatory powers, will weaken the ability of these agencies to forge a more functional health system. As a result, an effective forum for capturing diverse opinions on health system design faces possible extinction. Lave (1985) and Moyer and Calabria (1988) have acknowledged the advances in building a continuum of long-term care that have occurred because of CON and health planning. Without CON, the health system relied on institutional care. CON constraints, which slowed nursing-home construction and concomitant planning activities, promoted rethinking about long-term care delivery. As a result, many states now have noninstitutionally based models of long-term care in which many providers play pivotal roles in fulfilling the continuum.

CON's contribution to shaping health system development may ultimately lead to a well-defined and perhaps more stable base for health care organizations. Once providers are cognizant of their roles and have the inherent stability to accomplish their organizational missions, the potential for financial viability increases. Nursing homes encountering a completely unregulated market, for example, must invest considerable resources in monitoring the environment to detect and minimize adverse competitive influences. This challenge redirects resources from worthwhile investments, such as patient care or forging a continuum of care with hospital discharge planners, home health agencies, retirement centers, and assisted living centers, to less productive environmental scanning. In a regulated environment, the ability of nursing homes to respond to competition is enhanced and their survival thereby reinforced. Until there is a fully functional health system, however, society's and nursing homes' return on health resources may be suboptimal.

CON's Promotion of Competition

CON should also be recognized for its ability to promote competition although many opponents of CON would find such a proposition to be ludicrous. How can a well-structured regulatory process like CON promote competition? Simpson (1985) has suggested that the review process encourages competition. This occurs in several ways. First, CON proposals are filed by individuals or organizations that believe they can provide sufficient resources to deliver health care services or to complete construction. In effect, there is open competition in a bidding process. If a health agency's planning process identifies the need for an MRI in a community, for example, then a variety of applicants submit proposals to procure the imager and to deliver services. Admittedly, the market or competition-driven process ends when the CON is awarded thereby enfranchising only one applicant.

Second, CON promotes competition in terms of articulating and applying review criteria. In addition, CON facilitates discussion and definition of objective decision criteria. Once the prospective applicants know the prevailing criteria, they can formulate plans to meet the predetermined standards. Although not every applicant possesses sufficient resources to fulfill the criteria in the same fashion, each applicant has the same opportunity to address the criteria. Furthermore, the CON process can stipulate that competitive factors should be incorporated not only in the application process but also in the review criteria. A free market unfettered by CON regulation is susceptible to imperfections that could prevent equal opportunity for all competitors. In short, CON can foster competition through specific provisions and policies within the review process.

For health care organizations that are seeking to remain economically viable, CON provides incentives for wise financial decisions. CON applications are submitted in response to defined needs outlined in a local or state plan. This provides some assurance that sufficient demand for services is available. It is the responsibility of the health provider to translate that demand into financially secure operations. The CON application process encourages providers to develop sound projections of their ability to meet the financing, staffing, operations, and promotional aspects (among other considerations) of the project.

CON'S CONTRIBUTION TO A FISCALLY RESPONSIBLE HEALTH SYSTEM

The preceding overview suggests that CON is a successful regulatory policy. Although initial empirical evidence suggested that CON was ineffective, subsequent studies have shown that CON has encouraged prudent investments and resource allocations in the health care industry. Recent studies of CON indicate many beneficial results, including a heightened awareness of the implications of long-run capital investments, a more comprehensive outlook on designing service delivery efforts, and a commitment to programmatic efforts. Researchers not only have failed to provide conclusive proof that CON does not work, they have produced a growing body of literature substantiating the beneficial aspects of CON. Like many regulatory policies, CON will remain controversial because it allows some providers to offer services, acquire medical equipment, or build facilities that other providers cannot. A critical question that opponents of CON seldom address is whether or not CON is beneficial to the health system as a whole.

As we have seen, CON does promote competition during the application and review process. It offers incentives to providers to better manage and plan service delivery efforts. CON also helps to shape the health system and, in so doing, removes ambiguity about roles and assists health care organizations in making prudent capital investment decisions. In sum, CON has accomplished much considering its broad scope. In many situations, CON has functioned as an effective substitute for market mechanisms by restraining expansion or procurement when need has not been substantiated. In its early stages, CON could be criticized for devoting too much attention to cost control and perhaps not enough attention to quality of care or geographic and income-related accessibility issues (Shortell and Hughes, 1988; Hudson, 1990). These shortcomings have been rectified.

Ultimately, CON and similar regulations that address market malfunctions in health care benefit providers. CON can establish a well-planned health system in which scarce resources are allocated to the most deserving needs. Although the eventual result may be a short-run franchise for delivering services, CON can promote competition. For health care organizations, CON has helped to foster fiscally prudent decisions by providers consistent with the overarching design of health plans.

IS CON NEEDED IN A PROSPECTIVE PAYMENT ENVIRONMENT?

Having clarified the strengths of CON programs and, by implication, similar regulations addressing market weaknesses in the health care industry, there remains a question of relevance. Is CON needed when there are prospective payment systems? Don't prospective payment systems achieve everything that CON set out to do? Is there any practical benefit to maintaining CON in light of the powerful policy ramifications accompanying prospective payment systems? Are health care organizations concerned about capital investments they cannot afford because of prospective payment constraints?

Prospective payment systems appear to have helped regulate reimbursement and to have established some control over hospital-based health expenditures. However, a more comprehensive reimbursement strategy that incorporated outpatient service delivery, physicians, and other health services would help to fully develop cost containment. Although hospitals are a critical source of rising costs they are not the only source. Focusing on acute care reflects an incremental vision of health policy implementation. Prospective payment systems have helped to regulate revenues, but they have not provided an acceptable policy substitute for CON in urban and suburban settings.

Metropolitan hospitals (and other health care organizations) that face only prospective payment systems can respond by raising their levels of capital expenditures. CON formerly controlled building expansion and equipment such as MRIs. Without CON, providers are free to pursue strategies they believe will compensate for diminishing inpatient revenues. The result has been a dramatic rise in service diversification and vertical integration as hospitals strive to become full-service providers or to supplement falling inpatient revenues.

Hospitals and other organizations have widely embraced new diagnostic technologies such as CTs and MRIs. This trend has challenged health care organizations and planners to develop accurate forecasts of patient demand and to devise effective regulatory policies (Carnazzo, 1985; Hillman, 1986). Organizations that buy the equipment spend extraordinary amounts on capital investments and then face substantial yearly operating costs. Without commensurate revenue flow, the rate of return may decrease and financial well-being may deteriorate.

To ensure that operating income meets budget projections, some organizations have had to increase their use of new equipment. This practice raises the unresolved issue of how much unnecessary use accompanies these capital intensive investments. Unnecessary utilization might include use that could be handled by other diagnostic equipment in a more cost-effective manner, or it might include abuse from applying excessively sophisticated medical technology as a malpractice or palliative safeguard. Whatever the basis, the increase in utilization is needed to justify the equipment acquisition, to raise revenues, and to overcome the diminished cost-effectiveness of previous equipment that may now be idle or less intensively used.

Without CON, prospective payment systems have encouraged health facility expansion. In metropolitan areas, hospitals have progressively expanded their reach to patients through ambulatory clinics and urgent care centers. The result is investment in additional capital projects. Admittedly, the costs of constructing a clinic may not exceed inpatient facility costs, but the capital investment still must be covered. The precise purposes behind satellite facilities vary. Some hospitals raid the geographic area served by another hospital (e.g., through an ambulatory surgery center). Other hospitals use satellite facilities to adapt to population changes (Heller, 1988; and Richards, 1985). In the end, the outcomes are more health facility construction, more capital costs, higher operating costs, and more pressures to raise revenues.

A BALANCED PERSPECTIVE OF REGULATION

Prospective payment systems alone are not sufficient substitutes for CON or similar regulatory measures designed to control health costs. Although prospective payment has discouraged capital investments in rural areas, where almost half of all hospitals are located, the resolution of these facilities' long-term capital needs under prospective payment has not been addressed. In urban and suburban settings, prospective payment has been only partially effective in limiting capital investments.

It appears that a balanced perspective of regulation in the health care industry would recognize that multiple interventions may be needed. In essence, it is not an either/or proposition. A well-designed health system will incorporate and accommodate a workable ensemble of regulations and policies. CON is just one tool in the arsenal of policies used to forge a competitive, cost-efficient, effective, and accessible health delivery system. Prospective payment is yet another option that can be invoked to improve the functioning of the system.

Regulations like CON are necessary so that existing organizations can achieve returns adequate enough to ensure survival. Although such regulations may require years to refine and improve, ultimately they compensate for weak market restraints and improve on the overall ensemble of policies designed to create financially sound health care providers, accessible, low cost, and high quality medical care, and satisfied customers/clients.

REFERENCES

Abernathy, D. S., and D. A. Pearson. 1979. *Regulating Hospital Costs: The Development of Public Policy.* Ann Arbor, MI: AVPAA Press.

Bovjberg, R. R. 1980. "Competition vs. Regulation in Medical Care: An Overdrawn Dichotomy." *Vanderbilt Law Review,* 34(2): 965-1002.

Brown, J. B., and R. B. Saltman. 1985. "Health Capital Policy in the United States: A Strategic Perspective." *Inquiry,* 22(2): 122-131.

Burda, D. 1987. "Fear of Expansion Keeps CON Alive." *Hospitals,* 61(12): 76.

Burda, D. 1990. "Counting the Cost of Complying with Regulation." *Modern Healthcare,* 20(33): 40-52.

Carnazzo, J. S. 1985. "Demand Forecasting for Magnetic Resonance Imaging Services." *Hospital & Health Services Administration,* 30(2): 84-94.

Carpenter, E. S., and P. Paul-Shaheen. 1984. "Implementing Regulatory Reform: The Saga of Michigan's Debedding Experiment." *Journal of Health Politics, Policy, and Law,* 9(3): 453-473.

Cherskov, M. 1986. "Hospitals Hurdle CON Barriers Differently." *Hospitals,* 60(10): 89.

Enthoven, A. C. 1978. "Consumer-Choice Health Plan." *New England Journal of Medicine,* 298(12): 650-658A (Part 1) and 298(13): 709-720 (Part 2).

Feder, J., and W. Scanlon. 1980. "Regulating the Bed Supply in Nursing Homes." *Milbank Memorial Fund Quarterly/Health and Society,* 58(1): 54-88.

Feldstein, P. J. 1979. *Health Care Economics.* New York: John Wiley & Sons, pp. 232-233.

Fine, J. and K. E. Super. 1986. "Repeal of Some States' CON Laws Spurs Psych Hospital Construction." *Modern Healthcare,* 16(21): 74-76.

Hannan, E. L., R. L. Rouse, R. Barnett, and P. Uppal. 1987. "Methods for Developing Relative Need Criteria to Accompany a Health Care Capital Expenditure Limit." *Journal of Health Politics, Policy, and Law,* 12(1): 113-136.

Heller, D. L. 1988. "Structuring Ambulatory Care Projects to Minimize Problems with Regulatory Constraints." *Journal of Ambulatory Care Management,* 11(4): 23-27.

Hillman, A. L., and J. S. Schwartz. 1985. "The Adoption and Diffusion of CT and MRI in the United States: A Comparative Analysis." *Medical Care,* 23(11): 1283-1294.

Hillman, B. J. 1986. "Government Health Policy and the Diffusion of New Medical Devices." *Health Services Research,* 21(5): 681-711.

Horty, J. 1986. "Controversial Decisions on CONs Can Generate Lawsuits in Protest." *Modern Healthcare,* 16(6): 74.

Howell, J. R. 1984. "Evaluating the Impact of Certificate-of-Need Regulation Using Measures of Ultimate Outcome: Some Cautions from Experience in Massachusetts." *Health Services Research,* 19(5): 587-613.

Hudson, T. 1990. "CON 'Tailoring' Comes to a Head in Kentucky." *Hospitals,* 64(8): 106.

Kornblatt, E. S. 1985. "Mental Health in Health Planning Agencies." *Social Science and Medicine,* 21(4): 377-381.

Langwell, K. M., and S. F. Moore. 1982. *A Synthesis of Research on Competition in the Financing and Delivery of Health Services.* National Center for Health Services Research. U.S. Department of Health and Human Services, DHHS Pub. No. (PHS) 83-3327.

Larkin, H. 1987. "Deregulation Spurs Market Information Demand." *Hospitals,* 60(26): 58.

Lave, J. R. 1985. "Cost Containment Policies in Long-Term Care." *Inquiry,* 22(1): 7-23.

Luft, H. S. 1978. "How Do Health Maintenance Organizations Achieve Their Savings: Rhetoric and Evidence." *New England Journal of Medicine,* 298(24): 1336-1343.

Moyer, N. C., and J. A. Calabria. 1988. "Planning Long-Term Care Services for the 1990s: The Virtues and Limitations of State Regulation." *Family and Community Health,* 10(4): 58-66.

Neumann, B. R., and J. Kim. 1985. "Use of Cost Prediction Simulation Models for CON Affordability Review." *Health Care Management Review,* 10(1): 75-82.

Pauly, M. V. 1980. *Doctors and Their Workshops.* Chicago: University of Chicago Press.

Restuccia, J. D., S. M. C. Payne, G. Lenhart, H. P. Constantine, and J. P. Fulton. 1987. "Assessing the Appropriateness of Hospital Utilization to Improve Efficiency and Competitive Position." *Healthcare Management Review,* 12(3), 17-27.

Rhyne, L. C. 1986. "The Relationship of Strategic Planning to Financial Performance." *Strategic Management Journal,* 7(5): 423-436.

Richards, G. 1985. "Is This Overbuilding and Why Might It Occur?" *Hospitals,* 59(5): 70-72.

Robinson, J. C., D. W. Garnick, and S. J. McPhee. 1987. "Market and Regulatory Influences on the Availability of Coronary Angioplasty and Bypass Surgery in U.S. Hospitals." *New England Journal of Medicine,* 317(2): 85-90.

Rossiter, L. F. 1982. *Research on Competition in the Financing and Delivery of Health Services: Future Research Needs.* National Center for Health Services Research. U.S. Department of Health and Human Services, DHHS Pub. No. (PHS) 83-3328-2.

Salkever, D. S., and T. W. Bice. 1979. *Hospital Certificate of Need Controls Impact on Investment, Costs and Use.* Washington, D.C.: American Enterprise Institute for Public Policy Research.

Shortell, S. M., and E. R. X. Hughes. 1988. "The Effects of Regulation, Competition, and Ownership on Mortality Rates Among Hospital Inpatients." *New England Journal of Medicine,* 318(17): 1100-1107.

Simpson, J. B. 1985. "State Certificate-Of-Need Programs: The Current Status." *American Journal of Public Health,* 75(10): 1225-1229.

Steinberg, E. P., J. E. Sisk, and K. E. Locke. 1985. "X-Ray, CT, and Magnetic Resonance Imagers: Diffusion Patterns and Policy Issues." *New England Journal of Medicine,* 313(14): 859-864.

COUNTERPOINT

*Certificates of need and other regulations are **not** necessary to limit the number of competitors and facilities in a market so that existing organizations can achieve economic returns to ensure survival.*

JOHN D. BLAIR
Texas Tech University

John D. Blair is professor of management in the College of Business Administration and associate chairman of the Health Organization Management Department in the School of Medicine at Texas Tech University. Blair received a Ph.D. in sociology from the University of Michigan. He is program director for the Institute for Management and Leadership Research at Texas Tech. His most recent book, coauthored with Myron Fottler, is *Challenges in Health Care Management: Strategic Perspectives for Managing Key Stakeholders.* He is currently chairman of the Health Care Adminis-tration Division of the National Academy of Management. He has served as the associate editor of the *Journal of Management* and was a founding coeditor of the *Yearly Review of Management.* His current research focuses on developing strategic stakeholder management concepts as a way to link macrostrategic management and microorganizational behavior issues.

SUSAN MARIE LONG
Methodist Hospital

Susan M. Long is a Fellow in Health Organization Management at Methodist Hospital in Lubbock, Texas. As the Methodist Fellow, she works with the president/CEO and executive vice-president/COO of the largest hospital between Dallas and Los Angeles. Long received her MBA with a concentration in health organization management in 1991 from Texas Tech University. She has also been a research assistant in the Health Organization Management Program of the Institute for Management and Leadership Research at Texas Tech University and has served as a health care management consultant for the university's Center for Professional Development and the School of Medicine. She was formerly an account executive for an advertising agency in Baltimore. Her research and consulting interests have included the implications of impending changes in the physician payment system and analyses of the factors affecting length of stay in specific types of hospital units. Her current management focus is on strategic challenges for health care organizations facing dynamic environments.

Economic regulation of the health care sector was undertaken in the late 1960s and 1970s to curtail the rising costs of health care delivery. Regulations such as licensing and accrediting programs, utilization controls, and rate controls have imposed requirements on health facilities, particularly those participating in Medicare and Medicaid. Among the most controversial and expensive regulatory approaches are certificate of need (CON) programs, which were designed to restrain health care institutions from overinvesting in unneeded facilities and services. Some states have also used other regulations, such as moratoria and caps on capital spending, to control unneeded capital expenditures. Although all of these regulatory attempts have been effective to some degree, this essay will concentrate on certificates of need and their strategic impact in the health care market.

APPROACHING CERTIFICATES OF NEED STRATEGICALLY

In order to understand it as a strategic issue in health care, CON must be framed with two explicitly strategic points of view: *competitive strategy development*, using Porter's (1980) analysis, and *strategic stakeholder management* by Blair and Fottler (1990). The competitive strategy approach highlights the essentially self-serving nature of organizational strategy. By its very nature, strategic management is designed to give competitive advantage to the specific organization under consideration. In this case, each existing health care facility can be evaluated in terms of the strategic advantage that CON legislation provides or fails to provide. The strategic stakeholder management approach then identifies those individuals, groups, or organizations who have a stake in what the organization does as it attempts to gain competitive advantage.

Porter's analytical model identifies five key elements that affect the level of competition in an industry: the rivalry among existing competitors, the threat of new entrants, the bargaining power of suppliers, the bargaining power of buyers and consumers, and the threat of substitutes. These five potentially threatening competitive forces affect not only the intensity of the competition but also the strategic attractiveness of a particular industry.

Blair and Fottler (1990) have extended this analysis to include the stakeholder concept. Stakeholders are the individuals, groups, and organizations that have a stake in the decisions and actions of the organization and that may attempt to influence those decisions and actions. The support of stakeholders can be just as powerful, if not more so, as their threats and offers to bargain. Power either to threaten or to support is relevant here because stakeholders have a vested interest in the number of health care facilities and services that are available. Stakeholder support of new entry and expansion can affect the extent to which regulations affect the marketplace. Our analysis examines the various stakeholders that are affected by CON legislation.

Key buyer and consumer stakeholders in the health care industry include patients and their families, employers as purchasers of health care, and any managed-care organizations that are negotiating for contracts. Other potential key buyer stakeholders include federal, state, and local governments. Key supplier stakeholders include physicians who are currently practicing in the community, pharmaceutical suppliers, and managed-care organizations that have preferred provider arrangements (PPAs) with health care facilities already in the market.

In Figure 1 and Table 1, the competitive forces have been translated into specific stakeholders that, in the real world, make up those generic forces facing the organization. These stakeholders may be significantly affected by regulations like CONs. Certainly, CON regulatory actions affect the strategic attractiveness of the hospital industry in a local market. The effects of CONs on the level of competition are listed below.

1. The potential for threat from competitive rivalry is restricted through regulatory barriers to expansion/duplication of services.
2. The potential for threat from stakeholders that are potential new entrants into the industry is severely limited by regulatory barriers.

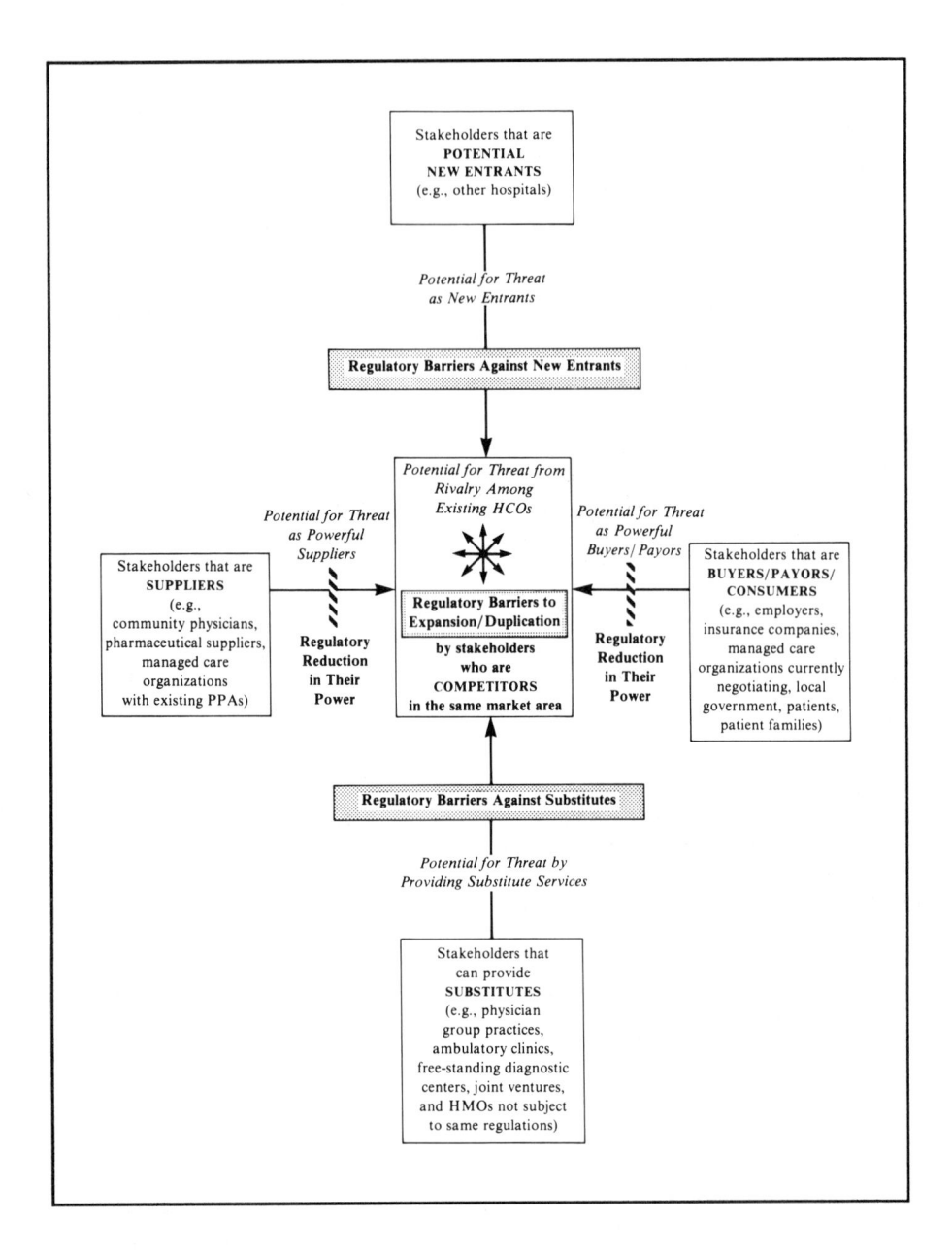

Figure 1 *Competitive Strategy and Strategic Stakeholder Management Implications of Certificates of Need*

Source: Adapted from M. E. Porter, *Competitive Strategy* (New York: The Free Press, 1980), p. 4, with stakeholder concepts from John D. Blair and M. D. Fottler, *Challenges in Health Care Management: Strategic Perspectives for Managing Key Stakeholders* (San Francisco: Jossey-Bass Publishers, 1990), p. 66. Revised and extended to show strategic impact of CON regulation on existing organizations in a local market.

TABLE 1 *Factors Affecting Stakeholders' Potentials for Threat and Cooperation*

	Increases or Decreases Stakeholder's Potential for Threat	Increases or Decreases Stakeholder's Potential for Cooperation
Stakeholder controls key resources (needed by organization)	**Increases**	**Increases**
Stakeholder does not control key resources	**Decreases**	**Either**
Stakeholder more powerful than organization	**Increases**	**Either**
Stakeholder as powerful as organization	**Either**	**Either**
Stakeholder less powerful than organization	**Decreases**	**Increases**
Stakeholder likely to take action (supportive of the organization)	**Decreases**	**Increases**
Stakeholder likely to take nonsupportive action	**Increases**	**Decreases**
Stakeholder unlikely to take any action	**Decreases**	**Decreases**
Stakeholder likely to form coalition with other stakeholders	**Increases**	**Either**
Stakeholder likely to form coalition with organization	**Decreases**	**Increases**
Stakeholder unlikely to form any coalition	**Decreases**	**Decreases**

3. The potential for threat from powerful supplier stakeholders is reduced because regulations limit the suppliers' market and reduce their bargaining power.
4. The potential for threat from powerful buyer stakeholders is reduced because purchasing power is restricted by regulation to a limited number of suppliers.
5. The potential for threat from stakeholders than can provide substitute products or services is restricted by the same barriers restricting new entrants, although not all substitutes are subject to regulation. Therefore, this regulatory barrier is permeable.

Certificates of need attempt to give an advantage to existing competitors by setting up barriers to new entrants and substitutes. In effect, existing health care providers are protected from the threat of new entrants and from the threat of expansion by existing providers who might compete with their services. CONs also reduce the bargaining power of suppliers and the purchasing power of consumers. Although CON regulations have potentially negative impacts on all the stakeholders involved, the extent of the impact is more severe for some than for others.

Certificates of need are based on four premises. The first premise assumes that competition, if left unchecked by regulation, will result in additional, unnecessary entry into the market and, therefore, excess capacity. The second premise is that excess capacity will result in inefficiency and thus raise the costs of health care. The third premise, which may not be well recognized, assumes that existing facilities are the only organizations that are needed and that they are capable of solving the overarching health care problems of cost, quality, and access. The last premise assumes that the only stakeholders affected by regulation are potential and existing competitors. This premise underestimates the importance of other key stakeholders. Because of these faulty assumptions and other failures inherent in the regulatory process, CON regulations have failed to contain costs in a fair and rational manner and have resulted in unanticipated consequences for many key stakeholders directly or indirectly involved in the decisions made.

STRATEGIC IMPACT OF CERTIFICATE OF NEED REGULATIONS ON KEY STAKEHOLDERS

In the sections that follow, we will continue the line of analysis presented visually in Figure 1. We will look at the strategic implications for other key stakeholders when CON is used not only in an attempt to contain costs but also to give significant competitive advantage to existing organizations. We will first look at the impact of CON regulation on the standard stakeholders — existing rivals, potential new entrants, and potential substitutes. Then, we will turn to two stakeholders not always included in the impact of CON regulation — suppliers and those who are going to buy, pay for, or consume health care services. Specifically, we will examine the impact CON regulation has on their power.

Strategic Impact on Existing Competitors

CON has protected existing organizations from new entrants and has preserved economic returns. In some instances, however, it has also served as a threat to the survival of other existing health care providers. Extremely powerful providers can use CON regulation to increase market share and drive other existing competitors from the market. Nowhere is this turnabout of using regulation against itself more evident than in the case of Humana Inc. in Louisville, Kentucky.

One of the biggest political battles in regulatory history occurred over changes in CON legislation in 1990. The war was waged between the Kentucky Hospital Association (KHA) and Humana Inc. in Louisville, Kentucky. KHA had initially supported streamlining CON legislation to reduce the time and paperwork required for hospitals going through the CON review process. KHA withdrew support, however, when an amendment was added that repealed CON review in Jefferson County (Jefferson County includes Louisville). The amendment would have allowed Humana to construct a $300 million "Center of Excellence." KHA refused support on the grounds that the Humana center would hurt rural hospitals and prevent providers in the rest of the state from updating technology and services. Wielding its political might, Humana threatened to build elsewhere and to move its insurance practice. This move would have cost Kentucky 3,000 existing jobs and another 3,000-5,000 new jobs that would be created by the new medical center (*Hospitals,* 1990). Four not-for-profit Louisville hospitals (all KHA members) refused to fight the amendment and weakened the political power of KHA. Humana won the political scuffle and is now protected from any large-scale competitors outside Jefferson County. This is a particularly good example of how providers can use CON legislation to their own benefit and to the detriment of existing competitors.

Although Humana is an extreme example of the failure of CON regulations to protect existing health care stakeholders, there are other, less extreme examples that support this ineffectiveness. CON regulations restrict the options available to existing stakeholders who are trying to grow. Decisions about new facilities and technologies often favor large urban hospitals that have a greater volume of patients to justify the expansion. Those competitors with greater resources will continue to become stronger through mergers, acquisitions, and other unregulated ventures and eventually will drive others from the marketplace. Buying a hospital and assuming its certificate of need is often the easiest way to grow. The Fort Sanders Alliance in Knoxville, Tennessee, for example, wanted to further penetrate the market in the western portion of the city. A CON application to transfer beds from their facility on the east side of the city to their facility on the west side was rejected. Fort Sanders eluded CON regulation by purchasing the Hospital Corporation of America's Park West Medical Center, thus increasing rather than stabilizing their market concentration in Knoxville (Nemes, 1991).

The CON process is also subject to considerable political manipulation by health care providers and other stakeholders, such as consumer constituents. In 1987, the trustees of Eastern Maine Medical Center, a nonprofit hospital in Bangor with 416 beds, were able to push a bill through the state legislature to raise the CON limit on the amount of money a hospital could invest in new facilities. (The limit was $6 million.) The bill enabled Eastern Maine to construct a new psychiatric facility that required more funds than the CON legislation allowed. The board hosted a special dinner for regional legislators, during which they listened to appeals by the trustees for the need to improve community mental health services. As a result of this presentation, legislators supported the bill. The day the bill was to be voted on, a breakfast meeting was held for the legislators. The bill was passed successfully, and Eastern Maine received approval to build its new facility (Berger, 1989).

Although CON regulation attempts to limit the growth of existing rivalries, stakeholders are finding new loopholes and methods of circumventing the regulatory process. New England Baptist Hospital had just finished a grueling battle with opposition over an approved CON when they discovered they needed an additional CON to operate their own cardiac disease detection, prevention, and rehabilitation program. To avoid the whole CON process, New England Baptist rented the renovated space to the New England Heart Center, which was a sole proprietorship owned by a cardiologist. No hospital employees work in the center. The hospital does not control services offered by the center, and, the center's patients are not billed by the hospital. These changes were not considered substantial enough to require CON, and the hospital now benefits from offering the service (Horty, 1986). Once again, the competitive advantage provided to existing rivalries through CON regulation failed to limit the true expansion of services. Providers remain threatened by new entrants who provide substitutes for regulated services.

Finally, the cost of complying with CON legislation can be very significant, especially if CON approval is contested by any interest groups. Health providers have the power to contest any and all regulatory decisions, often with the support of their primary stakeholders — buyers, purchasers, and consumers of health care. Because state agencies are confined to the rules of due process, the CON review can be delayed severely and incur exorbitant costs in lawyer and court fees (Kinzer, 1988). So-called easy CON applications that generate no opposition from the state or other providers can cost the hospital $10,000 to $15,000. Difficult CON applications that raise opposition from competitors or from the state can cost a hospital $150,000 or more (Burda, 1990). In the case of Franklin Square Hospital in Baltimore, Maryland, a CON application cost a whopping $600,000 in one year, largely because of litigation opposing the granting of CON approval to a competitor.

CON fails in its assumption that the barrier created by its legislation will provide an advantage for existing rivalries. Not only is the regulation extremely costly to implement for both regulators and providers, but it also favors larger existing competitors to the detriment of smaller ones.

Strategic Impact on Potential New Entrants

New entrants into the health care market are restricted by CON regulations. CON regulations assume these new entrants are threatening to stakeholders and detrimental to the economic survival of existing competitors. This is not always the case. New entrants into a market can introduce efficiency through up-to-date facilities and equipment, thus enabling the same volume of patients to be served in a less costly manner. Under CON regulations, new entrants into a market are often stuck in a quagmire of red tape before they can open their facilities. By the time they are allowed to enter the market, their competitive advantage has significantly diminished. This reduces the market's attractiveness for potential new entrants and perpetuates the inefficiencies of existing competitors.

In the *Rex Hospital* case, the for-profit Hospital Building Company (HBC) sought to enter the Wake County, North Carolina, health care market by buying an old facility with 49 beds and upgrading it with a new hospital having 140 beds. HBC was opposed during the CON approval process by two existing hospitals, Rex Hospital and Wake County Memorial Hospital. Although HBC eventually won the case and was given CON approval for its new facility, its entry into the market was delayed for five years. HBC claimed that the move was opposed by the other hospitals in order to block entry and reduce competition (Lynk, 1987).

Strategic Impact on Potential Substitutes

Health providers have found a number of ways to dodge the time-consuming, expensive process of CON approval. One way involves finding nonregulated substitutes for their services. Traditionally, CON regulation has failed to include a number of nonhospital health care providers. This has left the market wide open for the entrance of nonregulated substitutes: physician group practices, ambulatory surgery centers, health maintenance organizations, and so forth. Although a number of states have recognized this inequity and have amended CON legislation to include nonhospital providers, regulations in all states cannot keep up with the multitude and complexity of substitutes. In some states, health maintenance organizations (HMOs) and other nonhospital facilities have been exempted from controls on capital expenditures (Ford, 1986; and Kinzer, 1988). In fact, nonhealth care competitors have tended to benefit from CON regulations. For example, a venture capitalist who knows nothing about health care could purchase and install an MRI facility somewhere even though he or she had no health care experience. If a hospital wanted to provide the same service, the hospital would have to pass through several bureaucratic hurdles to provide service within its premises. The hospital could waste thousands of dollars and years of time going through the CON approval process while the entrepreneur captured the outpatient MRI market (Ford, 1986). In Massachusetts, for example, hospitals have been required to obtain a CON in order to operate a surgicenter, but HMOs have not. "The whole national trend toward corporate diversification of hospitals is in large part a process of building escape hatches from controls" (Kinzer, 1988, p. 22).

Even though CON regulation has attempted to set up a barrier to substitutes, these stakeholders have too much to offer and too much to gain to be kept from the marketplace. It would be impossible for regulators to devise an umbrella of CON review that would cover all possible substitutes for health care provision in the marketplace.

Strategic Impact on Suppliers

As stated before, large CON-regulated hospitals have more power than smaller hospitals because of the volume of patients they serve. This gives large hospitals a considerable competitive advantage and makes it easier for them to attract and retain physicians, nurses, and other health care professionals. This dramatically reduces the choice of desirable hospitals in which health care professionals wish to work and places certain regions of the country at a distinct disadvantage to others when trying to attract professionals. In areas that have no desirable alternatives, physician stakeholder power is reduced significantly through the reduction in choice. Other supplier stakeholders face similar reductions in their bargaining power. Even managed-care organizations with existing preferred provider arrangements to channel patients to a given facility have significantly reduced power to negotiate for the lowest rates.

Highly regulated areas are placed at other disadvantages. In a number of ways, CON regulation runs the risk of promoting technological obsolescence. Regulators who understand the technical impact and benefit of a new technology are not easy to find. Many times, the consumers involved in the CON process are unfamiliar with new technologies and have difficulty in determining what the technology's benefit to society would be. Consumers are often overwhelmed with technical jargon and spend considerable state time and resources having staff members explain what a particular CON application entails. Once they are prepared to make a decision, these consumers have little incentive for cost containment. They often side on making health care services more readily available (Havighurst, 1986; and Kinzer, 1988). Kinzer (1988) believes that better educated and more "sophisticated technocrats" are needed in place of direct consumer involvement in the CON process.

The decreased bargaining power of suppliers has increased their stake in the regulatory process. CON has forced suppliers to evaluate the market attractiveness of regional industries and to position their services in those environments that are most favorable. Professionals may choose to move their services and their patients to areas that are not regulated by CON. Unregulated areas are free to purchase state-of-the-art equipment and are free to respond to professional demands quickly and completely.

Strategic Impact on Buyers/Payers/Consumers

CON regulation has even more impact on stakeholders who are buyers, payers, and consumers of health care. The regulations decrease the bargaining power of buyers whose interests usually side with seeing more health care services available. One premise underlying CON regulations is that regulation will limit entry into a market, which will allow existing organizations to achieve economic returns adequate enough to ensure survival. Another is that regulation will reduce total health care costs by eliminating excess capacity. In actuality, by increasing the power of existing competitors and decreasing the power of buyers, payers, and consumers, CON establishes conditions favorable to price setting and collusive actions. Restricted supply and threats of collusion actually *increase* the cost of health care to buyer stakeholders and thus increase their stake in the regulatory process.

Unfortunately, CON does not significantly reduce health care costs. Therefore, the regulations reduce the bargaining power of buyers without having a justifying decrease in health care costs. Coyte (1987) found that CON regulations, when coupled with hospitals reimbursed by insurance plans on a per case basis, did not significantly alter the expected cost per patient.

Mayo and McFarland (1989) found that CON regulation in the state of Tennessee from 1980 to 1984 constrained hospital and bed growth and reduced both total variable costs and average variable costs. Increases in market concentration, however, tended to raise average costs per patient.

According to Havighurst (1982), CON cannot contain total hospital costs. If the preferences of hospital administrators, trustees, and doctors cannot be satisfied through the addition of new beds, alternatives will be found among less regulated options. CON has not attempted to constrain the resources available to the hospital. Instead, it is trying to control how those resources are spent. By limiting the *quantitative* improvements that hospitals can make in new buildings or services, CON has enabled providers to spend capital on *qualitative* improvements such as new furnishings, patient services, and others. The result is no overall reduction in costs attributable to CON because capital is redirected to other areas. If health care costs are going to be contained, regulators need to address the problem (resources available to the hospital), not the symptom (excess capacity and expansion) (Havighurst, 1982). Reducing the number of beds may not contribute to improved output. Constraints on beds increase the waiting time of patients, limit the number of patients who can be treated, and result in financial losses from patients who were not able to be treated (Havighurst, 1982; Kinzer, 1988). CON regulation can significantly limit access, another negative consequence for buyer stakeholders. A long-term bed reductionist strategy in New York City has added to the risk of dealing with unforeseeable increases in demand. Epidemics, such as AIDS, have the potential to use up any resources that may be labeled "unneeded."

Still another threat to buyer stakeholders is the possibility that highly regulated areas may experience more negative patient outcomes. An empirical study by Shortell and Hughes (1988) found that the presence of CON laws leads to decreases in morbidity rates for some services. Hospitals with stringent CON laws had significantly higher ratios of actual to predicted deaths than those in less regulated states. Shortell and Hughes found that hospitals faced with strict regulatory constraints respond in ways that *increase* mortality rates. These hospitals often cut costs by reducing staff, eliminating services, and postponing capital improvements. Stringent CON laws may lead to providing care with outdated facilities and technology. Hospitals may have to forego the development of new services and programs that could improve the quality of their care.

Whenever the access to care and the quality of care are threatened, buyer stakeholders react to counteract the negative influence. This has happened in the case of CON. Although buyer power has been reduced through regulation, buyers now often side with health care providers to fight CON rulings. Frequently, the combined power of existing providers and concerned buyers has been strong enough to have CON expenditure limits changed to suit individual providers and to meet the needs of the paying patient population.

Consumers and providers have always been participants in the CON decision-making process. By formalizing the role of the provider in the process, planning agencies are reinforcing the very problem that has existed in other industries: "the regulator's inability to act in the public interest without accommodating in substantial ways the private interests of the regulated" (Havighurst, 1982, p. 27). Those who are regulated often are unhappy with CON decisions. Hospital associations, trustees, and executives have considerable political lobbying power. Therefore, if a CON decision negatively impacts the health providers of a particular politician, for example, the politician may be pressured into threatening the regulators with budget cutbacks in order to appease constituents (Kinzer, 1988).

CONCLUSIONS AND MANAGERIAL IMPLICATIONS

Throughout this essay, we have presented the case against regulation to protect existing competitors in an existing market. Specifically, we have analyzed one of the most widely used and abused types of regulation, namely, certificates of need.

CON regulations have, in most cases, failed to operate in the systematic, fair way that they were envisioned. This is true in part because of political manipulation by powerful organizations that are pursuing their own interests.

CON regulations are supposed to contain costs. They have not. Consumer involvement in decision making has been ineffective in containing costs. Limits on the spending of resources is not the same as restricting the number of resources available. These resources have often been spent elsewhere.

The CON approach is based on an implicit model that builds in significant but unfair competitive advantages for existing competitors. The approach encourages existing competitors either to reduce or to maintain rivalries.

CON legislation also assumes that regulation will be relevant primarily for existing competitors. In actuality, there are many others who have strategic stakes in the regulations. As a result of the number of stakeholders and their many different interests, certificates of need have serious unanticipated consequences.

REFERENCES

Berger, Sally. 1989. "Trustees as Advocates: Selecting, Educating, and Deploying Trustees for Best Results." *Healthcare Forum Journal*, 32(3): 45-46.

Blair, John D., and M. D. Fottler. 1990. *Challengers in Health Care Management: Strategic Perspectives for Managing Key Stakeholders.* San Francisco: Jossey-Bass Publishers.

Burda, David. 1990. "Counting the Cost of Complying With Regulations." *Modern Healthcare*, 20(33): 40-52.

"CON 'Tailoring' Comes to a Head in Kentucky." 1990. *Hospitals*, 64(8): 106.

Coyte, Peter C. 1987. "Alternative Methods of Reimbursing Hospitals, and the Impact of Certificate-of-Need and Rate Regulation for the Hospital Sector." *Southern Economic Journal*, 53(4): 858-873.

Ford, Raymond L. 1986. "Regulations Can Hamper Competition." *Modern Healthcare*, 16(22): 86.

Havighurst, Clark C. 1982. *Deregulating the Health Care Industry: Planning for Competition.* Cambridge, MA: Ballinger Publishing Company.

Havighurst, Clark C. 1986. "The Changing Locus of Decision Making in the Health Care Sector." *Journal of Health Politics, Policy, and Law*, 11(4): 697-735.

Horty, John. 1986. "Controversial Decisions on CONs Can Generate Lawsuits in Protest." *Modern Healthcare*, 16(6): 74.

Kinzer, David M. 1988. "Our Realistic Options in Health Regulation." *Frontiers of Health Services Management*, 5(1): 3-40.

Lynk, William J. 1987. "Antitrust Analysis and Hospital Certificate-of-Need Policy." *Antitrust Bulletin*, 32(1): 61-84.

Mayo, John W., and D. A. McFarland. 1989. "Regulation, Market Structure, and Hospital Costs." *Southern Economic Journal*, 55(3): 559-569.

Nemes, Judith. 1991. "Not-for-Profits Like the Fit of Former For-Profits." *Modern Healthcare*, 21(1): 46-48.

Porter, M. E. 1980. *Competitive Strategy.* New York: The Free Press.

Shortell, Stephen M., and E. F. X. Hughes. 1988. "The Effects of Regulation, Competition, and Ownership on Mortality Rates Among Hospital Inpatients." *New England Journal of Medicine,* 318(17): 1100-1107.

> **ISSUE EIGHT**
>
> *Hospitals play an important role in meeting the goals of society by providing health care services to all people, regardless of their ability to pay.*

What is a hospital's role in contributing to social goals? Many people view low-cost, adequate health care as every citizen's right. It is the question of how to provide that care that has caused considerable debate. Over the years, the delivery of health care has become a complex system of interrelated institutions that include government, business, and a confusing array of profit and not-for-profit health care organizations. The social role of hospitals — a hospital's relationship and responsibilities to its community and patients — has become fuzzy. Have hospitals contributed to the goals of the public? Should hospitals contribute to these goals?

In the health care industry, the decades of the 1980s and 1990s have been marked by a significant increase in hospital strategies that are designed to increase revenues, spread risks, and control the flow of patients. At the same time, the growing number of uninsured and underinsured individuals has escalated concerns about runaway health care costs and raised questions regarding the quality of health care available to them. *The Future of Public Health* (1988), a report by the Institute of Medicine, notes that "this nation has lost sight of its public health goals and has allowed the system of public health activities to fall into disarray" (p. 1). Some groups advocate increased regulation to assure low-cost health care and universal access. Others argue that increased competition will provide a wide array of services and balance demand and supply. Still others posit that it is the responsibility of the hospital to assure adequate health care as a right to be enjoyed by all.

Throughout the past decade, health care organizations have engaged in a variety of strategies, including related and unrelated diversification and vertical integration, in an attempt to provide a wide array of services and to spread the risks of operation across several markets. Underlying many of these strategies is a strong profit motive. Have these strategies made hospitals stronger and thus better able to provide quality services? Are hospitals acting in a socially responsible manner? Have these profit-oriented strategies taken hospitals away from their primary mission — providing quality health care to those in need?

It is estimated that as many as 41 million people are without health insurance. In today's high-cost environment those without insurance do not have access to health care except through public health departments. Although some hospitals have chosen to serve indigent patients, many have refused and do not accept Medicaid reimbursement. Some hospital administrators feel that mixing paying patients with indigent patients is "bad for business." Which is more important, to provide services to needy patients or to promote an image congruent with paying patients' expectations?

Considerable controversy surrounds the question "Who is to blame for rising health care costs?" U.S. health care costs are about $650 billion, or 12 percent of the gross national product (GNP). Has competition contributed to health care cost escalation? Have hospitals concentrated too much on margins and the bottom line rather than on the needs of the public?

In a recent survey of consumers, employers, physicians, and hospitals, 24 percent of the consumers and 29 percent of the employers said that they believed the quality of hospital care had deteriorated in the past five years (Kenkel, 1990). Many studies cite incidents of unneeded procedures and inconsistent treatment. In addition, consumers have come to expect crowded conditions, long waits, uncompassionate care, and inconsiderate attitudes. Why is there a perception of declining quality? Have hospitals abandoned their basic purpose and mission?

What is the social responsibility of hospitals? What role should they play in seeing to the goals of society? In examining the issue of social responsibility, Stephen S. Mick, of the University of Michigan, argues that hospitals have had problems but are important parts of a community's social systems, representing and fostering local values and norms. On the opposing side, Rueben R. McDaniel, of the University of Texas at Austin, suggests that hospitals are not servants of society but actual threats to society because of their inefficient and inequitable use of society's resources.

REFERENCES

The Institute of Medicine. 1988. *The Future of Public Health.* Washington, D.C.: National Academy Press.

Kenkel, Paul J. 1990. "Pointing the Finger: Who's to Blame for High Healthcare Costs?" *Modern Healthcare,* 20(48): 22-25.

POINT

Hospitals play an important role in meeting the goals of society by providing health care services to all people, regardless of their ability to pay.

STEPHEN S. MICK
University of Michigan

Stephen S. Mick is an associate professor in the Department of Health Services Management and Policy at the University of Michigan. Mick earned a B.A. in psychology from Stanford University in 1965 and a Ph.D. in sociology from Yale University in 1973, specializing in organization theory. Before joining the faculty at the University of Michigan in 1989, he taught at Middlebury College, Yale University, the University of Oklahoma, the University of Washington, and the Johns Hopkins University. His teaching interests include medical care organization, health care management, and organization theory. His research interests include work on rural hospital management and innovation, vertical integration, and medical manpower with specific reference to foreign medical graduates. He is the editor and co-author of *Innovations in Health Care Delivery: Insights into Organization Theory.*

THE PROBLEM

The American hospital — voluntary, community-based, public, or investor-owned — may well be at a critical juncture in its history and evolution. Although some might date the beginning of the American hospital's current troubles to an earlier time, most would agree that since the early 1980s, the hospital has been buffeted by insurer and payer restrictions on reimbursable costs, squeezed by certain states' rate-setting commissions, and subjected to more careful quality reviews of outcome measures, including mortality. For some hospital critics, these woes are just retribution for the hospital's transgressions, and the sooner the hospital can be made to pay for its sins, the better. Thus, the number of recent hospital closures — from 1980 to 1990, 431 urban and 330 rural (American Hospital Association, 1991) — is regarded by critics as a healthy sign. Hospitals — those usurpers of scarce health care dollars, purveyors of authoritarian control over the availability of health services, and laboratories of iatrogenesis — are in decline.

The American hospital has been criticized for being a hegemonic entity, voraciously devouring weaker hospitals and raiding the domains of community-based organizations such as visiting nurses associations and home health agencies. Its expenditures consume $0.39 of every $1.00 spent on health services, the largest single institutional share (Lazenby and Letsch, 1990). It has been pilloried as an unhealthy place in which infection is inadequately controlled and iatrogenic diseases are rampant. To iatrogenesis, Illich (1976) adds the paradox that medical practice in hospitals has so surpassed reasonable technological limits of effectiveness that any net change due to treatment leads to decrements in health. The hospital has received the wrath of those who see it as nothing more than a physician workshop, exploited by the medical profession in the interest of its own goals and objectives. In short, the American hospital has been, and continues to be, decried as an organization that has lost its basic mission — to care for the sick and injured — in a maze of organizational self-interest, professional profiteering, and contradictory processes that produce as much illness as they cure.

These are serious criticisms that cannot be easily brushed aside. Yet, in the end, I view hospitals as benefiting society more than harming it. I will make my case not in a point-by-point rebuttal of the negative views outlined above, but by presenting two arguments of my own. The first suggests that the organizational entities called hospitals exist for good reason. If one thinks of a hospital as a nexus of exchanges among a bewildering array of complex and simple goods and services, one must consider what is the most efficient way to plan, coordinate, monitor, and control those exchanges. I contend that the hospital is the preferred choice. My second argument is that any major institutional sector, especially the hospital, both reflects and contributes to society's values and norms, hopes and fears, and aspirations and disappointments. As such, hospitals have a central place in the life of communities and society. The remainder of this essay develops these two themes.

THE HOSPITAL AS A VERTICALLY INTEGRATED SYSTEM

What is it that we gain by having care delivered in hospitals? In view of the complex nature of most health care, particularly as it becomes more technologically based, the answer relies on certain economizing features of organizations when compared to nonorganizational modes of care.[1] A key operating assumption of this

---

[1] Unlike some, I see no necessary evil in high-technology medicine. Certainly its abuse occurs, but that hardly requires its wholesale repeal. As Ginzberg (1990) notes, one can question the assumptions that high technology medicine is disliked by Americans, is responsible for severe cost escalation, or is dysfunctional for patients.

argument is derived from an idea central to transaction-cost economics: When the cost of market exchanges increases beyond what it would cost the organization itself to produce or control needed inputs and outputs, the organization should integrate the relevant entities into its own structure (Williamson, 1975). What makes transaction costs high for an organization are the expenses of finding, bidding, securing, monitoring, and assuring predictable, stable, quality supplies in the face of uncertainties in markets or the environment.

Put another way, as the uncertainty and complexity of the health care environment increases, so do the transaction costs associated with the care that takes place among independent and autonomous organizations in the environment. A logical way to reduce these costs is to bring together, or integrate, the separate smaller organizations into a single organizational entity. This action allows managers, through the cost-minimizing control systems at their command, to replace the market in affecting exchanges. Thus, by vertical integration, I mean the provision of a service or product inside the hospital that could, in fact, be provided outside the hospital but at different transaction costs.

Looked at this way, hospitals are really nothing more than extensively integrated vertical structures (Mick and Conrad, 1988). It is hard to think of any service in a hospital that is not in some sense vertically integrated. Even nursing services, traditionally seen as part of the essence of a hospital, are actually vertically integrated services. The opposite case, vertical de-integration, existed earlier in the century when private duty nurses, whose services were ordered by the patient or the physician, were used. Today, we have nurse registry agencies that supply nurses for a hospital on demand. There is nothing written in stone that requires nurses to be full-time, salaried (vertically integrated) inputs for patient care. But, the benefit of their integration is the reduction of transaction costs in the provision of that care. The point is made nicely by Roemer and Roemer (1982):

> The operations of virtually all programs of organized health care delivery are further demonstrations of the high cost and inefficiencies of multiple separate transactions [that would occur in nonhospital, market-like situations]. (p. 118)

Their examples are drawn from a wider spectrum of care needs (e.g., rehabilitation for disabilities, which would include physician services, drugs, hospitalization, physical and occupational rehabilitation, prosthetic appliances, occupational retraining, and job placement) than those one would see within a hospital, but the point is the same. How would one propose to offer the set of services required for much hospital-based care outside the confines of a hospital? In almost any emergency or elective surgical procedure, the staff and personnel (technicians, nurses, surgeons, and others) must be present; the facilities must allow quick preoperative preparation for and coordination with the actual surgical activities, as well as timely, coordinated, immediate postoperative care and observation, often in an intensive care unit; the laboratory and imaging services that may be involved need to be present; and postoperative care and recovery needs must be met. Imagine if there were no hospital organization with these services integrated? Could one expect to have a predictable, timely, stable, quality response in providing these outside the hospital? Or, perhaps less extreme, could one expect the same level of coordination, timeliness, predictability, and quality if these services were done in separate places by nonhospital organizations and patients were shuttled from one place to another, from one provider or group of staff to another?

It is entirely possible to organize care on this basis, and, for much care, this sort of thing already occurs. For Medicare recipients, the substitution of ambulatory services for inpatient services, prompted largely by the prospective payment system (PPS), shows that one must not draw hard and fast conclusions on the limits of inpatient vertical integration. One must wonder, however, how far this de-integration can go. When will quality issues finally make themselves known in poorly supervised ambulatory surgical clinics, in the increasing number of nonhospital-based laboratories, and in the proliferating home-health industry that has virtually no oversight? Under de-integration like this, the transaction costs incurred to assure minimal standardization and quality would undoubtedly be far greater than those incurred in a hospital.

There is no need for hospitals as we currently know them. In fact, the history of the hospital throughout the twentieth century clearly belies the notion that there is an *absolute entity* called the hospital. The boundaries of a hospital fluctuate over time. They are subject to technological, professional, political, and social forces. There are many instances of de-integrated care, including nonhospital-based care for the mentally impaired and mentally ill. These instances are confined mostly to long-term, chronic conditions that require low technological intervention. The town of Geel, Belgium, for example, is a complete therapeutic community that has existed for centuries and grew out of the medieval pilgrimages of the mentally ill who sought cures from the cult of St. Dymphna (Roosens, 1979). In Geel, a mentally ill patient attempting to lead as normal a life as possible, stays with a local family, sometimes for years. Roosens notes that any "average, medium-sized community" can adopt hundreds of mentally ill or feebleminded persons. There are no overwhelming technical problems to overcome. The key is the community's desire and will to undertake the venture. If the community's wish is to experience life and prosperity without the presence of the mentally ill, then the community is signaling that it does not want such an arrangement (Roosens, 1979).

As the oddity of Geel reveals, such largess is rare anywhere, but it is particularly rare in the United States, where the results of nearly twenty years of deinstitutionalization and dismantlement of mental hospitals have led to a truly scandalous situation in which the mentally ill have been left to fend for themselves in hostile communities and now constitute a large segment of the homeless population. The hospital, viewed as evil and satirized in films such as *Titicut Follies*, has given way to a far worse nonhospital evil: neglect, indifference, destitution.

We might be able to do without hospitals, but what society forfeits in closing hospitals may be much more than it bargained for. In fact, there is more at stake than economizing on transaction costs.

THE HOSPITAL AS A SOCIAL INSTITUTION

My premise is simply that a hospital is more than the sum of its parts or, if you will, that a hospital is more than an economic organization of vertically integrated pieces. Hospitals have more to do with communities, however defined, than merely being places in which physicians and other practitioners meet and treat patients under the administrative guidance of hospital managers. A hospital is more than the "doctors' workshop" (Pauly and Redisch, 1973). One needs to recall the vast literature on the hospital as a "social system," an internally dynamic structure that not only mirrors the social system within which it is embedded but also extends its influence beyond its own boundaries into other facets of a community's life (Freidson, 1963; and Croog and Ver Steeg, 1972). Hospitals, especially voluntary community hospitals, are obvious care centers, but at a more abstract level, they are also social institutions. A social institution is a vehicle that embodies and melds society's material and technological capacities with its normative and value-laden or symbolic features. In today's business-oriented health care rhetoric, which emphasizes organizational efficiencies and competitive stances, we seem to have forgotten earlier research and writing that posited that hospitals were miniature social systems embedded within larger social systems and that the configuration of services and organization were not coincidental to larger social configurations. Despite the business rhetoric of the 1980s, hospitals remain the small social systems they have always been.

If hospitals represent an organizational distillate of the surrounding community's hopes and values, this does not mean that because they have existed for decades, they must be good or that they are somehow necessary for society's survival (the functionalist viewpoint). Rather, one can view the hospital as a particularly visible organization that makes tangible the value and norm constellations of the social system in which it is located. That a society may or may not need hospitals for survival (although many would argue that it is hard to imagine why else they exist) is not the point. The point is that hospitals provide public places where what people affirm as important is important, allowing values and norms to survive.

The plight of America's rural communities illustrates this point (Davidson, 1990). For many rural communities in the 1980s and 1990s, the hospital is very nearly their last social institution. The others have disappeared. Small businesses have been driven out of existence by national franchise outlets. Local churches often have been displaced by regionally oriented fundamentalist congregations that have no strong community connections (Ploch, 1990). School districts have consolidated local schools into regional learning centers. The list could be extended. But, the rural hospital has been a mainstay of community values, a center of community activity that encompasses more than the sheer delivery of health care (Margolis, 1989). The closures cited earlier underscore the changes that are happening to these institutions and suggest that the 1990s will produce continued diminution in their numbers. For rural communities, the question is, What social institutions will be left to act as "centering" forces of community life, to transmit values and norms, and to provide a material locus for the intangible, sometimes ceremonial, expression of important social symbols?

There is an economic problem as well. Hospital closures wreak havoc with local, often already weakened, economies (Doelker, 1989). Christianson and Faulkner (1981) have estimated that the direct and indirect total community income generated by the local hospital varied between $700,000 to $1,000,000. Doeksen, Loewen, and Strawn (1990) have documented the effect of a hospital closure in rural Oklahoma: 51 people unemployed out of a total population of about 2,600. They concluded that "policymakers must examine the social costs of reduced economic viability in rural communities as well as the social costs of reduced levels of service" (p. 64). For rural communities, and for more of our urban and suburban areas than we may realize, hospitals are more than organizations that provide places for people to be healed or to die.

Hospitals also reflect both the good and the bad that a person finds in society generally, sometimes in startling ways. Duff and Hollingshead (1968), for example, showed in a celebrated case study of a major teaching hospital that quality of care was negatively related to socioeconomic status. Twenty-two years later, Wenneker, Weissman, and Epstein (1990) rediscovered the enduring relationship between socioeconomic status and features of care in an examination of cardiac procedures in five Massachusetts hospitals: privately insured patients had odds 80 percent higher than Medicaid recipients of receiving angiography, 40 percent higher for bypass grafting, and 28 percent higher for angioplasty. Society itself is highly stratified with a wide range in the distribution of income and wealth and deep rifts among racial, ethnic, and religious groups. These divisions are often reflected internally in the hospital. In fact, hospitals can even contribute to these very divisions in their own way. One study revealed that the stratified relationships among teaching hospitals in the training of foreign medical graduates versus U.S. medical graduates were recapitulated in the subsequent medical practices of these physicians (Mick, 1987). Why would one expect hospitals to be impervious to these larger social characteristics? This is not a defense of social inequality, limits on opportunity, or any other untoward, usually unspoken, social norm. Rather, I question the extent to which any social institution can maintain incongruent social patterns or values and norms and remain integrated into its larger societal context.

Yet, on a more positive note, as Rosner (1988) pointed out, hospitals can and have made deliberate efforts to enact moral objectives within the hospital's wards to inculcate certain values held as good by hospital owners, managers, and trustees. Sometimes these values are somewhat out-of-step with what is current. In the late nineteenth and early twentieth centuries, for example, "many trustees understood the inclusion of a wide range of religious, racial, and ethnic groups to be an important indication of the usefulness of the institution" (Rosner, 1988, p. 99). At their best, hospitals can and do contribute to positive social goals; as one of my students recently noted, hospital care is the first step in guaranteeing equality of opportunity for the poor (Goold, 1991). Finally, who cannot be moved by Renée Fox's study of the bravery and humor of both patients and clinicians in the early experimental days of hemodialysis and renal transplants (Fox, 1959)? Moving and inspirational stories abound in hospitals for those who care to look. In sum, hospitals embody society's best and brightest hopes of renewal, healing, birth, and rebirth. They harbor society's worst fears of illness, injury, deterioration, and death. They act as witnesses to courage, happiness, and humor as well as sadness, disappointment, turmoil, grief, and agony.

In general, however, the values and norms of the larger society are the critical causal forces that guide the stance of hospitals. Stevens (1989) has clearly demonstrated that hospitals are creatures of their environment, and she shows how, decade to decade, hospitals have reacted to broad social signals. The body of organizational writing called "institutional theory" makes explicit the historical phenomenon Stevens revealed. Alexander and D'Aunno (1990), for example, have written that organizational change follows change in the definition and elaboration of externally imposed normative criteria that emanate from important environmental sources. In the case of health care, one counts the various levels of government, insurers and payers, professional groups, the judiciary, and organizations conveying more authority.

The improvement in hospital performance that happened in Maryland in 1974 following the inception of the Health Services Cost Review Commission (HSCRC), a mandatory hospital rate setting agency is a prime example of the powerful effect of environment on hospitals. The HSCRC established the following guidelines:

1. Similar services at similar hospitals should cost about the same.
2. Patient charges should be related to actual costs.
3. Nonpatient revenues should not subsidize wasteful operations.
4. Profitable patient services should not subsidize unprofitable ones.
5. All payers should share bad debt and charity care equally.

A review of the seventeen-year experience of hospitals under this system found hospital costs are now 7 percent below the national median (the state began with costs 24 percent above the national median); that $1 billion has been saved since 1974; and that little "downsizing" of the health care sector has occurred (Merson, 1991). Other relevant outcomes include high access for all people to hospital services, virtually no patient "dumping," only a modest level of uncompensated care, no cost shifting, diminished duplication of tertiary care technology and programs, and good public perception of quality.

I do not intend to laud mandatory state rate-setting systems. Rather, I underscore the point that hospitals respond to environmental and societal forces just as other institutions do. But, in all circumstances, hospitals represent new life and rebirth as well as decline and death.

CONCLUSION

The two themes — hospitals as vertically integrated organizations and as social institutions — are actually entwined. The rationale for minimizing transaction costs by vertical integration is not solely an economic rationalization. Close reading of transaction-costs literature reveals an emphasis on so-called governance structures, that is, organizational systems of authority and control that replace the autonomous, faceless discipline of the marketplace in allocating resources. These governance structures are precisely the mechanisms that reduce transaction costs and make organizations an appealing alternative to market exchanges (Ouchi, 1980). These organizational governance structures consist of managers, governing boards, and professional groups, such as medical staff organizations. In short, governance structures are the same agencies that sociologists identify as those that implement action to maintain both the manifest and latent norms and values of the hospital as a health care delivery organization and as a social institution. We have two sides of the same coin, two mutually reinforcing functions, one economic, the other sociological.

I believe it would be unimaginably difficult, inefficient, and dangerous to provide modern health care in radically de-integrated, decentralized, "dehospitalized" alternatives, such as clinic- or home-based services, controlled by a myriad of small agencies. Although it could be done, one would forfeit most of the good that centralized control systems and high technology clinical science achieve. In addition, it is difficult to think of modern society without such social institutions as hospitals. It is true that large bureaucratic organizations — like many hospitals — squeeze the life out of interpersonal relationships. It is to be hoped that sensitive managers and clinicians do not allow this to happen. But, would we prefer the atomized, disjointed option of de-integrated care? Would the de-integrated delivery system provide an equivalent symbolic substitute for our hopes and fears surrounding illness and cure? It is true that not long ago, most medical care was given to people in their homes by physicians who made house calls; babies were born and people died in their homes. Certainly today some conditions do not always require hospitalization, but for the most part, I suspect that without it, most of us would worry about the quality of the care and whether or not families were equipped for the task.

I conclude, therefore, that the hospital, for all its frailties and foibles, is a critical and important part of the social fabric and more efficient than nonhospital-based alternatives. Hospitals have their weaknesses and dark sides; so do all human organizations and institutions. Still, we need hospitals, and we must make the best of them that we can.

REFERENCES

Alexander, Jeffrey A., and Thomas A. D'Aunno. 1990. "Transformation of Institutional Environments: Perspectives on the Corporatization of U.S. Health Care." In Stephen S. Mick and Associates, eds., *Innovations in Health Care Delivery: Insights for Organization Theory.* San Francisco: Jossey-Bass Publishers, pp. 53-85.

American Hospital Association, Hospital Data Center. 1991. *Hospital Closures 1980-1990: A Statistical Profile.* Chicago: American Hospital Association.

Christianson, Jon B., and Lee Faulkner. 1981. "The Contribution of Rural Hospitals to Local Economies." *Inquiry,* 18(1): 46-60.

Croog, Sidney H., and Donna F. Ver Steeg. 1972. "The Hospital as a Social System." In Howard E. Freeman, Sol Levine, and Leo G. Reeder, eds., *Handbook of Medical Sociology,* 2d ed. Englewood Cliffs, NJ: Prentice-Hall, pp. 274-314.

Davidson, Osha Gray. 1990. *Broken Heartland: The Rise of America's Rural Ghetto.* New York: The Free Press.

Doeksen, Gerald A., Ron A Loewen, and David A. Strawn. 1990. "A Rural Hospital's Impact on a Community Economic Health." *Journal of Rural Health,* 6(1): 53-64.

Doelker, Richard E., Jr. 1989. "Impact of Rural Hospital Closings on the Community." *Social Work,* 34(6): 541-543.

Duff, Raymond S., and August B. Hollingshead. 1968. *Sickness and Society.* New York: Harper and Row.

Fox, Reneé C. 1959. *Experiment Perilous: Physicians and Patients Facing the Unknown.* New York: The Free Press.

Freidson, Eliot, ed. 1963. *The Hospital in Modern Society.* New York: The Free Press.

Ginzberg, Eli. 1990. "High-Tech Medicine and Rising Health Care Costs." *Journal of the American Medical Association,* 263(10): 1820-1822.

Goold, Susan. 1991. "Need Versus Demand for Health Services: The Moral Argument." Paper submitted in partial fulfillment of course requirements in HSMP 601, University of Michigan.

Illich, Ivan. 1976. *Medical Nemesis: The Expropriation of Health.* New York: Pantheon Books.

Lazenby, Helen C., and Suzanne W. Letsch. 1990. "National Health Expenditures, 1989." *Health Care Financing Review,* 12(2): 1-26.

Margolis, Richard J. 1989. "In America's Small-Town Hospitals, a Patient Isn't 'Just a Number'." *Smithsonian,* 10(6): 52-67.

Merson, Michael R. 1991. "Managing in Maryland." *Health Management Quarterly,* 13(1): 24-28.

Mick, Stephen S. 1987. "Sector Theory, Stratification, and Health Policy: Foreign and U.S. Medical Graduates in Medical Practice." *Journal of Health and Social Behavior,* 28(1): 74-88.

Mick, Stephen S., and Douglas A. Conrad. 1988. "The Decision to Integrate Vertically in Health Care Organizations." *Hospital & Health Services Administration,* 33(3): 345-360.

Ouchi, William G. 1980. "Markets, Bureaucracies, and Clans." *Administrative Science Quarterly,* 25(1): 129-141.

Pauly, Mark, and M. Redisch. 1973. "The Not-for-Profit Hospital as a Physicians' Cooperative." *American Economic Review,* 63(1): 87-99.

Ploch, Louis A. 1990. "Religion and Community." In A. E. Luloff and Louis A. Swanson, eds., *American Rural Communities.* Boulder, CO: Westview Press, pp. 125-150.

Roemer, Milton I., and John E. Roemer. 1982. "The Social Consequences of Free Trade in Health Care: A Public Health Response to Orthodox Economics." *International Journal of Health Services,* 12(1): 111-129.

Roosens, Eugeen. 1979. *Mental Patients in Town Life: Geel — Europe's First Therapeutic Community.* Beverly Hills, CA: Sage Publications, Inc.

Rosner, David. 1988. "Heterogeneity and Uniformity: Historical Perspectives on the Voluntary Hospital." In J. David Seay and Bruce C. Vladeck, eds., *In Sickness and in Health: The Mission of Voluntary Health Care Institutions.* New York: McGraw-Hill Book Company, pp. 87-125.

Stevens, Rosemary. 1989. *In Sickness and in Wealth: American Hospitals in the Twentieth Century.* New York: Basic Books.

Wenneker, Mark B., Joel S. Weissman, and Arnold M. Epstein. 1990. "The Association of Payer with Utilization of Cardiac Procedures in Massachusetts." *New England Journal of Medicine,* 264(10): 1255-1260.

Williamson, Oliver E. 1975. *Markets and Hierarchies: Analysis and Antitrust Implications.* New York: Free Press.

COUNTERPOINT

*Hospitals do **not** play an important role in meeting the goals of society because they do not provide health care services to all people, regardless of their ability to pay.*

REUBEN R. McDANIEL, Jr.
University of Texas at Austin

Reuben McDaniel teaches strategic management, organizational behavior, and policy analysis in the Graduate School of Business at the University of Texas at Austin. McDaniel received an Ed.D. degree from Indiana University. His current research focuses on understanding organizational strategic decision-making making processes and those factors that lead to effective organizational designs, particularly in health care delivery systems and other professional organizations. His articles have appeared in *Management Science, Journal of Applied Behavioral Sciences, The Academy of Management Journal, Organizational Behavior and Human Decision Processes, The Journal of the National Medical Association, Health Services Research,* and *Health Progress*. He has acted as a consultant to the Catholic Health Care Association, the Texas Department of Human Services, IBM, and Microelectronics and Computer Technology Corporation. He serves on the board of the Daughters of Charity Health Services of Austin.

An earlier version of this essay was given as the Van Zile Scott Lecture at the University of Alabama at Birmingham on January 24, 1991. The author would like to thank Ruth Anderson, Donde Ashmos, and Judith Smith for comments on an earlier version of this paper. Thanks are also due to Angie Austin for assistance in the literature review.

Hospitals and the other components of our country's health care system are not servants of society, but threats to society. Those who deliver and manage health care often argue that hospitals have served society by providing health care to all who have needed their services. The evidence, however, suggests that hospitals have been neither effective, efficient, nor equitable users of society's resources. As we examine the efficacy of the health care system, it becomes clear that the system has failed society and, in fact, now poses a direct threat to society's future.

What does it mean to say that society is threatened? A society is threatened when it is faced with a situation that creates a hazard for its members that puts them in jeopardy. As noted by Richard Darman, the director of the Office of Management and Budget, "Runaway health care costs are jeopardizing the nation's long-term economic stability and sinking the federal government into deeper debt" (Zaidivar, 1991, p. A4). The hazard posed by the health care system has created a sense of anxiety and feelings of frustration. In order to relieve these feelings, people engage in approach-avoidance behavior. In describing society's feelings about health care, Wildavsky (1979) notes "[we are] doing better and feeling worse" (p. 285). To relieve their anxiety in threatening situations, individuals, groups, and organizations tend to restrict their attention to critical information, repress conflicts, and simplify responses to events (Staw, Sandelands, and Dutton, 1981). These behaviors serve to reduce performance, increase the actual danger, and thereby increase the real risk. If the threat is sustained, people feel insecure and experience extreme helplessness. In these situations, people resort to increased centralization of authority and appeals to demagoguery. They attempt to reduce the threat by imposing simple rules of behavior that may not address the real problem.

Hospitals are important to everyone. If hospitals were not important, their present way of operating would not be a threat and they could be safely ignored. However, because the activities that take place in hospitals are treated seriously by all members of society, the behavior of hospital leaders cannot be ignored. In every community, hospitals are the buildings that more people go into alive and come out dead than any other building in town. Almost everyone starts life in a hospital, and many will end life there as well. These facts make the relationship between hospitals and society difficult to understand and manage. As noted by Ehrenreich and Ehrenreich (1974), "The expansion of the medical system has been accompanied by a deepening public dependency on the system" (p. 31). Because hospitals are important to the overall well-being of society, hospital managers do not have a free hand. They must be socially responsible. The remainder of this essay will show the extent of the threat posed by the health care system, suggest a hypothesis about its causes, and present some ideas for change.

SOME OBSERVATIONS

The State of the System

Our country's health care system threatens society because it consumes society's resources without achieving society's goals. The United States has the world's highest per capita expenditure for health care but the health status of the nation's people is among the lowest in the industrialized world (Schieber, 1990; The Pepper Commission, 1990). Monheit (1990) found that

> In 1987 Americans spent $2051 per person on health care, almost double the $1033 average for other industrialized countries. . . . [yet] there is diminished access to health care as socioeconomic status and ability to pay decline and health status worsens. (pp. 7-11)

It is projected that by the year 2000, health care will consume 15 percent of the country's annual output of goods and services (American Medical Association, 1989).

Spending on this country's health care system is sustained by a public relations campaign that is designed to convince Americans they should be grateful for the meager health care services they receive and should not question the wisdom or good will of those entrusted with its management and delivery. No other nation tolerates a system in which people pay so much and get so little.

The Disenfranchised

The system threatens society because all those who need services are not served. Access to medical care is uneven across income groups. An individual's access to care is often determined by his or her income (Patrick, et al., 1988; Fleming, 1990; The Pepper Commission, 1990). Because public hospitals carry much of the burden of serving the poor, their resources are being strained to the limit (Luggiero, 1991). "The average emergency room wait for a bed in the nation's public hospitals is now more than five and a half hours and in the worst cases 3 to 10 days" (Hilts, 1991).

The uninsured pose a particularly difficult problem for our society. Although estimates vary, there are approximately 35 million Americans without health care coverage. This is an alarming fact because the evidence suggests that being uninsured is dangerous to your health. If a person is uninsured, he or she is three times more likely to die in a hospital than if he or she is insured ("Uninsured Hospital Patients," 1991). In 1988, 17 percent of the nation's children, ages 17 and under were not covered by either a private-pay health plan or Medicaid. The number of children without health insurance went up 40 percent in the ten years between 1977 and 1987 ("Uninsured Rate," 1991).

Despite the historical relationship between health care and charitable institutions, such as the church, many not-for-profit hospitals are ignoring many of the needs of the poor. According to the General Accounting Office (GAO), the value of the uncompensated and charity care in many not-for-profit hospitals is less than the value of their federal and state tax-exempt status ("House Proposal," 1990). In making recommendations to providers in response to the GAO's findings, Fahey and Murphy (1990) do not suggest that hospitals might give more charity care. Instead, they suggest monitoring developments, highlighting flaws in minimum charity care standards, and determining the adequacy of methods for documenting the provision of care.

The Dissatisfied

A health care system threatens society if those who use the system are dependent on it but are dissatisfied with it. The American consumer is significantly less satisfied with the present U.S. health care system than either the Canadians or the British are with their systems (Citizens Fund, 1990). Most Americans want fundamental changes in the direction and structure of the health care system (Families USA Foundation, 1990). Although Americans normally express satisfaction with the health care that they personally receive, they are not satisfied with the system of health care delivery and they are particularly dissatisfied with the use and distribution of resources (Harvey and Shubat, 1989). According to Jensen (1991), 86 percent of the consumers surveyed believe that hospitals charge more than it actually costs to provide services. Consumers have good reasons to be suspicious of health care charges. Health care inflation has been about twice the general rate of inflation for the past decade, and excessive health care price increases account for about one quarter of health care inflation (Families USA Foundation, 1990). Most Americans believe that by the time they are eligible for benefits, programs like Medicare will offer them significantly less than they offer today ("Americans Fear," 1990).

Not only are consumers concerned about health care issues, a majority of physicians and hospital administrators believe that health care costs are the nation's number one problem (Jensen, 1991). About two-thirds of all physicians surveyed believe that hospitals charge more than it actually costs to deliver services.

Health care is also a major concern for America's business community because health care costs are a major source of corporate expenses. In 1990, fully 26 percent of the average company's net earnings went for medical costs, and the average cost per worker was $3,217 (Freudenheim, 1991).

All sectors of the society are dissatisfied, and they should be. "Studies have failed to discern a strong relationship between the quantity of health resources expended and improvement of health status" (Monheit, 1990, p. 9). In addition, there are wide, unexplainable disparities among the charges for the same services in different parts of the country. For example, the average median charge for an artery bypass graft with cardiac catherization varies from $53,160 in California to $25,744 in New York (Kenkel, 1991). In health care, it is quite possible to spend money and not get anything for it (Fleming, 1990).

The Beneficiaries

A system is a threat to society if it inequitably benefits some segments of the society. In spite of its cries of economic trouble, the health care industry is considered by many to be one of the best investments in America. *Business Week,* reporting in 1991 on the state of America's industries, stated, "Health care is this year's favorite. The health care services group set investors' hearts thumping last year. This group of companies posted a huge 60 percent jump in market value" ("Health Care," 1991, p. 16). The health care industry itself recognizes that health care organizations are making a lot of money and that it is one of the best performing industries financially. As Cerne (1991) reports in the *AHA News,* "The same factor that made health care stocks potent performers in 1990 — strong earnings growth —

is likely to continue this year, some financial analysts predict" (p. 1). Hospitals seem to be able to resist recessionary pressures, which makes them good investments even in a volatile market (Tokarski, 1990).

This remarkable financial strength is not a response to demand-side pressures. According to *Business Week*, "Each day, 35 percent of the nation's 1 million hospital beds lie empty" (Garland, 1991, p. 69). According to a study by the Department of Health and Human Services, about 800,000 Medicare patients were hospitalized unnecessarily in 1985 (Rich, 1988). Hospitals are capturing markets by driving other providers out of business and then "creaming" the market. Hospital managers know how to make money for their owners. The total gross hospital charges (i.e., the prices hospitals charged for services) rose at a faster rate than operating revenues and expenses, suggesting that hospitals are raising their prices more than necessary (Burda and Tokarski, 1990).

All of this has happened while the health care system of the United States has paid the highest proportion of administrative costs in the world — on the average, 18 percent of its total expenses (Families USA Foundation, 1990). Many hospitals have seven to nine management layers and a manager-employee ratio as low as one-to-five (Burda, 1990). One way that hospitals mask their prosperous state is through the traditional indicators of hospital activity. Traditional indicators, such as occupancy rates in an era when bed occupancy is not an indication of hospital prosperity, may be misleading if, for example, the hospital has emphasized growth in outpatient treatments and diagnostic services. The hospital may have had strong economic growth while experiencing decline in traditional measures of occupancy. The use of traditional measures may make the performance of hospitals seem worse than it really is (Phillip, 1990). Hospitals now act as businesses, businesses that are concerned about stockholder wealth and not patient health. These businesses threaten to consume the resources that society needs to be stable and prosperous.

The Neglect of Other Needs

A system is a threat to society when it prevents other societal needs from being met. As a greater and greater proportion of the nation's resources are spent on health care, other pressing societal needs go unmet. Federal health programs consumed 14.7 percent of federal expenditures in 1989 and the proportion seems to be continuing to rise in the 1990s ("HHS Releases," 1991).

> If health care costs [during the 1980s] had consumed the same level of real economic growth in America as in Japan and Germany, the United States would have had $70 billion more each year to invest in areas such as domestic plant expansion, research and development. . . . If the United States had spent the same share of our [Gross Domestic Product] as our international competitors, we would have saved $158 billion in [1987] alone. (Citizen Fund, 1990, pp. 5-7)

The money spent by the federal government for health care has resulted in less money being available for enhanced educational opportunities at all levels. It has meant that the industrial infrastructure, including roads, bridges, rail systems, and communication linkages, has deteriorated to such a point that international competitiveness has been compromised. Funds that might have been available for the improvement of cities have been spent on overpriced and, sometimes ineffective, health care. Because of the excessive profits to be made in health care, many of the best minds in the country have been drawn to the field, perhaps draining human resources needed to address issues in other sectors of the society.

HOW DID THIS HAPPEN?

This situation is not the result of maliciousness. There has been a failure of both policy and management, and this failure has led to a situation in which "the medical care system is now ranked last of a dozen major institutions in terms of public support — far behind business and industry in general, the press, the court system, public schools, labor unions, and the U.S. Congress" ("Disgruntled Consumers," 1991, p. 6). Gail R. Wilensky, the chief of the Health Care Financing Administration, states the problem this way, "We've set up a system that in no way rewards prudent behavior" (Garland, 1991, p. 69). When she was the director of the Congressional Budget Office, Alice Rivlin (1983) suggested that politicians could not sensibly control the rapidly growing costs of medical care so they should, "put the money on the stump and run" (p. 6).

It is entirely possible that this situation has occurred because of faulty paradigms that drive our thinking about health care. A person's ability to act in a given situation is a function of the paradigms that drive his or her thought processes. Everyone is a victim of the models he or she uses to look at the world. Our present models of health care tend to focus on the idea of competitive markets. Unfortunately, using a market paradigm as the central paradigm for health care does not work for either the hospital or society. The leadership of the country has attempted to develop health care policy and to manage health care organizations as if the service provided were an individual good, subject to rational control through the market, when, in fact, health care is a social good.

Health care systems do not respond to competitive conditions in the classical fashion because of the economics of imperfect information, which suggest that "consumer uncertainty about product quality can make even the most price-competitive markets behave in unusual and socially undesirable ways" (Robinson, 1988, p. 479). Competition among hospitals usually does not involve price competition because of the paucity of information about the real cost (as opposed to charges) for services and the industry's ability to engage in essentially undetectable cost shifting. To date, empirical studies suggest that nonprice competition such as high touch, high tech, facility, and prestige, drives up prices (Robinson, 1988; Higgins, 1989, 1991). Robinson and Luft (1987) in a study of 5,732 hospitals found that costs per admission were over 25 percent higher in hospitals that were in more competitive environments. The idea of competition as a solution to health care issues is often tied to the idea of privatization. Regardless of the theoretical promise of privatization, when it has been tried, it has not led to improved health care in terms of either quality of services or cost of services (Gardner and Scheffler, 1988).

Perhaps hospitals and other health care delivery systems should be treated as professional organizations rather than as businesses that respond to market forces in much the same way as McDonald's or Pepsico (Weick and McDaniel, 1989).

Professional organizations are those organizations in which the work of the core technology is performed by professionals — workers who possess special expertise and values. This expertise and these values must be brought to bear in the development of strategies for the reform of the health care system (Schultz, 1991). In hospitals, physicians and other health care specialists are critical task specialists who are important sources of strategic information (Ashmos and McDaniel, in press). New strategies must be invented in order for the variety of professionals in the health care system to join forces with nonmedically trained administrators and turn the system around (Schultz, 1991). Because these two groups view their worlds differently, this will be difficult (Ashmos and McDaniel, 1990; Weiner, Boyer and Farber, 1986). It will require redesigning the future and inventing ways of bringing it about; it will require planning to do better in the future than it presently appears possible to do (Ackoff, 1974).

SOME SPECIFIC SUGGESTIONS

There are numerous suggestions for fixing the health care system. Most of them involve governmental policy options and major initiatives that are designed to reduce or eliminate the threats the health care system poses to society. Rather than repeat those here or attempt to develop new options, I am going to offer eight suggestions that can be implemented by hospital administrators to assist in reducing the hospital's contribution to the problem.

We often see problems on such a grand scale that we become psychologically paralyzed and unable to engage in a suitable course of action (Weick, 1984). When we look for those things that changed the relationships between races, for example, we often see the Civil Rights Act or Martin Luther King's "I Have a Dream" speech rather than Rosa Parks refusing to sit in the back of the bus. This causes us to be overwhelmed and perhaps miss the essential elements of social change. The refusal to sit in the back of the bus may be more pivotal in social progress than more publicized events. Not many of us can pass a piece of legislation or make an immortal speech, but all of us can refuse to sit in the back of the bus. Rosa Parks provided a model of behavior that was within every person's reach.

So it is in health care. Small wins are needed to turn around the present situation (Weick, 1984). The suggestions listed below are techniques for hospital administrators who want to achieve small wins. They are techniques for managing nonroutine information in turbulent, complex environments. They are techniques for increasing the probability that an organization will develop appropriate responses to the environment — responses that benefit both the organization and society. Each is theoretically and empirically justifiable, and they are presented here without the normal academic undergirding but as ideas worth trying.

1. *Seek to balance the demands for effectiveness, efficiency, and equity.* Historically, managers have been concerned with effectiveness and efficiency, and they have believed that an invisible hand would take care of equity issues. Equity in health care today is a concern of patients, providers, and payers.

2. *Create closer alliances between third-party health care providers, patients, managers of health care systems, and third-party payers.* The assumption of classical economics is that everyone should look out for himself. It is a "let the buyer beware" approach. Neither the technology nor the financing of medicine is such that self-focused behavior can lead to satisfactory outcomes.
3. *Pay attention to both the interpretation and the decision-making functions of management.* Interpretation involves giving meaning to events, while decision making involves choosing between alternative courses of action. Often, attention is given to choosing without adequate attention to meaning. Organizational problems are not things to be found but are the conceptual creations of the members of the organization. A primary function of managers it to give meaning to the work of others.
4. *Develop strategies for bringing both the expertise and the values of health care providers to bear on the functions of interpretation and decision making.* The scientific basis for medicine has reduced the attention given to value issues in the delivery of health care, but because medicine is a social good, it is the value system of medicine that gives health care organizations their legitimacy.
5. *Enhance the participation of all health care providers, including physicians, nurses, and pharmacists, in organizational strategic decision making.* Increase both the scope and intensity of participation because participation in strategic decision making goes far beyond "how many people are involved in making the decision."
6. *Decentralize decision making by moving it closer to the task and expect more individual responsibility for the quality and quantity of work.* Do not confuse decentralization with participation. Decentralization involves relinquishing authority and responsibility. Participation involves sharing authority and responsibility. Expect people to take responsibility, and you will discover that one of the best predictors of performance is managerial expectation.
7. *Decouple decentralization, control, and coordination through the use of advanced information technologies.* We used to believe that decentralization, control, and coordination were tied together in organizational design decisions. If one wanted to coordinate, one had to centralize; if one decentralized, one lost control; and if one controlled, one would be able to coordinate. Advanced information technologies allow the manager to decouple these functions because they allow the separation of hierarchical lines of authority from lines of communication.
8. *Take more responsibility for what is happening in the hospital and in the environment.* Health care executives, like most other people, tend to credit others with their failures and acknowledge their own successes. Being accountable means assuming responsibility for the problems in the system and trying to do something about them. Health care executives and the organizations they lead cannot recapture the respect and confidence of society unless they take control in both the good times and the bad.

A VISION OF THE FUTURE

We can envision a hospital in which the corporate culture is such that the concerns of the organization and of society amplify each other rather than threaten each other. We can envision a hospital in which cooperation, not conflict, is the dominate characteristic of the relationship between the organization and society. We can envision hospital executives who are redirecting the environment rather than reacting to it. As Joseph A. Califano, Jr. (1989), the former secretary of Health, Education and Welfare, has noted:

> Fortunately, the money needed to [avoid a disaster] is already allocated to health care. We need only to spend that money wisely. If we do, we can provide higher quality health care for all our citizens at the same price we're now paying to provide a declining quality of care for only some. (p. A25)

REFERENCES

Ackoff, R. L. 1974. *Redesigning the Future.* New York: John Wiley and Sons.

American Medical Association. 1989. *The Environment of Medicine.* Chicago: The American Medical Association.

"Americans Fear Future Medicare Reductions." 1990. *Healthcare Financial Management,* 44(7): 7.

Ashmos, D. A., and R. R. McDaniel. (in press). "Understanding the Participation of Critical Task Specialists in Strategic Decision Making: The Case of Physicians and Hospitals." *Organizational Science.*

Ashmos, D. A., R. R. McDaniel, and D. Duchon. 1990. "Differences in Perception of Strategic Decision Making Processes: The Case of Physicians and Administrators." *Journal of Applied Behavioral Science,* 26(2): 137-156

Burda, D. 1990. "Untangling Management Structures." *Modern Healthcare,* 20(17): 11. Quoted in *Medical Benefits.*

Burda, D., and C. Tokarski. 1990. "Hospitals Are Under Pressure to Justify Cost Shifting." *Modern Healthcare,* 20(45): 28-35 Quoted in *Medical Benefits.*

Califano, J. A., Jr. 1989. "Billions Blown on Health." *The New York Times,* p. A25.

Cerne, F. 1991. "Continued Growth in Health Care Stocks Predicted." *AHA News,* p. 1.

Citizens Fund. 1990. *Spending More and Getting Less: A Comparison of the Cost and Quality of Health Care in the United States and the World.* Washington, D.C.: Citizens Action.

"Disgruntled Consumers Want Reform Soon." 1991, April 15. *The Public Pulse.* In *Medical Benefits,* p. 6.

Ehrenreich, B., and J. Ehrenreich. 1974. "Health Care and Social Control." *Social Policy,* 5(1): 26-40.

Fahey, T. M., and A. M. Murphy. 1990. "Tax Exemption and Charity Care — What Can Hospitals Expect?" *Trustee,* 43(11): 6-8.

Families USA Foundation. 1990. *To the Rescue: Towards Solving America's Health Cost Crisis.* Washington, D.C.: Families USA Foundation.

Fleming, S. T. 1990. "The Relationship Between the Cost and Quality of Hospital Care: A Review of the Literature." *Medical Care Review,* 47(4): 487-502.

Freudenheim, M. 1991, January 29. "Health Care a Growing Burden." *The New York Times,* pp. C1, C17.

Gardner, L. B. and R. M. Scheffler. 1988. "Privatization in Health Care: Shifting the Risk." *Medical Care Review,* 45(2): 215-253.

Garland, S. B. 1991, April 22. Terminating the Medical Arms Race. *Business Week,* p. 69.

Harvey, L. K., and S. C. Shubat. 1989. *Physician and Public Attitudes.* Chicago: American Medical Association.

"Health Care Is This Year's Favorite." 1991. *Business Week,* Special Issue: 16.

"HHS Releases U.S. Healthcare Spending Figures for 1989." 1991. *Healthcare Financial Management,* 45(2): 6.

Higgins, C. W. 1989. "Competitive Reform and Nonprice Competition: Implications for the Hospital Industry." *Health Care Management Review,* 14(4): 57-66.

Higgins, C. W. 1991. "Myths of Competitive Reform." *Health Care Management Review,* 16(1): 65-72.

Hilts, P. J. 1991, January 30. "Public Hospital Wait for Bed Can Be Days, U.S. Study Says." *The New York Times,* p. A10.

"House Proposal Would Link Charity to Tax-Exempt Status." 1990. *Healthcare Financial Management,* 48(8): 7.

Jensen, J. 1991. "Consumers Trail Other Groups in Concern over Healthcare Costs, but Interest Is Rising." *Modern Healthcare,* 21(9): 50, 52.

Kenkel, P. J. 1991. "DRG Study Shows Disparity Among Hospitals." *Modern Healthcare,* 21(4): 18.

Luggiero, G. 1991. "Uncompensated Care Strains Public Hospitals." *AHA News,* p. 1.

Monheit, A. C. 1990. "Returns on U.S. Health Care Expenditures." *The Journal of Medical Practice Management,* 6(1): 7-13.

Patrick, D. L., J. Stein, M. Porta, C. Q. Porter, and T. C. Ricketts. 1988. "Poverty, Health Services and Health Status in Rural America." *The Milbank Quarterly,* 66(1): 105-136.

The Pepper Commission (U.S. Bipartisan Commission on Comprehensive Health Care). 1990. *A Call for Action: Executive Summary.* Washington, D.C.: U.S. Government Printing Office.

Phillip, J. 1990. "New Yardsticks." *Health Management Quarterly,* 12(4): 14-17.

Rich, S. 1988. "Unneeded Admissions to Hospitals Cited: Cost to Medicare Seen as $1 Billion a Year." *The Washington Post,* p. A3.

Rivlin, A. M. 1983. "An Intelligent Politician's Guide to Dealing with Experts." In *The Rand Graduate Institute Commencement Addresses.* Santa Monica, CA: The RAND Corporation.

Robinson, J. C. 1988. "Hospital Quality Competition and the Economics of Imperfect Information." *The Milbank Quarterly,* 66(3): 465-481.

Robinson, J. C., and H. S. Luft. 1987. "Competition and the Cost of Hospital Care, 1972-1982." *Journal of the American Medical Association,* 257(23): 3241-3245.

Schieber, G. J. 1990. "Health Care Expenditures in Major Industrialized Countries, 1960-87." *Health Care Financing Review,* 11(4): 159-167.

Schultz, H. 1991. "Health Policy: If You Don't Know Where You're Going, Any Road Will Take You." *American Journal of Public Health,* 81(4): 418-420.

Staw, Barry M., Lance E. Sandelands, and Jane E. Dutton. 1981. "Threat Rigidity Effects in Organizational Behavior: A Multilevel Analysis." *Administrative Science Quarterly,* 26(4): 501-524.

Tokarski, C. 1990. "Health Spending Eludes Recession." *Modern Healthcare,* 20(2): 4. Quoted in *Medical Benefits.*

"Uninsured Hospital Patients Found Far More Likely to Die." 1991, January 16. *The New York Times,* p. A13.

"Uninsured Rate for U.S. Children Is Skyrocketing." 1991, January 28. *AHA News,* p. 2.

Weick, K. E. 1984. "Redefining the Scale of Social Problems." *American Psychologists,* 39(1): 40-48.

Weick, K. E., and R. R. McDaniel. 1989. "How Professional Organizations Work: Implications for School Organization and Management." In T. J. Sergiovanni and J. H. Moore, eds., *Schooling for Tomorrow: Directing Reforms to Issues that Count.* Boston: Allyn and Bacon, pp. 330-355.

Weiner, J. L., E. G. Boyer, and N. J. Farber. 1986. "A Changing Health Care Decision-Making Environment." *Human Relations,* 39(7): 647-659.

Wildavsky, A. 1979. *Speaking Truth to Power: The Art and Craft of Policy Analysis.* Boston: Little, Brown and Co.

Zaidivar, R. A. 1991. "Medical Bills Threaten U.S. Economic Health." *Austin-American Statesman,* p. A4.

> **ISSUE NINE**
>
> *Rural hospitals are important parts of their communities and provide essential health care services not otherwise available, therefore federal and state governments should provide the support necessary to ensure their survival.*

Rural hospitals are financially troubled, and many are failing. Within the health care industry, government, and the affected communities, people debate who or what is to blame for the financial problems of rural hospitals and what should be done about them. A rural hospital is any hospital that is not located within a metropolitan statistical area (MSA), which is defined by the U.S. Bureau of the Census as a large population nucleus together with the adjacent counties that have a high degree of social and economic integration with that nucleus. Currently, there are more than 2,700 rural hospitals in the United States.

In a rural area, the hospital is a symbol of the community and often the community's largest employer. Many rural hospitals were constructed under the Hospital Survey and Construction Act of 1946 (the Hill-Burton Act). Lister Hill's dream was to ensure health care for all rural Americans. Between 1947 and 1971, more than $3.7 billion were distributed by the Hill-Burton Act to individual states to build hospitals, primarily in rural areas. The federal standard of 4.5 hospital beds per 1,000 population was followed (Starr, 1982).

In the 1960s and 1970s, health care costs escalated far more rapidly than costs in any other segment of the economy. The shortage of health care professionals, the aging rural population, the increased cost of technology, and some believe even the introduction of cost-containment measures, including prospective payment systems (PPS) using diagnosis related groups (DRGs) in 1983, added to the increase in costs for hospitals. The result has been a decrease in inpatient services and further pressure on operating margins.

Rural hospitals have been especially hard hit. The federal reimbursement system has paid lower amounts to rural hospitals because their costs are lower according to a 1981 study made prior to the introduction of PPS and DRGs. Recent research, however, indicates that rural hospitals with few beds and low occupancy rates have higher costs (Gianfrancesco, 1990). Unfortunately, as more patients travel to urban areas for care, more beds are not utilized, and costs for rural hospitals continue to escalate. Because Medicare patients are less able to travel for care than private-pay patients, rural hospitals have little opportunity to use the revenue from private-pay patients to make up for the lower reimbursement provided by Medicare (a common practice for large urban hospitals).

As their costs rise and their reimbursements fall, rural hospitals find they cannot compete with urban hospitals in terms of salaries to attract the most qualified health care professionals. Rural hospitals also cannot afford the expensive new technologies that are in demand. They do not have the capability to raise the capital required to buy the technology, nor do they have sufficient demand to achieve economies of scale in operation. Some argue that investment in large, regionalized centers will yield better results.

Others argue that unprofitable rural hospitals should be closed because of the quality of their care. Some research indicates that rural hospitals do not perform certain procedures frequently enough to develop and maintain an adequate level of care. Open heart surgery, comprehensive oncology services, and organ transplants are seldom provided by rural hospitals. Infrequent surgical need and the lack of full-time surgical specialties for follow-up patient care are the major reasons for poor outcomes. Although rural hospitals usually provide obstetrics, pediatrics, general medical services, emergency medical services, and surgical services, is this access to what may be poor quality care enough (Moscovice, 1989)?

If rural hospitals serving sparsely populated areas are closed, will any kind of health care be available to these communities that are increasingly older and poorer? Can urban hospitals with higher volumes achieve greater efficiencies and lower health care costs? Deaths from cardiovascular disease, cancer, occupational accidents, and chronic illnesses related to pesticides and chemicals are higher in rural areas (Mullner, 1990). Infant and maternity mortality are higher for rural areas that lack appropriate resources. The question may become: Is health care a right or a privilege? Arguing for federal and state support of rural hospitals is Gerald A. Doeksen, of Oklahoma State University. Arguing against efforts to save failing rural hospitals is James E. Rohrer, of the University of Iowa.

REFERENCES

Gianfrancesco, F. D. 1990. "The Fairness of the PPS Reimbursement Methodology." *Health Service Research*, 25(1): 1-19.

Moscovice, I. 1989. "Rural Hospitals: A Literature Synthesis and Health Services Research Agenda." *Health Service Research*, 23(6): 891-929.

Mullner, R., R. Rydman, and D. Whiteis. 1990. "Rural Hospital Survival: An Analysis of Facilities and Services Correlated with Risk of Closure." *Hospital & Health Services Administration*, 35(1): 121-137.

Starr, P. 1982. *The Socialization of American Medicine.* New York: Basic Books, pp. 348-351.

> **POINT**
>
> *Rural hospitals are important parts of their communities and provide essential health care services not otherwise available, therefore federal and state governments should provide the support necessary to ensure their survival.*

GERALD A. DOEKSEN
Oklahoma State University

Gerald A. Doeksen is regents professor and extension economist in the Department of Agricultural Economics at Oklahoma State University, as well as adjunct professor at Oklahoma University. Doeksen earned a master's degree and a Ph.D. in agricultural economics at Oklahoma State University. He has served as editor of the *Southern Journal of Agricultural Economics* and chairman of the Publication of Enduring Quality Committee for the American Agricultural Economics Association. He has received numerous awards for his involvement and research in rural economics from such organizations as the United States Department of Agriculture, the American Agricultural Economics Associa-tion, the American Rural Health Association, and the Southern and Western Agricultural Economics Associations.

Decision makers in sparsely populated rural areas are extremely concerned about the viability of their communities' economies. Over the past several decades, these decision makers have witnessed many changes and have observed the impact of these changes on their communities. They have watched the economies of their small communities decline as public and private services, such as schools, implement dealers, and lumber companies, have consolidated. As they have consolidated and moved to county seats or to trade centers, the small communities have lost jobs, income, and eventually, population. Now, these county seats or trade centers also face decline as other public and private services face consolidation. Rural hospitals are also facing financial problems, and many experts predict hospital closures. Rural areas, which have a high and growing proportion of the elderly, need health services if the elderly are going to have minimum quality of life. Few would dispute that health services and hospitals are needed for the health of these residents. The rural hospital, however, is also important to the economic health of the community. The objective of this essay is to demonstrate and discuss the importance of the hospital to the rural economy. This will be accomplished by reviewing the basic concept of community economics and reviewing several recent studies that have measured the impact of a hospital on a community's economy.

COMMUNITY ECONOMICS

To discuss the economic impact of a hospital closing in a community, it is important to understand community economics. Figure 1 presents an overview of the community economic system. The flow chart presented in Figure 1 illustrates the major flow of goods, services, and dollars within a community's economic system which is comprised of three components: basic industries, households, and services. Basic industries are usually the industries that export goods from the community. These may include agriculture, mining, and manufacturing. To produce these goods for export, the basic industries purchase inputs from outside the community, which is illustrated by the arrow in the upper left corner showing inputs coming into the industry. The industries also purchase labor from households of the community and inputs from service industries located within the community. The flow of labor, goods, and services in the community is completed by households using their earnings to purchase goods and services from the community's service industries as well as from outside the community. The flow chart illustrates that any change in the economy will reverberate throughout the community's entire economic system.

The total impact on an economy of a change in an industry consists of direct, indirect, and induced impacts. Direct impacts are changes in the activities of the industry. If the industry changes its purchases of inputs as a result of the direct impact, it will produce an indirect impact in the business sector. Both the direct and indirect impacts change the flow of dollars to the community's households. The households then alter their consumption of goods and services accordingly. The effect of this change in household consumption on businesses in a community is referred to as an induced impact.

The relationship between the direct impact and the sum of the direct, indirect, and induced impacts is referred to as the *multiplier effect*. This relationship indicates the number of jobs or amount of income created or lost due to a one unit change in employment or income. An employment multiplier of two, for example, indicates that for any direct job created by a firm, another job is created to support that job. The size of the multiplier depends upon the amount of economic activity occurring within the community. If inputs and labor are purchased outside the community, then the multiplier will be low. Because the flow of goods, services, and labor is different for every community, the impact of a hospital closure will be different for every community.

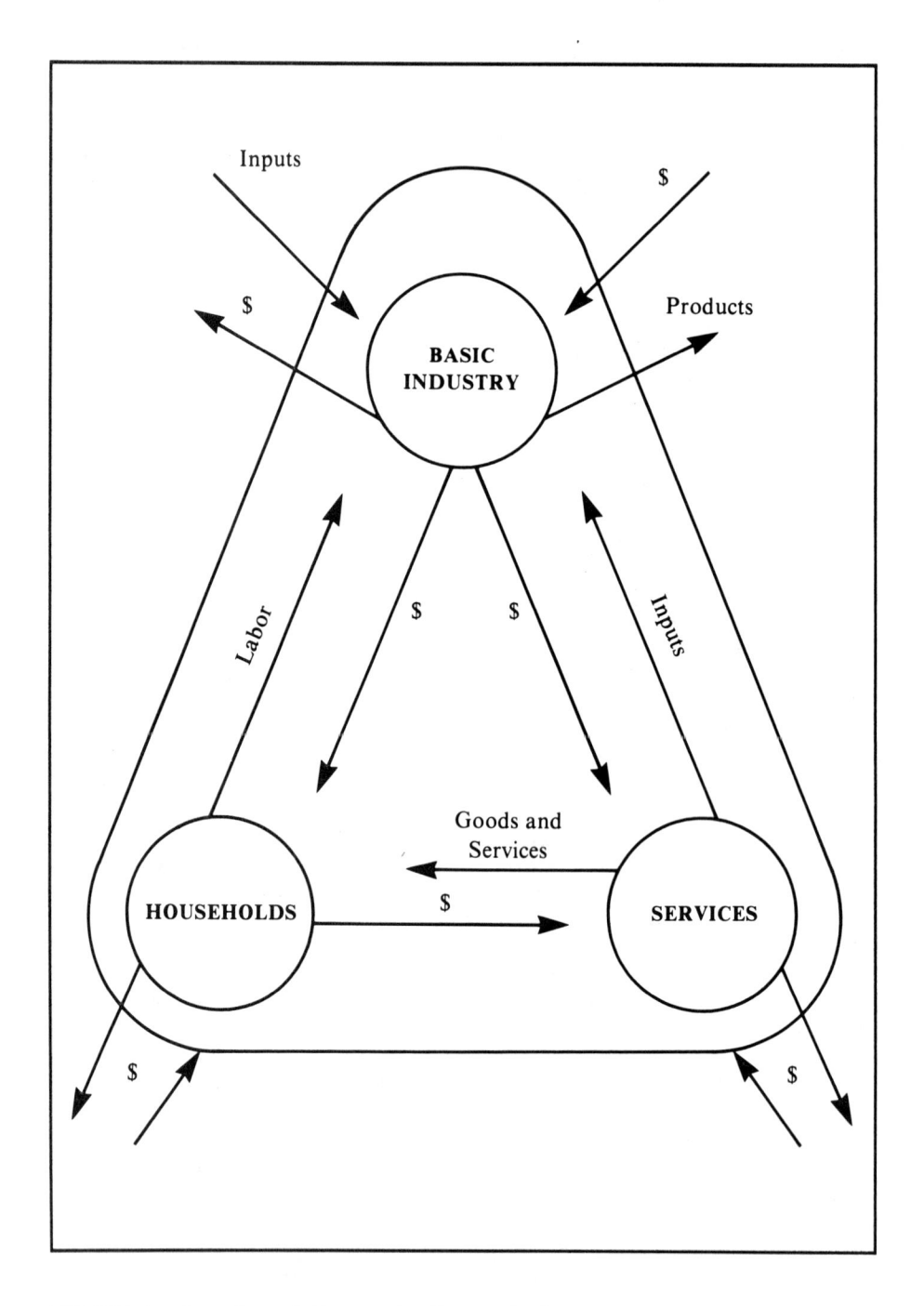

FIGURE 1 *Overview of Community Economic System*

RECENT STUDIES OF HOSPITAL CLOSURES

Few studies have been completed that attempt to qualitatively measure the impact of a hospital closing on the community's economy. One study in northeastern Minnesota used an economic forecasting model for a seven-county area and projected that the closure of a single rural hospital would cost the regional economy more than $100 million and 8,000 jobs in a seven-year period (Lichty, Jesswein, and McMillan, 1986). A Florida study estimated that for each full-time job lost when a hospital closed, another 0.587 jobs were lost in the local economy due to the multiplier effect (Sharpe, 1987). An Oklahoma study measured the impact of one hospital closing in eastern Oklahoma (Doeksen, Loewen, and Strawn, 1990). A Texas study measured the impact of three hospitals closing (Doeksen and Altobelli, 1990). The results of the Oklahoma and Texas studies will be summarized in the following section.

The Oklahoma Study

In 1988, we completed a study measuring the impact of a hospital closing on Stigler, Oklahoma. Stigler is the county seat and the largest community in the county. The 1988 community population was 2,617 and the county population was 12,012. The hospital had forty-five beds and employed forty-three full-time equivalent employees in 1988. There are no other hospitals in the county.

The community simulation model was a recursive system of equations built around an input-output model (Woods and Doeksen, 1983). The model estimates such community economic variables as employment, income, and population. The model was run the first time on the assumption that current conditions would continue. That is, the projection for the next five years reflected the conditions that had occurred in the past five years. The model was run the second time on the assumption that the hospital would close in 1988. The difference between the two runs of the model is the impact of the hospital closure.

The results are presented in Table 1. If the hospital closed, many of the hospital's employees would have to move out of the community. Doctors, administrators, and other personnel would move with their families. Because some of the employees are second-income wage earners, they would not move. The closure of the hospital with its forty-three jobs would cause another eight jobs to be lost in other businesses in the community (a total of fifty-one jobs). Projections showed that thirty people would move and that income would be reduced by $659,800. The impact on businesses in Stigler would be a reduction in retail sales of $171,500. The city's sales tax collection would be reduced by $3,400.

This impact increases over time, as families who do not move immediately but cannot find local employment move outside the area. As less money is spent locally, other businesses will reduce their employment. It was projected that by 1992, the hospital closure would result in a reduction in population of 154, in employment of 78, in annual income of $1,724,800, in annual retail sales of $452,100 and in annual sales tax collection of $9,100. These are significant economic impacts on the economy of Stigler.

TABLE 1 *Impact of Hospital Closing on Population, Employment, Income, Retail Sales, and Sales Tax Collections*

YEAR	POPULA-TION	EMPLOY-MENT	INCOME	STIGLER RETAIL SALES	STIGLER SALES TAX COLLECTION
1988	30	51	$ 659,800	$171,500	$3,400
1989	60	56	901,400	234,400	4,700
1990	91	63	1,161,500	301,900	6,000
1991	122	69	1,441,700	374,800	7,500
1992	154	78	1,724,800	452,100	9,100

Source: Gerald A. Doeksen, Ron A. Loewen, and David A. Strawn. 1990. "A Rural Hospital's Impact on a Community's Economic Health." *The Journal of Rural Health*, 6(1): 62.

The Texas Study

The Texas study employed the same simulation model as the Oklahoma study. Three communities were selected in central Texas: Crowell, Breckenridge, and Graham. Crowell, a community of 1,500, was selected because its hospital, which had twenty-four beds, closed in December 1987. Breckenridge, a community of 6,900, had a hospital with forty beds that was experiencing significant economic stress. Graham, a community of 9,700, had a hospital with forty-three beds that was economically sound.

The economic impact created by the hospital closure in Crowell is presented in Table 2. When the Crowell hospital closed in 1987, it had twenty-three employees. The total estimated impact in 1987 was a loss of twenty-eight jobs and $337,000 in income. By 1994, the projected impact was even greater: a loss of thirty-three jobs and an annual income loss of $533,000. Population was projected to decline by ten and retail sales by $73,000.

The results for the projected impact of the Breckenridge hospital and the Graham hospital are also presented in Table 2. The projected closure of the Breckenridge hospital with its fifty-four jobs in 1989 would cause another fifteen jobs to be lost in other businesses of the community. Similarly, the closing of the Graham hospital would put 100 people out of work and cause the loss of another twenty-eight jobs in the community. Because of the larger initial loss of jobs in both communities, the total loss of jobs, income, sales taxes, population, and retail sales is greater than for Crowell.

TABLE 2 *Impact of Hospital Closing on Employment, Income, Retail Sales, Population, One-Cent Sales Tax, and Unemployment Rate in Crowell, Breckenridge, and Graham, Texas from 1987 through 1994*

YEAR	EMPLOY-MENT	PERSONAL INCOME ($000)	RETAIL SALES ($000)	POPU-LATION	ONE-CENT SALES TAX ($)	UNEM-PLOYMENT RATE
Crowell						
1987	28	337	46	0	460	7.1
1988	28	361	49	2	490	7.0
1989	29	387	53	4	530	6.9
1990	30	413	56	5	560	6.8
1991	30	441	60	6	600	6.7
1992	31	470	64	7	640	6.6
1993	32	500	68	9	680	6.5
1994	33	533	73	10	730	6.4
Breckenridge						
1989	69	975	532	4	5,320	8.1
1990	70	1,061	579	8	5,790	8.0
1991	72	1,150	628	14	6,280	7.9
1992	72	1,246	679	22	6,790	7.8
1993	75	1,344	733	30	7,330	7.8
1994	77	1,448	790	37	7,900	7.7
Graham						
1989	128	2,045	803	5	8,030	6.8
1990	131	2,209	867	9	8,670	6.5
1991	133	2,382	935	19	9,350	8.1
1992	135	2,565	1,007	29	10,070	5.9
1993	137	2,756	1,082	39	10,820	5.6
1994	140	2,958	1,161	49	11,610	5.3

Source: Gerald A. Doeksen. 1989. "The Economic Impact of Rural Hospital Closings: A Case Study of Three Texas Communities." Monograph. Department of Agricultural Economics, Oklahoma State University.

SUMMARY AND CONCLUSIONS

The Oklahoma and Texas studies clearly demonstrate how economic variables such as employment and income will decline if a hospital closes. The impacts in these studies are low because the studies assumed that related medical services would remain in the community. This probably is not true. Some physicians, for example, would relocate to communities with hospitals. Pharmacists would experience difficulties and might move or close. If a hospital closes, the total impact in downsizing the medical services is much greater than depicted in these studies. Whatever the final estimate is, few would argue the fact that the closure of a hospital and the downsizing of other medical services would be devastating to the economy of a rural community.

Rural communities built hospitals with federal Hill-Burton funds when the facilities were needed. Today many of these hospitals are in financial trouble because admissions are declining, hospital payments are depressed due to Medicare's fixed-rate diagnosis related group system (DRG), and because of weak economies in their communities. As with most services, the rural health sector must change to meet the needs of the community.

Federal and state governments should provide the support necessary for the survival of the rural health care system. Survival, however, does not necessarily mean a hospital retains its current framework. Jeffrey Bauer (1989), in hearings before the joint economics committee of the U.S. Congress, has argued that many rural hospitals should be changed from acute care facilities to rural primary care hospitals with three to six short-stay observation beds for infirmary-level care. In addition, the rural area should have an outstanding emergency medical service system that can transport critical patients directly to secondary and tertiary care facilities. Because rural residents are made up of a large number of elderly people, any restructuring should include providing more services for the elderly. Rosenberg and Runde (1989) have argued that restructuring some rural hospitals to skilled nursing homes, may help the hospitals to survive and still provide a specific level of health care in their communities.

Some federal and state government programs that might aid in the restructuring include innovative grant programs that can demonstrate that restructured facilities can survive and the creation of state data banks and technical assistance centers. The technical assistance centers would be able to evaluate what services a community needed and determine what services could be provided profitably. The data bank would include the information needed to assist with the technical studies.

For many local decision makers who are concerned about the impact of a hospital closing on the local economy, restructuring may ease their concerns. In many cases employment remains constant or increases when a hospital is restructured, and there may be no impact or even a positive net economic impact on the community itself. The bottom line is that the health sector must change to survive. If local leaders desire the changes to be neutral or positive in relation to their local economies, they must work with federal and state officials to design a health care system that meets the needs of the local residents and also provides jobs and income for the community. By working together, health and economic benefits can be provided, and the quality of life in their community can be maintained.

REFERENCES

Bauer, Jeffrey. 1989. "The Safe and Appropriate Level of Health Services in Rural America." In *Better Health Care for Rural America.* Joint Economics Committee, 101st Congress, 1st session, pp. 8-15.

Doeksen, Gerald A. 1989. "The Economic Impact of Rural Hospital Closings: A Case Study of Three Texas Communities." Monograph. Department of Agricultural Economics, Oklahoma State University.

Doeksen, Gerald A., and Joyce Altobelli. 1990. "The Economic Impact of Rural Hospital Closure: A Community Simulation." Research Report. The University of North Dakota Rural Health Research Center.

Doeksen, Gerald A., Ron A. Loewen, and David A. Strawn. 1990. "A Rural Hospital's Impact on a Community's Economic Health." *The Journal of Rural Health,* 6(1): 53-64.

Lichty, R., W. Jesswein, and D. McMillan. 1986. "Estimated Medical Industry Impacts on a Regional Economy." *Medical Care,* 24(4): 350-362.

Rosenberg, Steve, and Denise Runde. 1989. "Restructuring Rural Hospitals." In *Health Issues in Rural America.* Washington, D.C.: National Governors' Association, pp. 11-33.

Sharpe, H. 1987. "Florida's Rural Hospitals — The Prognosis is Not Good." Florida Office of Comprehensive Health Planning. Tallahassee, FL: Florida Department of Health and Rehabilitative Services, November (Bulletin).

Woods, M., G. A. Doeksen. 1983. "A Simulations Model for Rural Communities in Oklahoma." Oklahoma Agricultural Experiment Station Bulletin, B-770. Oklahoma State University, Stillwater, OK.

COUNTERPOINT

Rural hospitals are important parts of their communities but they do not provide essential health care services not otherwise available, therefore federal and state governments should not provide the support necessary to ensure their survival.

JAMES E. ROHRER
University of Iowa

James E. Rohrer is associate professor and head of the Graduate Program in Hospital and Health Administration and the Center for Health Services Research at the University of Iowa. Rohrer received a Ph.D. in health services organization and policy from the University of Michigan. His two main research interests are planning and monitoring patient outcomes.

Dr. Rohrer has been involved in rural health planning projects periodically since his arrival at the University of Iowa in 1985. In addition, he is principal investigator for two NIH-funded projects investigating the outcomes of nursing home care. Dr. Rohrer has published more than twenty articles in the past five years. These have appeared in journals such as *Medical Care, Health Services Research,* and *Social Science and Medicine.* He serves on the editorial board of the *Journal of Public Health Policy* and is a member of the The American Public Health Association.

An argument against subsidization of rural hospitals is essentially an argument in favor of a rational health care delivery system. To subsidize unneeded providers of inpatient care while failing to guarantee delivery of other important services is quite simply irrational. Irrationality is a luxury we cannot afford if we are to develop a cost-effective system for delivering personal health services.

The argument presented below begins by establishing the fact that many rural hospitals are not needed. Next, some of the other services that are needed are documented. Finally, the notion of regionalization is developed as an alternative to subsidization of rural hospitals.

NEED FOR RURAL HOSPITALS

Modern hospitals provide acute inpatient medical care and related services. Some defenders of rural hospitals evade the issue of their irrelevance by saying that a hospital remains a hospital even if it divests itself of its acute care inpatient role. Technically, this may be true. However, most people in and out of the health system regard a hospital as a place where patients stay overnight so that they may safely receive medical services too complex to be delivered at home. For the purposes of this essay, the conversion of a rural hospital into a clinic will be regarded as the elimination of the hospital and the establishment of an alternative, and often more necessary, community resource.

In 1987, there were four community hospital beds for every 1,000 people in the United States (National Center for Health Statistics, 1989, Table 96). On average, only 65 percent of those beds were occupied. Occupancy rates have been declining for a generation (National Center for Health Statistics, 1989, Table 97), and with good reason. Changes in reimbursement and medical technology have permitted shorter hospital stays and outpatient treatment for some conditions that otherwise would have required inpatient care. Third-party payers, both government and private insurance companies, have begun to reimburse hospitals in ways that encourage more efficient use of hospital services. In addition to changes in financial incentives, hospitals have been forced to respond to more aggressive external management of care in the form of utilization reviews, preadmission screenings, and the like.

Hospitals have been the focus of rate regulation and micromanagement by third-party payers because hospital care is expensive and obvious inefficiencies seem to exist. Third-party payers have concluded that the fastest way to reduce health care expenditures per capita is to reduce hospital admissions per capita. To support the claim that hospital inefficiencies exist, third-party payers have offered three major arguments. First, small independent hospitals (many of which are rural) do not achieve economies of scale. This argument can be countered by the observation that costs per case are lower in small rural hospitals. In the absence of perfect severity adjustment, it is difficult to be sure how much difference scale economies really make.

The second argument rests on the potential problems that arise from excess hospital capacity. Excess hospital capacity mitigates against rationing of hospital services. The hospital industry in the United States has a propensity to provide more services than are needed and to overinvest in bricks, mortar, and new pieces of equipment. This conclusion, which is shared by many in the field of public health, is based on epidemiological evidence that investment in expensive medical technology is not the most cost-effective way to maintain and improve population health status. One needs only to point to health maintenance organizations, whose enrollees are less likely to be admitted to hospitals, and to the United Kingdom, where the population is healthier and per capita expenditures are low to prove this point.

Critics of the British National Health Service describe it as rationing and second-class care. Certainly, patients in Great Britain are more likely to face waiting lists for inpatient care than patients in the United States, and this is indeed rationing. Any public service must be rationed, however, and scarce medical resources are no exception. Great Britain has simply demonstrated that constraining hospital expenditures does not have to lead to declines in population health status. Because health expenditures per capita in the United States are nearly double the British rate, we could reduce expenditures a great deal before we were in danger of offering a health system as constrained as the British National Health Service.

The United Kingdom has not used controls on hospital bed supply to limit health expenditures. In fact, there are more hospital beds per capita in Great Britain than in the United States (Anderson, 1989). The British government is able to control expenditures more directly by not budgeting very much for new equipment or medical services. Our government cannot do this because our financing systems must reimburse private vendors for services rendered to eligible populations. However, we can discourage aggressive, and therefore expensive, use of medical resources by building incentives for efficiency into our reimbursement systems, and we can micromanage the use of those resources. Unfortunately, these indirect controls have limited impact. This conclusion is supported by our continued high rate of medical inflation.

Limiting hospital capacity will reduce hospital expenditures per capita. Just as a hose will only permit a certain flow of water, fewer hospital beds will have to treat fewer people. Because occupancy rates are quite low, a lot of beds will have to be eliminated before this strategy can have an effect. The fastest way to reduce beds is to allow entire hospitals to close, and the easiest hospitals to close are those in financial trouble.

Critics of the foregoing argument can assert that utilization reviews have already reduced hospital utilization to minimum acceptable levels. The fat has been cut, they argue, and we are down to the bone. Further cuts may adversely affect population health status. Until a test region is chosen and unnecessary hospitals are selectively winnowed out, it will be impossible to say that health status will not suffer. In short, we have a *Catch-22* situation: We can't prove bed reduction is not harmful until we try it, and we can't try it until we have proven it is safe. This kind of reasoning can be disregarded, of course, because it precludes ever taking any action to improve the organization of health services.

In short, the strongest argument for bed reduction rests on allocative efficiency. That is, there are more cost-effective uses for many of the buildings, personnel, and subsidies now employed for providing acute inpatient care in small rural hospitals. Unless hospital defenders can prove that acute inpatient care is more necessary and less costly than primary care, resources should be reallocated from inpatient care to primary care.

NEED FOR PRIMARY CARE

The allocation of scarce medical resources to unnecessary inpatient capacity is bad policy not only because it is wasteful but also because those resources could be used for other purposes. Consider the following facts:

- The proportion of mothers who began prenatal care in the first trimester of pregnancy has not improved since 1980 (National Center for Health Statistics, 1989).
- The percentage of low-birth-weight infants has not changed since 1980 (National Center for Health Statistics, 1989).
- The infant mortality rate in 1987 was 10.4 deaths per 1,000 live births. The United States now ranks above countries such as Spain, Singapore, Italy, and Northern Ireland in infant mortality rates (National Center for Health Statistics, 1989).
- Health status is actually worse in rural areas than in cities, partly because the rural population is more elderly and thus suffers from more chronic illness and partly because unemployment is greater, per capita income is lower, educational levels are lower, and more people live in substandard housing (Ermann, 1990).
- Many rural residents are at risk of potentially life-threatening delays in receiving emergency medical services (Office of Technology Assessment, 1989a).
- Mental health services are less accessible in rural areas than in urban or suburban areas (Office of Technology Assessment, 1989b).
- Many rural communities lack access to physician services (Ermann, 1990).

These facts point to the pressing need for expanded health services in rural areas. Not surprisingly, rural hospitals have found that diversification into services other than acute inpatient care is financially advantageous. These services may include outpatient surgery, nonsurgical outpatient care (hospices, emergicenters, primary-care units, diagnostic imaging centers, clinical laboratories, end-stage renal disease services, specialty clinics, adult day care, and rehabilitation), home health care, swing beds, and nursing-home care.

Local delivery of such services is more necessary for rural populations than local delivery of acute inpatient care. In fact, the ideal would be a conversion of rural hospitals into providers of comprehensive primary-care services. Unfortunately, reimbursement may be too low to attract the requisite health professionals to rural communities. If this is the case, subsidies from state and county government may be required. Because many rural hospitals may eventually require subsidies to stay open, it may be possible to require use of the subsidies for the delivery of services that are needed more than acute inpatient care.

REGIONALIZATION

One of the most important characteristics of modern society is the belief that management improves organizational performance. Although this may seem like a trite observation, it has fundamentally changed the structure of modern society. Large corporations have replaced small businesses; governments have assumed responsibilities formerly left to individuals; and individuals contract with attorneys, physicians, accountants, and social workers for the management of their personal affairs.

All of these changes reflect widespread belief in the three basic principles of classical management. Specialization increases performance. The activities of specialists must be coordinated if they are to optimize organizational objectives. Effective coordination depends on giving a single manager a general knowledge of how the work of the specialists aids in accomplishing organizational objectives, timely and accurate information about the performance of the various specialized workers, and the authority to influence the behavior of the workers. The implementation of these principles results in the creation of hierarchical organizations in which work is allocated, monitored, and controlled as rationally as possible.

Large businesses and corporations are organized hierarchically. Successful corporations have tended to spread geographically and to diversify into related product lines, approaching monopoly status whenever possible. The net result has been reduced unit costs. According to the noted business historian Alfred Chandler, the modern business enterprise has replaced the invisible hand of the market with the visible hand of direct management (Chandler, 1977). Adding to the hierarchy has been proven to increase efficiency and effectiveness (Chandler, 1990). Government efforts to impede these developments through antitrust action have had little impact.

It is precisely these improvements in performance arising from greater organizational scale and scope that have prompted American hospitals to form coalitions, networks, consortia, and systems. Although systems have generally failed to live up to performance expectations, this is probably due to halfhearted adherance to the hierarchical model.

If we define the health system as an entity with the over-arching mission of cost-effective maintenance and improvement in community health, then organizational theory suggests that it should be organized in classical bureaucratic form. This, of course, is an accurate description of the British National Health Service. Such a wholeheartedly socialistic strategy is not an option in the United States. When unregulated markets have failed to produce essential goods and services at affordable prices, U.S. policy has tended to prefer public regulation of privately owned enterprises over direct ownership. In either case — regulated private enterprise or public monopoly — large bureaucracies result.

Historically, acute inpatient care has been the primary mission of the community hospital, but rural health systems are not currently meeting public needs for comprehensive primary care. Failure to convert production facilities into priority services is a direct result of the absence of public policies making the local hospital accountable for community health. Until rural hospitals are organized into regional health systems responsible for community health, reallocation of hospital resources toward comprehensive primary care is not likely to occur.

The establishment of a regionalized health system with a broad mission would allow the activities of local health care organizations to shift into more urgently needed product lines. However, the creation of comprehensive, regionalized, publicly accountable health systems is not much more likely than nationalization of the hospital industry. The reallocation of resources from acute inpatient care will have to be accomplished in some other fashion.

The financial distress of rural hospitals is an opportunity in disguise. Rather than receiving subsidies either directly or in the form of preferential reimbursement, these hospitals should be given incentives to change their missions. Subsidies could be offered in exchange for conversion into comprehensive primary-care clinics that would refer patients to regional hospitals. This would allow jobs that would be lost if a hospital went bankrupt to be kept within the community, and it would increase the degree of regionalization. Administrative costs would be reduced because administrative functions could be centralized at the regional centers. Most importantly, the needed reallocation of resources from acute inpatient care into comprehensive primary care would be accomplished.

Rural hospitals are the focus of bed reduction strategies not because they are rural, but because their communities can no longer afford the luxury of maintaining the capacity for the unneeded local delivery of acute inpatient care. Residents of rural communities will not bear the brunt of reduced inpatient utilization if their local hospitals are converted into clinics. When inpatient care is needed, rural residents will be referred to regional hospitals, which will ration their resources according to client needs. Many rural residents are already choosing to use rural referral hospitals rather than local facilities.

CONCLUSION

Rural communities and their elected representatives have only a few choices. The first choice is to continue the present situation: limited access to needed services and financially distressed rural hospitals. The second choice is to subsidize rural hospitals that provide unneeded hospital capacity while the real access problems remain unresolved. The third choice is to subsidize comprehensive primary care independently of the existing organizational capacity. In this situation, the hospital would continue to struggle, and the providers of new services would not be integrated into a regional structure. The last, and best, option is to offer rural hospitals subsidies if they will abandon their role as providers of acute inpatient care.

The federal government has taken tentative steps in all four directions. Grants are available for community and migrant health centers. The National Health Service Corps (NHSC) places health professionals in areas that need them. Preferential reimbursement is provided to sole community hospitals, essential access community hospitals (EACHs), and hospitals that are willing to convert into primary-care hospitals (PCHs). PCHs are essentially clinics with a few holding beds. The federal government also provides so-called transition grants to rural hospitals to aid in strategic planning.

The seeds of regionalization are sown in these funding programs. They remain fragmented, however, because there is no overt commitment to coordinate them for the purpose of working toward rational regional systems. Because these programs employ different criteria for the designation of some hospitals as essential, they often may be working at cross-purposes. Transition grants, for example, may help hospitals change their missions and the EACH/PCH networks may offer preferential reimbursement for hospitals choosing to do so, but sole community hospital reimbursement may permit a faltering hospital to hang onto inpatient care for an indefinite period. Even if a hospital chooses the PCH option, comprehensive primary care may not become available in the community unless a community health center grant is acquired. In short, a planning program is needed to coordinate the other federal programs. Without this, transition to a rational rural health care system will be delayed.

Although this essay has argued that many rural hospitals are not needed for the inpatient care capacity they provide, the wholesale conversion of these hospitals into comprehensive primary-care clinics is neither wise (because some rural inpatient capacity is needed) nor politically feasible. Furthermore, it is possible that hospital closures will make the recruitment of health professionals even more difficult than it is for rural communities.

For these reasons a prudent planning program would first build a primary-care support system. A primary-care support system would consist of shared administration, coordinated back-up to permit time off, and, if possible, an income floor. This essentially constitutes a dispersed, but highly organized, group practice. At present, no federal program is directed at developing such networks.

The second task of a planning program would be the development of standardized methods for designating some hospitals as essential. This would permit the development of regional plans that could serve as blueprints to guide decisions about the allocation of health-center grants, transition grants, EACH/PCH and sole-community hospital preferential reimbursement, and NHSC personnel.

Critics will protest that areawide planning has been tried and found wanting. Health Systems Agencies (HSAs), however, were hampered by provider-dominated boards (even though consumers were technically in the majority) and lack of political support. Furthermore, the major task of the HSA was to prevent unneeded expansion of capacity. Today, planning agencies would be in much stronger positions. Instead of impeding privately financed expansion, their task would be to allocate federal funds to providers who comply with need-based plans. Third-party payers and major employers are now less willing to subsidize high per capita medical expenditures than they were. Therefore, political support for planning may be greater now in some states than it was a decade ago.

The time is ripe for another attempt at rationalization of the health system. Indeed, planning is the only way scarce medical resources can be effectively reallocated from inpatient care to primary care. Such a reallocation is necessary if we are to begin to control our appetites for medical gadgetry and to take strides toward improving the public's health.

REFERENCES

Anderson, Odin W. 1989. *The Health Services Continuum in Democratic States.* Ann Arbor, MI: Health Administration Press.

Chandler, Alfred. 1977. *The Visible Hand: The Managerial Revolution in American Business.* Cambridge, MA: Belknap Press.

Chandler, Alfred. 1990. *Scale and Scope: The Dynamics of Industrial Capitalism.* Cambridge, MA: Belknap Press.

Ermann, Dan A. 1990. "Rural Health Care: The Future of the Hospital." *Medical Care Review,* 47(1): 33-73.

National Center for Health Statistics. 1989. *Health United States, 1989.*

U.S. Congress, Office of Technology Assessment. 1989a. *Rural Emergency Medical Services–Special Report,* OTA-H-445. Washington, D.C.: U.S. Government Printing Office.

U.S. Congress, Office of Technology Assessment. 1989b. *Rural Health Care: Defining Rural Areas: Impact on Health Care Policy and Research.* Staff paper. Washington, D.C.: U.S. Government Printing Office.

U.S. Congress, Office of Technology Assessment. 1990. *Health Care in Rural America: Summary,* OTA-H-434. Washington, D.C.: U.S. Government Printing Office.

> **ISSUE TEN**
>
> *The shortage of allied health professionals is due to relatively low salaries, long working hours, fear of infectious diseases, and the inability of physicians to create a health care team.*

One of the more difficult aspects of this issue is determining who is to be considered an "allied health professional." According to the Council of Medical Education (1990), allied health professionals are all those who complement, facilitate, or assist physicians and other health care specialists in their work and have chosen to be identified as a part of the allied health cluster. Allied health professionals comprise the majority of health care workers. They have diverse levels of training and are found in all types of care, from acute to primary to tertiary to chronic. Some organizations include nurses, dental hygienists, and others as allied health professionals although other organizations do not. The definition is organization specific and needs to be assessed before identifying shortages.

The health care sector is the third largest employer in the United States. Only government and retailing employ more people (Ginzberg, 1990). It has been projected that by the year 2000, there will be more than 10 million jobs in health care. Where crucial shortages do exist, they must be resolved in order to ensure access to health care and to maintain the quality of care. More students need to be recruited and more attention must be given to retaining workers. The shortages of allied health professionals can cause further deterioration in the work environment and may impact the quality of patient care.

Prospective payment systems (PPS) have added further strains to the health care system by discouraging hospital inpatient treatment. The result is a sicker patient at admittance who then requires more medical and nursing care (Donley and Flaherty, 1989). Thus, there are increased demands on allied health professionals to give more attention and to perform more services for hospitalized patients. Although the number of patient days has decreased, the patients' need are greater. The number of intensive care beds, for example, doubled between 1973 and 1988. The number of nurses needed for intensive care compared to other inpatient treatment (four to six times as many nurses per bed) only increases the demand for nurses (Aiken, 1989).

As inpatient days have decreased, there has been a 15 percent increase in hospital outpatient services, including day surgery, emergency centers, birthing centers, and health education centers (Department of Health and Human Services, 1990). These changes in the delivery of health care will continue the current escalating demand for allied health personnel. Further adding to the demand is the presence of increasing numbers of elderly individuals who tend to require higher levels of care. As the incidence and complexity of disease, the sophistication of treatment (e.g., open heart surgery, transplants, and so on), and prospective payment systems increase, the demand for health care professionals will also increase. Unfortunately, alternative career opportunities, perceptions concerning a health career, and the work environment are frequently cited as factors reducing the supply of allied health professionals.

Not all allied health professions have critical shortages. Some geographic regions and some specific health care institutions have few problems in recruiting workers. Research on the shortage of allied health professionals is quite limited although the shortage of nurses has been well documented. Ginzberg (1990) suggests that many of the shortages in the nursing profession can be generalized to the allied health field. Using that generalization, Barbara A. Mark, of Virginia Commonwealth University, states that the shortage of health professionals has been created by us through low salaries and the failure to implement the team concept of medical care. R. Scott MacStravic, of St. Anthony Health Center in Denver and the University of Colorado, provides an equally clear argument that it is the increase in demand for all aspects of health care that has led to the shortages of allied health professionals.

REFERENCES

Aiken, Linda H. 1989. "The Hospital Nursing Shortage: A Paradox of Increasing Supply and Increasing Vacancy Rates." *The Western Journal of Medicine,* 151(1): 87-92.

Council on Medical Education. 1990. "Allied Health Personnel Shortage: A Report of the Council on Medical Education." *AARC-Times,* 14(4): 26-30.

Donley, Sr. Rosemary, and Sr. Mary Jean Flaherty. 1989. "Analysis of the Market Driven Nursing Shortage." *Nursing and Health Care,* 10(4): 183-187.

Ginzberg, Eli. 1990. "Health Personnel: The Challenges Ahead." *Frontiers of Health Services Management,* 7(2): 3-20.

U.S. Department of Health and Human Services. 1990. *Seventh Report to the President and Congress on the Status of Health Personnel in the United States.* Washington, D.C.: U.S. Government Printing Office.

> **POINT**
>
> *The shortage of allied health professionals is due to relatively low salaries, long working hours, fear of infectious diseases, and the inability of physicians to create teams.*

BARBARA A. MARK
Virginia Commonwealth University

Barbara A. Mark is currently associate professor and chair of the Department of Nursing Administration and Information Systems at the School of Nursing, Medical College of Virginia/Virginia Commonwealth University. Mark received a Ph.D. in nursing and organizational behavior from Case Western Reserve University. She has published widely in nursing and health services literature, with articles appearing in *Nursing Economics, Nursing and Health Care,* and *Health Services Research.* She is a coauthor with Howard Smith of *Financial Management for Nurse Executives.* Her research interests continue to be in evaluating the usefulness of structural contingency theory in health care organizations and the development of a framework to predict patient and administrative outcomes in nursing. She has been active for ten years in the Academy of Management and served as chair of the division in 1989.

The alarm rings. It's 4:45 A.M. and pitch dark outside. Raining, too. Ten more minutes of sleep would be nice — maybe tomorrow. Right now, just enough time to grab some coffee, get the baby to day care, and arrive at 6:00 for a twelve-hour shift on 6 East — Medical Oncology.

It's still dark when the nursing report begins. One RN has called in sick — family emergency; another has been pulled to cover the unit upstairs. Unit occupancy is down a bit — three empty beds today. On the whole, patients seem reasonably stable. Maybe the day will pass without too many crises. Maybe.

12:00 P.M. Noon, lunchtime — what a joke! Nabs crackers and more coffee. Mr. Allen, the thirty-eight year old father of two kids, who's been in the unit a month, getting worse the whole time, is in real trouble. Mr. Allen — the man who reminds you of your healthy husband, the man who, through his illness, has taught you about living, really living — Mr. Allen is dying. And there's nothing you or anyone else can do but hold his hand. Afterwards, you spend some time with his wife, holding her while she cries. Or, is she holding you?

3:00 P.M. Fatigue is more than settling in. It's taking command. Five straight days of twelve-hour shifts. Craziness. For how much money? Not nearly enough.

5:30 P.M. A new patient is being admitted, and you thought you might get off work at some reasonable hour. She arrives at the unit with her physician, someone you haven't worked with too much. Starts barking orders at you to do things that you knew an hour ago would need to be done, things you've taken care of, and arrangements you made an hour ago.

7:00 P.M. Finally, the work is done. Or rather, the work is done enough. At home, you wonder what you should have done that you simply didn't have time to do. Even then, the worry doesn't stop, the concern doesn't go away.

THE ISSUES AND THE MYTHS: ECONOMICS AND THE NURSING SHORTAGE

Most who have analyzed the nursing shortage have concluded that, although there have been other cyclical shortages, this one is different and of critical magnitude and projected duration. A variety of reasons for the scarcity of nursing resources has been reported: more career options for women; decreasing enrollments in schools of nursing; and the poor public image of nursing. Within the hospital itself, dissatisfaction with salaries and working conditions, increasing levels of patient acuity, unsatisfactory nurse-patient ratios, unrewarding relationships with physicians, and the inability to truly practice professional nursing are also cited (Institute of Medicine, 1983; National Commission on Nursing, 1983; and Secretary's Commission on Nursing, 1988).

In a series of articles and speaking engagements, Linda Aiken (1987, 1988, 1989a, 1989b, 1990) has addressed some of the misperceptions that abound in the explanations of the nursing shortage. First, through the years, the "intuitive" response to the nursing shortage has been to increase the supply of nurses. However, simply increasing the supply of professional nurses obviously has been an ineffective solution to the problem. Note the following statistics:

1. Nurse-to-population ratios have grown by more than 100 percent in the past thirty years.
2. In the past ten years, the number of employed nurses has risen by 50 percent.
3. Even states in which the ratio of number of employed RNs per 100,000 population is high (1166 in Massachusetts compared to 411 in Louisiana, for example), make no claim to lower than average vacancy rates.

Second, there is the perception that the shortage is caused by nurses leaving the profession in large numbers. In fact, the labor force participation rate for nurses is nearly 80 percent, which is almost double the participation rate for women as an occupational group and approaches the participation rate of American men. In other words, four out of every five individuals educated as nurses still work as nurses and only 5 percent leave health care for other careers. A third misperception is that the shortage has been brought about by nurses fleeing the acute care setting for ambulatory care settings, insurance companies, and other nonhospital jobs. In fact, the proportion of nurses who work in hospitals today (two-thirds) is the same as the proportion who worked in hospitals in 1966. The vast majority of nurses who do resign their positions in hospitals take jobs in other hospitals. Since 1980, more than 140,000 full-time nurses have been added to hospital staffs, even though inpatient days have fallen by 51 million annually over the same period. The fact is that more nurses are working in hospitals than ever before.

Because the actual supply of nurses does not seem to warrant the conclusion of a nurse shortage, Aiken began looking into the demand side of the equation, rather than focusing solely on the supply side. On the surface, there are a variety of reasons why the demand for nurses has increased. Changing patterns of hospital practice explain some of the increased demand. Discretionary admissions have decreased as a result of preadmission screening programs and noninvasive diagnostic technology among other things. Balancing this decrease, however, is the increase in patient acuity and the concomitant increase in the number of nursing hours required overall. The dramatic expansion in ICU beds, which require four nurses per bed for twenty-four hour staffing rather than the one nurse per bed required in general units, has also boosted demand for nurses. Still, these factors only partly explain the increased demand.

Aiken has also documented the existence of an inverse relationship between nurses' relative wages and hospital vacancy rates over the past 25 years. When nurses' wages fail to keep pace in real dollars with inflation or with the rate of escalation in other health care sectors, vacancy rates rise. Prior to prospective payment systems (PPS), nurses' salaries were increasing faster than the salaries of other occupational groups in the hospital industry. Following the introduction of PPS, however, nurses' salaries increased at a much slower rate than other hospital employees. Even with more nurses being hired, the nursing budget has continued to average 17 percent of the total hospital budget.

The artificially depressed wages in a captive labor market are easy to recognize when comparisons are made with other professional groups. Over a lifetime, nurses can expect to increase their salaries by 36 percent while secretaries will increase their salaries by 72 percent, accountants by 193 percent, and attorneys by 226 percent. For nurses, twenty years of experience have been estimated to have a salary premium of about 5 cents per hour (McKibbin, 1988 cited in Aiken, 1989b).

Increased demand and artificially depressed wages have given rise to further demand and the phenomenon of substitution of RNs for LPNs and aides. In 1968, approximately one-third of nursing service personnel were nurses; today more than 60 percent are nurses. Between 1979 and 1982, hospitals employed 3.2 RNs per LPN, while by 1986, they were using 5 RNs per LPN. After the introduction of prospective payment, hospitals reduced the non-RN, non-LPN work force by more than 300,000 full-time equivalents. At the same time, they increased the number of full-time equivalent RNs by 40,000. Clearly, hospitals increased their reliance on RNs, while minimizing their dependence on other non-RN workers. Given the narrow difference between RN and LPN market wage rates and the fact that nurses "perform a wide range of functions in addition to nursing care and require little supervision," hospitals clearly prefer to have more RNs (Aiken, 1989b, p. 88). In other words, RNs provide more work for not much more money.

As the case vignette at the beginning of this chapter illustrates, whether or not there is a real nursing shortage and whether the shortage is supply or demand driven, the unit nurse feels it acutely. Nurses consistently lament their inability to practice their profession — caring for patients. Partly as a consequence of the substitution of RNs for non-RN workers and partly as a result of administration and physician failure to recognize the contribution of nursing to both the quality and economics of hospitals, professional nurses spend a substantial portion of their time in non-nursing activities that could be done by others. Time and motion studies show that nurses spend only 25 to 35 percent of their time in direct care of patients. The remainder of the time is spent in indirect patient care activities, including charting and clerical work, administrative functions, patient transport, and communication. Aiken has even suggested that the nursing shortage would be over if the time nurses spent on direct care were doubled to between 50 and 70 percent (Aiken, 1989b).

RELATIONSHIPS WITH PHYSICIANS

Although the quality of their relationships with physicians has always been an issue for nurses, the importance of nurse-physician relationships did not begin to receive more serious attention by non-nurse health professionals until a 1986 research report indicated that outcomes in a multicenter study of ICU effectiveness were dependent upon the quality of nurse-physician coordination and communication (Knaus, et al., 1986). Even with this knowledge, the "doctor-nurse game," first described by Stein (1967) in an article that has become somewhat of a classic in nursing, still exists. The original doctor-nurse game was based on the assumption of a hierarchical relationship between physician and nurse. The cardinal rule was that open disagreement should be avoided at all costs. Consequently, nurses who made recommendations to physicians had to so phrase the suggestions that they appeared to be initiated by the physician. Nurses who communicated openly and directly were barely tolerated by either physicians or other nurses and were frequently labeled "bitches" or worse. Physicians who failed to understand the subtleties of the game were labeled "stupid," "inept," or "clods" or worse.

Stein (1990) has suggested that the game endures but external forces have changed how it is played. The shortage of nurses, decreased public esteem for physicians, an increase in the number of female physicians, and an overall glut of physicians have led to alterations in the game's dynamics. "What is happening now is that one of the players (the nurse) has unilaterally decided to stop playing that game and instead is consciously and actively attempting to change both nursing and how nurses relate to other health professionals" (Stein, 1990, p. 547).

In a *Newsweek* editorial, George Will (1988) has suggested that nurse-physician relationships are deteriorating because "many physicians cannot understand, or will not accept, that nurses can, should, and want to do more than just carry out doctors' orders . . . . Physicians are an episodic presence in the life of a patient. Nurses control the environment of healing" (p. 80). Nurses' attempts to become autonomous health professionals who work cooperatively as equal partners with physicians have left some physicians with feelings of "puzzlement . . . and confusion, and not infrequently . . . with feelings of betrayal and anger" (Stein, 1990, p. 548). The perhaps unprecedented collective denouncement of the AMA's proposal for a new class of health care worker — the registered care technician — illustrates how far the profession of nursing has come. It is almost as if the profession of nursing, which is made up mostly of women, announced that it was well aware of its problems and let it be known that it did not need the profession of medicine, made up mostly of men, to help fix it. If, however, nurses want physicians to work cooperatively with them and to treat them as equal partners, physicians must also be treated as equal partners by nurses.

NURSING PRACTICE AND AIDS

Acquired immune deficiency syndrome (AIDS) has changed the face of health care in America. Hospitals, in particular, are feeling the shock. Although early reports indicated that it was unlikely that the disease could be spread from an infected health care worker to a patient or from an infected patient to a health care worker, the first six months of 1991 have seen a remarkable increase in television and print reporting about such transmissions. Despite media attention and Kimberly Bergalis's plea to Congress, epidemiologic studies continue to report otherwise. The risk of HIV seroconversion in hospital workers receiving a needlestick injury involving a patient known to have AIDS was found to be 0.36 percent in one study (Stock, Gafni, and Bloch, 1990) and 0.3 percent in another study (Henderson, et al., 1990). The risk after skin and mucous membrane exposure to blood or other body fluids of AIDS patients was 0.00 percent (Stock, Gafni, and Bloch, 1990; and Henderson, et al., 1990).

The fact that patients with AIDS are often more severely ill than other hospitalized patients simply adds to nurses' concerns about the illness. AIDS patients frequently have multiple system infections — *Pneumocystis carinii* pneumonia, dementia, and cryptosporidiosis diarrhea. One study found that hospitalized AIDS patients required 28 percent more nursing time than did non-AIDS patients and twice the amount of time as a person with leukemia. The needs of patients with AIDS range from "multisystem physical care to needs for psychological support, teaching, advocacy and caring" (Grady, 1989, p. 7).

Despite their ethical obligations to care for all patients, nurses have grave concerns about caring for AIDS patients. In one study of over 1,000 nurses, 23 percent indicated that they would not take a position that involved caring for AIDS patients (Servellen, 1988). In another study, over one-half of the responding RNs said that they would refuse to take care of a patient infected with the AIDS virus if given the choice (Wiley, et al., 1990). In that same study, nearly 30 percent indicated that they had considered leaving nursing because of the risk of AIDS.

No one knows how many nurses have left the profession because of their fears of contracting AIDS. Even if nurses resolve their fears, the youth and acuity of the patients, the psychosocial complexities of their frequently inadequate support systems, the stigmatization that patients (and nurses working with them) face, and the fatality rate all combine to contribute to enormous psychological stress. Hospital nursing services are struggling to develop programs that will help to ease nurses' fears and assist them in managing recurrent and sometimes overwhelming grief.

It is clear that hospitals must create programs to help nurses and other health care workers cope with their fears and increase their competency in caring for patients who have a disease for which there currently is no cure. The need to provide appropriate psychosocial support for nurses as they attempt to maintain a sense of professional and personal integrity and self-esteem in the face of constant death and disfigurement is equally important. The extent to which hospitals are able to meet this challenge is directly related to the success they will have in providing empathic and technically skilled nursing care to patients who are in desperate need of it.

SUMMARY

This article has demonstrated that the shortage of nurses is demand, not supply driven, and that it results primarily from the substitution of RNs in non-RN positions and compressed wage scales. Other factors that may have contributed to the shortage are the difficulty of creating cooperating physician-nurse teams and the fear of AIDS. Until physicians and nurses are able to work cooperatively, patient care is likely to suffer. Finally, hospitals need to develop programs to support nurses who deal daily with the difficult task of caring for AIDS patients.

REFERENCES

Aiken, L. 1987. "The Nurse Shortage: Myth or Reality?" *New England Journal of Medicine,* 317(10): 641-646.

Aiken, L. 1988. "Assuring the Delivery of Quality Patient Care." *Nursing Resources and the Delivery of Patient Care.* U.S. Department of Health and Human Services, Pub. No. 89-3008.

Aiken, L. 1989a. Keynote Address. Third National Conference on Nursing Administration Research. Richmond, Virginia.

Aiken, L. 1989b. "The Hospital Nursing Shortage: A Paradox of Increasing Supply and Increasing Vacancy Rates." *Western Journal of Medicine,* 151(1): 87-92.

Aiken, L. 1990. "Charting the Future of Hospital Nursing." *Image: Journal of Nursing Scholarship,* 22(2): 72-77.

Grady, C. 1990. "Acquired Immunodeficiency Syndrome: The Impact on Professional Nursing Practice." *Cancer Nursing,* 12(1): 1-9.

Henderson, D. K., et al. 1990. "Risk of Occupational Transmission of Human Immunodeficiency Virus Type 1 (HIV-1) Associated with Clinical Exposures: A Prospective Evaluation." *Annals of Internal Medicine,* 113(10): 740-746.

Institute of Medicine. 1983. *Nursing and Nursing Education: Public Policies and Private Actions.* Washington, D.C.: National Academy Press.

Knaus, W., et al. 1986. "An Evaluation of Outcome from Intensive Care in Major Medical Centers." *Annals of Internal Medicine,* 104(3): 410-418.

McKibbin, R. C. 1988. "Analysis of Career Earnings in Nursing and Other Occupations." Paper presented at the American Nurses Association meeting March 11, 1988, Kansas City, MO.

National Commission on Nursing. 1983. *Summary Report and Recommendations.* Chicago: Hospital Research and Educational Trust.

Servellen, G. 1988. "Nurses Responses to the AIDS Crisis: Implications for CE Programs." *Journal of Continuing Education in Nursing,* 19(1): 4-8.

Stein, L. 1967. "The Doctor-Nurse Game." *Archives of General Psychiatry,* 16: 699-703.

Stein, L., D. Watts, and T. Howell. 1990. "The Doctor-Nurse Game Revisited." *New England Journal of Medicine,* 322(8): 546-549.

Stock, S. R., A. Gafni, and R. F. Bloch. 1990. "Universal Precautions to Prevent HIV Transmission to Health Care Workers: An Economic Analysis." *Canadian Medical Association Journal,* 142(9): 937-946.

U.S. Department of Health and Human Services. *Secretary's Commission on Nursing.* 1988. Washington, D.C.: DHHS.

Wiley, K., et al. 1990. "Care of HIV-Infected Patients: Nurses' Concerns, Opinions and Precautions." *Applied Nursing Research,* 3(1): 27-33.

Will, George. 1988. "The Dignity of Nursing." *Newsweek,* 111: p. 80.

ADDITIONAL REFERENCES

American Journal of Nursing. 1987. "AIDS Patients Need More Nursing Time." *AJN,* 87(12): 1540.

Boland, B. 1990. "Fear of AIDS in Nursing Staff." *Nursing Management,* 21(6): 40-44.

Carroll, S. 1987. "Impact of AIDS on Hospitals: A Challenge for the Nurse Manager." *Nursing Management,* 18(9): 82-84.

Mark, B. A., and J. T. Turner. 1990. "Economic Trends Influencing the Nurse Executive's Role." *Aspen's Advisor for Nurse Executives,* 5(5): 1, 3, 6, 7.

Newschaffer, C., and J. Schoenman. 1990. "Registered Nurse Shortages: The Road to Appropriate Public Policy." *Health Affairs,* 9(1): 98-106.

Prescott, P. 1987. "Another Round of Nurse Shortage." *Image: The Journal of Nursing Scholarship,* 19(4): 204-209.

COUNTERPOINT

The shortage of allied health professionals is due to relatively low salaries, long working hours, fear of infectious diseases, and inability of physicians to create teams.

R. SCOTT MacSTRAVIC
*Provenant Health Partners and
University of Colorado*

R. Scott MacStravic is adjunct professor at the University of Colorado and vice-president for marketing and strategic planning at St. Anthony Healthcare Corporation in Denver, Colorado. He earned a Ph.D. in hospital administration from the University of Minnesota after completing his undergraduate work at Harvard University. He teaches a course in tactical health services marketing, and his current research interest is patient loyalty. Before moving to Colorado, Dr. MacStravic was vice-president for planning and marketing at Health and Hospital Services, Inc. in Bellevue, Washington and has served on the faculty at the University of Washington and the Medical College of Virginia in the graduate programs in health administration. He is the author of nine books and over 100 articles on health care marketing and strategy. He currently serves on the editorial boards for *Health Progress, Inquiry, Health Care Strategic Management,* and *Health Care Supervisor.*

The antithesis of this thesis statement, strictly speaking, would be created by placing the word *not* between the words *is* and *due*. In this case, however, let us consider the statement from two perspectives. The assertion that the shortage "is due to" suggests that the listed factors are *the* cause of the problem. It may be argued that there are other equally, perhaps more important, causes. In such a case, the antithesis to this statement could be that the shortage is due to some, perhaps many, other factors in addition to those cited.

An alternative reading of the statement would be that if the shortage is due to these factors, then reducing or eliminating the shortage can be accomplished by correcting these factors. Given the state of affairs that are likely to affect health care in the future, such an interpretation might well lead to pessimism and resignation. With increasing pressures on payment, how can we increase salaries and reduce working hours? How can we eliminate fear of infectious diseases? We have been trying to promote equality of status and teamwork between physicians and allied health professionals for decades. Do we see significant improvement in the immediate future?

In addressing the counterpoint to the thesis statement, I shall argue that an entirely different approach should be taken to eliminate the shortage of allied health professionals (AHPs), *regardless of what its causes may be.* The essence of this argument is that we must focus our attention on getting the most possible out of our allied health professionals, rather than simply dealing with shortages. Getting the most out of those we have in terms of productivity and efficiency can reduce the shortage. It can also make working in health care organizations more attractive to current allied health professionals, which will help to reduce the shortage further. Finally, it can make allied health professions more attractive to new entrants and career changers in the job market, thereby increasing the size of the labor pool and reducing the shortage still further.

Allied health professionals can contribute significantly to the success and survival of health care organizations through eight distinct role categories: suppliers, customers, donors, volunteers, political allies, advisers, ambassadors, and governors.

Not all employees are capable of adopting all eight roles well, but all roles can be adopted by some employees, and the more employees adopt more roles, the greater overall contribution to the organization. These eight roles are defined and illustrated below:

Supplier: Allied health professionals function primarily as suppliers of professional services to patients and the organization. How well they supply such services determines productivity and efficiency, clinical quality, service quality/customer satisfaction, and mission achievements.

There are countless ways in which the behavior of AHPs contribute to or detract from the kinds of productivity and efficiency that all health care organizations must strive for. When AHPs can function as self-governing teams, they can eliminate the need for (and costs of) managers (Umiker, 1988). Self-managed teams have been termed the productivity breakthrough of the 1990s (Dumaine, 1990). Employees at St. Mary's Health Center in St. Louis, Missouri, for example, were able to find ways to reduce the average length of stay by a full day (Brice, 1990). Furthermore, several studies have noted the use of AHPs in quality circles and similar devices to monitor and improve quality (Helmer and Gunatilake, 1988; and Dutkewych and Buback, 1982).

Other studies have noted that AHPs are key to promoting service quality and customer satisfaction. In one hospital, nurses organized a physician-dedicated unit, devoted to four admitting endocrinologists and their patients, to promote both physician and patient satisfaction (Ventura, 1988). How patient and other customer contact personnel interact with customers largely determines service quality (Keaveney, 1987).

Finally, AHP contributions can extend beyond the walls of the health care organization to promote its mission and reputation in the community. One hospital's staff provided technical support to community groups and helped to obtain a grant to deliver health care to inner city schools (Adams, 1988). A psychiatric hospital's staff transferred to community centers and thus vastly increased the number of clients served (Herskowitz and Curtis, 1977).

Customer Contributions: In at least two senses, AHPs are key customers in the health care organization itself. As users of health care themselves, they significantly affect the health insurance and health care costs of health care organizations. They can be prudent or profligate in their use of health care (Bartlett, 1988). If they dedicate themselves to controlling or reducing the organization's health care costs, they can make a significant difference (Posner, 1989). When they become patients, they can use the health care organization's services or those of competitors. It can save money when they use their own health care organization, as Mid Valley Hospital discovered ("Innovations," 1983). When employees use their own health care organization's services, they promote its reputation; when they use a competitor, they undermine it.

Donors: AHPs and other employees can be significant donors to fund-raising efforts by health care organizations that employ them. This fact has long been recognized by hospital fund-raisers (Reynolds and Hilary, 1989). When employees are motivated, they have been known to contribute over half the costs of particular projects (Powills, 1989).

Volunteers: While there seems to be a contradiction between paid AHP employees and volunteers, there need not be. In one hospital, for example, employees volunteered to help feed patients with spinal cord injuries during a period of staff shortages and did so during their own lunch hours (Teschke, 1989). Employees of Group Health of Puget Sound, Washington, have even volunteered to transport home-bound patients to clinics and outpatient service sites (MacStravic, in press). One hospital's employees regularly volunteered to serve in community agencies and outreach programs (Kramer, 1988).

Political Ally: Although this may occur rarely, AHPs can be significant allies in political issues affecting the health care organization. Employee testimony at zoning, certificate-of-need, or rate-setting hearings can make a difference (Boscarino, 1988). Their canvassing efforts and votes in local or state referenda also can be crucial (Hudson, 1990). One health care organization's employees are frequently called upon to give expert testimony to state legislators (Group Health of Puget Sound, 1989).

Adviser: In addition to their direct efforts, AHPs can be valuable sources of advice and information. They can generate wide-ranging ideas on new sources of revenue (Tucker, 1987; and Tzirides, 1988). They are excellent sources of advice on how to improve service quality, and they are invaluable sources of suggestions on how to improve productivity and patient care (Barger, et al., 1987; and "1,100 Cost-Cutting

Ideas," 1989). AHPs also can supply useful ideas on how to screen new recruits (Pickens, 1988).

Ambassadors: AHPs and other employees can be among the most effective and efficient means of advertising a health care organization. One hospital's "Baptist Brigade" enlisted 500 employees as volunteer outreach canvassers of neighborhoods where the hospital's new primary-care centers were opening (Grossi, 1988). Another hospital's "Ambassador Club" includes employees who volunteer for health fairs and video commercials ("Innovators Catalog," 1987). One hospital's employees attracted new patients through networking with handicapped children and caregiver support groups for the elderly (Mourning, 1988). The opposite is equally true. Employees can devastate a hospital's reputation in the event of a strike (Cerne, 1989). The employees of one nursing-home chain sent out direct mail brochures urging citizens not to send their loved ones to any of the chain's facilities (Sussman, 1987).

Governors: In addition to their contributions as suppliers, customers, donors, volunteers, allies, advisers, and ambassadors, AHPs can contribute to the governance of health care organizations. In some cases, they have participated in employee stock ownership plans that have enabled health care organizations to continue operating with the employees as owners (Nemes, 1989). They have also proven effective on formal decision-making bodies (Kennedy, 1988). Some hospitals have found shared governance systems for nursing more than satisfactory ("Shared Governance System," 1989).

EXPLOITING THE POTENTIAL

Given the great range and potential value of AHP contributors to health care organizations, the next question to address is how to realize such potential in practice. Judging from the literature, there are eight approaches that have worked in specific instances. To date, no organization seems to have even attempted, much less succeeded, in realizing the full potential of all eight of the described contribution roles.

The most obvious, and sometimes most effective, approach is to ask employees to join in. This simple approach rests on the fact that people are more likely to do something if invited than if left entirely alone. Most people have a latent potential for responding to requests although the potential varies according to the personality of the requestee, the relationship with the requestor, the nature of the request, and the circumstances. As Tom Peters (1989) has pointed out, people may add to the contributions they make out of sheer boredom with the limited scope of their activities. Austin (1989) has noted that merely asking employees for ideas is often enough to stimulate their efforts, especially when tradition has expected ideas to come only from managers.

Sometimes it is necessary to persuade employees to join in. This goes a little bit beyond simply asking employees to make a particular contribution. Ascito and Ford (1980) have described an indirect approach to persuasion frequently referred to as the "Avis Effect." It involves using advertising to show or describe how employees behave with the expectation that properly motivated employees will live up to their billing. This is a risky practice if employees are not motivated to do so. One hospital used a systematic "Why Bother" campaign to persuade employees to prove that the hospital cares ("Why Bother Employees," 1985).

Going beyond persuasion, education and training programs are also ways to enable employees to contribute and convince them that they should. Education and training programs can include building skills in guest relations (Fisk, 1990). One clinic used grand-round style sessions at lunch hours to promote improved customer service (Droste, 1989). Another clinic cross-trained employees to enable them to fill in for shortages (Salahuddin, 1989). Discovering and exploiting latent skills and interests among employees can greatly improve productivity (Peters, 1987).

Recruiting new employees and attracting new customers are similar challenges as are retaining employees and keeping customers. Wise employers will deal with employees as if they were customers. This means the health care organization must know enough about their employees to know their distinct individual personalities and their basic human needs (Waterman, 1987; Yura, 1986). The organization must be willing to tailor the experiences employees have to their unique traits (Waterman, 1987). Conducting regular customer satisfaction surveys of employees will help the organization to understand the employees' attitudes and to get the most from them (Hoffman, 1987). One of the best ways to have an optimally contributing AHP staff is to select people who are both motivated and skilled in contributing (Thompson, 1989). Current employees, particularly those who are already contributing, can be effective advisers and participants in the new employee selection process (Pickens, 1988).

Rewarding employees also encourages them to contribute. It is well known that what gets rewarded is what gets done (LeBoeuf, 1986). Rewards can be as simple as written or oral praise from peers, such as the "Aloha-Grams" used at the Queen's Medical Center in Honolulu ("Promoting Healthy Employee Attitudes," 1988), formal performance appraisals to reward employees who are making the most contributions (Browdy, 1989). This may require reexamining wage structures that pay the least to those who have the most customer contact (Herzlinger, 1989). On the other hand, focusing on the intrinsic rewards of task value, autonomy, and goal achievement is more likely to promote the kind of organizational commitment that is conducive to maximizing employee contributions (Alpander, 1990). It is possible that extrinsic rewards will stifle productivity, innovation, and teamwork (Kohn, 1988).

In order to realize the full potential for employee contributions, it may be necessary to restructure health care organizations. Restructuring may be seen in the change in the names used for AHPs — from "employees" to "team members," from "managers" to "team directors" — as Irvine Medical Center did ("Radical Redesign of Hospital Organization," 1990). Another hospital now contracts with nursing group practices rather than hiring individual nurses ("St. Joseph Likes Nursing Group Practice," 1991). One way of turning the organizational structure upside-down is to have employees evaluate their supervisors and managers (Kiechel, 1989). Establishing formal structures for promoting specific contributions is another way (Fonvielle, et al., 1985).

To realize fully employee contribution potential, health care organzations must learn how to empower their employees through new relationships that go well beyond traditional employer-employee models. Empowered employees essentially manage themselves. Supervisors and managers serve in supportive, "coaching" roles, rules are minimized, and individual initiative is promoted (Peters, 1987; and Austin, 1989). Employees participate in setting goals and developing strategies (Waterman, 1987). Relations with employees are based on trust and common goals rather than power (Bice, 1990). Traditional hierarchies are replaced by horizontal networks of colleagues engaged in collaborative efforts (Pate, 1991). These types of organizations frequently offer extra support to their employees such as providing stress management programs and chores and day care support for working parents (Williams, 1989). Empowered employees contribute out of a strong commitment to transcendent values rather than self-interest (Haddock, 1989).

Perhaps the greatest advantage in addressing AHP shortages through convincing employees to give more lies in what is known as a positive feedback loop. In systems dynamics, a positive feedback loop describes a situation in which the operative factors work on each other in such a way that when change begins to happen in a particular direction, the factors tend to keep change going in that direction. If the change is bad, we call the loop a vicious cycle. If the change is good, however, it is known as a virtuous circle (Stearns, et al., 1976). In the case of AHP shortages, employees with higher levels of commitment to the organization tend to contribute more. At the same time, employees who contribute more tend to develop higher levels of commitment and are less likely to leave the organization. This has been demonstrated with respect to customer loyalty, hospital donations, and volunteering (Parasuraman, et al., 1985; and deCombray, 1987).

This phenomenon may be due to cognitive dissonance, i.e., people feel that something must be important if they are contributing to it. It may reflect B. F. Skinner's findings that behavior influences attitudes and attitudes influence behavior. In any case, the virtuous cycle exists although it is not an example of perpetual motion. Both commitment levels and contribution behavior need to be encouraged to supplement the effect they have on each other. If they are not, inertia, friction, and competition from other interests can diminish and even destroy the cycle's effect.

Fortunately, many of the contributions employees can make are intrinsically rewarding; they help promote and reinforce commitment. Participating in an advisory role and in governance is a way to motivate employees as well as realize their potential (Waterman, 1987). When employees benefit as patients, they can develop the same sort of gratitude toward a health care organization as its other patients. Employees proud enough of their health care organization to recommend it can enjoy the sense of helping a friend as well as their organization.

The challenge to health care organizations is to identify and recognize publicly the value of the contributions their employees make and to estimate the value of the additional contributions they might make. The former is part of contribution engineering, stimulating and maintaining high current levels of contributions by employees. The latter is essential to developing new contribution engineering strategies that will deliver worthwhile returns on investment.

Making significant and well-recognized contributions to an organization is at least partially a self-rewarding, and thereby self-sustaining, activity. The more we can get employees to contribute, the more they are likely to identify and engage in new forms of contribution. The more they contribute, the more we can afford to recognize and stimulate such contributions. The more rewarding the employee experience becomes through this process, the more attractive the profession, or at least the health care organization will be, and therefore shortages will tend to diminish.

REFERENCES

Acito, F., and J. Ford. 1980. "How Advertising Affects Employees." *Business Horizons*, 23(1): 53-59.

Adams, C. 1988. "Urban Hospital's Innovations Save Money, Win Support." *Health Progress*, 69(1): 56-58, 62.

Alpander, G. 1990. "Relationship between Commitment to Hospital's Goals and Job Satisfaction." *Health Care Management Review*, 15(4): 51-62.

Austin, N. 1989. "You Don't Find Many Patients in In-Boxes." *Hospitals*, 63(3): 60-61.

Barger, G., et al. 1987. "Improving Patient Care Through Problem-Solving Groups." *Health Progress*, 68(7): 42-45.

Bartlett, E. 1988. "Uncovering an Untapped Resource." *Business and Health*, 5(12): 16-18.

Bice, M. 1990. "Employees Can Be Your Competitive Edge." *Hospitals*, 64(14): 40.

Boscarino, J. 1988. "Hospital Planners as Political Activists." *Health Care Strategic Management*, 6(12): 10-12.

Brice, J. 1990. "Threefold Leadership Approach Encourages Worker Initiative, Creativity, and Continuous Quality Enhancement at SSM Health Care System." *Healthcare Productivity Report*, 3(11): 1-7.

Browdy, J. 1989. "Performance Appraisal and Pay-for-Performance Start at the Top." *The Health Care Supervisor*, 7(3): 31-41.

Cerne, F. 1989. "Employees: A Hospital's Goodwill Ambassadors." *Hospitals*, 63(5): 39.

deCombray, N. 1987. "Volunteering in America." *American Demographics*, 9(3): 50-52.

Droste, T. 1989. "Well-Informed Employees Are A Valuable Resource." *Hospitals*, 63(17): 54.

Dumaine, B. "Who Needs a Boss?" *Fortune*, 121: 52-60.

Dutkewych, J., and K. Buback. 1982. "Quality Circles — The Henry Ford Hospital Experience." *Dimensions in Health Services,* 59(12): 20-25.

Fisk, T. 1990. "How to Make Nurses Marketing's Allies." In *Vision 2000.* Chicago: American Marketing Association, pp. 99-103.

Fonvielle, W., et al. 1985. "How to Stimulate Innovation." *Hospital Forum,* 28(1): 53-57.

Grossi, P., and S. Rhodes. 1988. "Employee Volunteerism . . . A Natural Extension of Customer Relations." *Hospital Entrepreneurs' Newsletter,* 3(12): 1, 5-7.

Haddock, C. 1989. "Transformational Leadership and the Employee Discipline Process." *Hospital & Health Services Administration,* 34(2): 185-194.

Helmer, F., and S. Gunatilake. 1988. "Quality Control Circles." *The Health Care Supervisor,* 6(4): 63-71.

Hershkowitz, J., and W. Curtis. 1977. "The Psychiatric Hospital Employee: A Resource for Social Change." *Health Care Management Review,* 2(1): 95-102.

Herzlinger, R. 1989. "The Failed Revolution in Health Care." *Harvard Business Review,* 67(2): 95-103.

Hoffman, B. 1989, March. "Employee Surveys Key to Attitudes." *Quirk's Marketing Research Review,* pp. 53-54.

Hudson, T. 1990. "Executives Learn (Sometimes the Hard Way) How to Handle Public Referendums." *Hospitals,* 64(1): 44-47.

"Innovator's Catalog." 1983. *Hospital Forum,* 26(2): 31.

"Innovator's Catalog." 1987. *Healthcare Forum Journal,* 30(5): 16.

Keaveney, S. 1987. "Add Value to Services Through Contact Personnel." In C. Suprenant, ed., *Add Value to Your Service.* Chicago: American Marketing Association, pp. 169-173.

Kennedy, M. 1988. "Would An Employee Advisory Board Help You Manage?" *Physician Executive,* 13(6): 36.

Kiechel, W. 1989. "When Subordinates Evaluate the Boss." *Fortune,* 119(13): 201-202.

Kohn, A. 1988. "Incentives Can Be Bad for Business." *INC.,* 10(3): 93-94.

Kramer, J., and C. Schmalenberg. 1988. "Magnet Hospitals: Part I Institutions of Excellence." *Journal of Nursing Administration,* 18(1): 13-24.

LeBoeuf, M. 1986. *The Greatest Management Principle in the World.* New York: Berkeley Books.

MacStravic, S. In press. "Getting the Most From Your Members." *MGMA Journal.*

Mourning, S. 1988. "Networking Strategies for Hospitals." *Topics in Health Care Financing,* 14(3): 56-61.

Nemes, J. 1989. "Healthcare Stocking Up on ESOPs." *Modern Healthcare,* 19(28): 24-26, 30.

"1,100 Cost-Cutting Ideas from Employees Will Save El Camino Hospital $5 Million in Five Years." 1989. *Healthcare Productivity Report,* 2(7): 1-6.

Parasuraman, A., V. Zeithaml, and L. Berry. 1985. "A Conceptual Model of Service Quality and Its Implications for Future Research." *Journal of Marketing,* 49(4): 41-56.

Pate, J. 1991. "Holding On To What You've Got." *Health Texas,* 46(8): 10-11, 14-15.

Peters, T. 1989. *The Leadership Alliance.* Palo Alto, CA: TPG Communications, p. 16.

Pickens, J. 1988. "Marketable Staff the Result When Marketing Personnel Cooperate." *Health Care Marketing Report,* 6(11): 1, 7-9.

Posner, B. 1989. "Preventive Medicine." *INC.,* 11(3): 131-132.

Powills, S. 1989. "The Hospital Cafeteria That Employees Built." *Hospitals,* 63(17): 56.

"Promoting Healthy Employee Attitudes." 1988. *Healthcare Marketing Report,* 6(1): 18-20.

"Radical Redesign of Hospital Organization and Patient Care Management is Outgrowth of Shared Leadership Approach at Irvine Medical Center." *Healthcare Productivity Report,* 3(12): 1-8.

Reynolds, P., and C. Hillary. 1989. "Employee Giving: Personalization is the Key." *NAHD Journal,* 26(8): 26-28.

"St. Joseph Likes Nursing Group Practice." 1991. *Catholic Health World,* 7(1): 4.

Salahuddin, M. 1989. "Cross-Training Eases Worker Shortages, Hospitals Find." *HealthWeek,* 3(8): 6.

"Shared Governance System Gives Nurses More Authority." 1989. *Healthcare Productivity Report,* 2(8): 7-8.

Staff of Group Health of Puget Sound, Seattle, Washington. 1989. Personal communication with author.

Stearns, N., et al. 1976. "Systems Intervention: New Help for Hospitals." *Health Care Management Review,* 1(4): 9-18.

Sussman, D. 1987. "Both Sides Dig in Heels in Connecticut Nursing Home Salary Fight." *HealthWeek,* 1(15): 7.

Teschke, D. 1989. "Employee Volunteers Can Alleviate Temporary Staff Shortages." *Healthcare Financial Management,* 43(3): 117.

Thompson, A. 1989. "Customer Contact Personnel: Using Interviewing Techniques to Select for Adaptability in Service Employees." *Journal of Services Marketing,* 3(1): 57-65.

Tucker, T. 1987. "Trying to Survive: Hospital Encourages Employees to Find New Sources of Revenue." *Marketing News,* 21(10): 34.

Tzirides, E. 1988. "Health Outreach Program: Marketing the 'Health Way'." *Nursing Management,* 19(4): 55-57.

Umiker, W. 1989. "The Health Care Supervisor: Dinosaur or Superstar?" *The Health Care Supervisor,* 6(4): 39-44.

Ventura. 1988. Personal communication with author.

Waterman, R. 1987. *The Renewal Factor.* New York: Bantam Books.

"Why Bother Employees Question." 1985. *Healthcare Marketing Report,* 3(6): 1, 8-9.

Williams, L. 1989. "Too Many Chores? Help is at the Doorstep." *New York Times,* pp. C1, C8.

Yura, H. 1986. "Human Need Theory." *The Health Care Supervisor,* 4(3): 45-58.